PHILOSOPHICAL ESSAYS.

PHILOSOPHICAL

ESSAYS.

IN TWO VOLUMES.

By THOMAS GORDON, Esq.

VOL. II.

THERE ARE MORE THINGS IN HEAVEN AND EARTH
THAN ARE DREAMT OF IN OUR PHILOSOPHY.

SHAKESPEARE.

London:

PRINTED FOR THE AUTHOR,

BY C. ROWORTH, BELL-YARD, TEMPLE-BAR.

1809.

CONTENTS.

VOLUME SECOND.

ESSAY VI. *Continued.*

CONTENTS.

ESSAY VII.

ESSAY VIII.

ERRATA.——VOL. II.

Page 16, line 4th from the bottom, *for* entertain *read* certain.

    47,   3, *for* have *read* has.

    54,   26, *for* a *read* as.

  105,   30, *after* to *insert* be.

  128,   -   1, *for* bar *read* bars.

  211,   -   10, *for* $1 - + \frac{1}{4} = \frac{-3}{4}$ *read* $\frac{1}{4} - 1 = \frac{-3}{4}$.

  251,   -   31, second word, *for* decreased *read* increased.

  226,   .   11, *after* induced *insert* a comma.

               12, *after* just *dele* the comma.

               13, *after* conclusion *dele* the comma.

               15, *after* amount *for the* point *insert* a comma, *and dele* for these two propositions.

INTRODUCTION.

———

THE observing, collecting, and recording of physical phenomena and facts constitute the HISTORY OF NATURE. And in the discovery and knowledge, as rationally deduced from the phenomena and facts thus observed and collected, of those pre-established, undeviating, and determinate mutual relations and dependencies which subsist between things, commonly distinguished by the name of the laws of nature, does SCIENCE consist.

SCIENCE is either theoretical or practical; and the practical part of science differs from art, as consisting in the discovery and establishment of rules according to which practice to be successful necessarily must be regulated. In the application of these scientific rules to practice, with dexterity and address sufficient for obtaining by their means the purposes intended, does ART consist.

The ultimate end and object of PHILOSOPHY is the attainment of the greatest possible degree of human happiness, by the enlargement of human power, and the proper regulation of human conduct.

PHILOSOPHY may be defined—*Knowledge of things and of the powers of nature or physical causes of things in as far as things and the causes of things are discoverable and determinable from phenomena by human reason; and consequently of the laws of nature, or the different modes of operation and different degrees of energy or force with which these causes or powers act for each particular case as influenced by different circumstances.*

From this definition it is manifest, that philosophy furnishes the means not only of discovering the phenomena and effects which necessarily must result from the operations of these different causes or powers of nature, as influenced in their respective modes of action and degrees of force by different known circumstances and thereby the means of foreseeing events and providing for futurity, but also of discovering methods whereby these powers may in many cases by human ingenuity and exertion be rendered subservient to man so as to be applied by him to purposes of the greatest utility to him, and which are highly conducive to his comfort and happiness.

Philosophy, in the full and proper acceptation of the term, is of very comprehensive signification, as including every kind of human knowledge acquired by means of *rational* investigation, whether that knowledge respects the laws of physical or of moral action; whether those laws which, by rational investigation from phenomena have been discovered to regulate the course of natural events, or the actions of inanimated substances; or which, by the same means, have been ascertained to regulate and determine moral conduct or the actions of animated beings; or as it respects the use and application of the powers of nature or causes of events agreeable to their various different modes of action, that is to the laws of nature with regard to the accomplishment of those ends intended to be obtained by their means, and which are obtainable by no other means and according to no other laws, that is every kind of human knowledge that is not the result of mere observation and memory, or that is not the offspring of the sportings of fancy; so that philosophy comprehends every kind of useful knowledge except that of languages, nomenclatures, geographical, historical, &c. facts; and a knowledge of the rules and practice of many of the arts and sciences without a knowledge of the reasons on which that practice and these rules are founded.

It is upon philosophical knowledge that the well-being, power, and happiness of rational beings principally depends, as their conduct is in every case in a great measure necessarily regulated by the degrees of it they respectively possess, and as the degree of success attending their conduct also necessarily depends upon it whatever the object of that conduct may be, whether the attainment of some physical or of some moral end; whether the applying of the physical powers of nature, as that of gravity for the attainment of some useful purpose, the applying the principles of mechanics to the construction or improvement of some instrument or machine,

or

or those of astronomy to the improvement of navigation: or whether the attainment of moral good or excellence, or of virtue and happiness in the individual, in the state, or in mankind in general, is the object. In it are included all the sciences properly so called, those of jurisprudence, government, political œconomy, &c. as well as those of metaphysics, morals, and mathematics, and those which are usually denominated, and are often regarded as exclusively physical mechanics, chemistry, astronomy, &c.

But though the extending of philosophical knowledge must on the above mentioned accounts undoubtedly be an object of great importance to mankind, yet it is not so much so as the establishing of it on a solid and permanent basis by freeing it from any erroneous and delusive principles, from any chimerical entities, any illogical deductions and conclusions, and from any unfounded and visionary theories on which it may in part be established; since these must necessarily render the knowledge of it not only unprofitable and vain, but also deceitful and prejudicial in a high degree: error and disappointment ever being the inevitable consequences of proceeding on principles unfounded, and the precepts of an imaginary philosophy.

As there are many facts from which it may be inferred, so there are many reasons which evince a probability at least of philosophy having been cultivated with much success and of its having attained a very high degree of perfection in some very remote period of antiquity, and in some country now unknown, though most probably situated in the east. That the arts and sciences, and many most profound and enlightened philosophical doctrines, were introduced into Greece either directly from the east, or, in a more corrupted state, through the medium of Egypt, are facts well ascertained. To Cadmus a Phœnician the Grecians were indebted for the first knowledge of letters. Thales of Miletum, the founder of the Grecian philosophy, travelled into Egypt and the east for the express purpose of acquiring the wisdom of the east, and was the first European who predicted an eclipse of the sun:---a fact he must have become acquainted with in Egypt or the east, as not possessing instruments proper for making such a discovery himself. Vetruvius informs us that astronomy was introduced into Greece immediately from Babylon itself by Berosus a Babylonian who opened an astronomical school in the isle of

Cos: and Pliny says the Athenians in consideration of his wonderful predictions erected him a statue in the gymnesium with a gilded tongue. According to Herodotus it was from the Babylonians that the Greeks first learned the Pole, the Gnomon, and the twelve divisions of the day.

Pythagoras the son of a Phœnician, and, according to some authors, a Phœnician himself as being born at Sidon in Syria, but according to others a native of Samos educated in Phœnicia, travelled into the east for instruction; some say even into India. Among other profound and sublime doctrines introduced into Greece by Pythagoras were those of the obliquity of the zodiac; that the sun is in the center of the universe; that the earth is round, and people have antipodes; that the earth moves both round the sun and also round its own axis; that the moon reflects the rays of the sun and is inhabited like the earth; that comets are a kind of wandering stars disappearing in the further parts of their orbits; that Lucifer and Hesperus are not, as was then supposed, two different stars, but the same, being the planet Venus, and that the movements of the planets are in harmony: meaning, perhaps, that they all harmonize or accord in describing areas about the sun which are proportional to the times in which they are described. The common multiplication table is also ascribed to him; and he either invented or introduced into Greece several geometrical theorems of great importance in that science. He also unfolded the fundamental principles of music, and gave the several parts their proper names. Like the Brachmans of India he and his disciples abstained from all animal food.— Knowledge, both in the sciences and in the arts, was introduced into Greece from the east by many others, both foreigners and natives, besides those mentioned above.

Euclid, the celebrated mathematician, author of the Elements of Geometry, and Data, which are still extant, and of other geometrical works on Conics, Porisms, &c. which are lost, was a native of Alexandria in Egypt, and taught mathematics there under the reign of Ptolemy Lagus; and there it was that all the eminent mathematicians from that time till the conquest of Alexandria by the Saracens were either born or studied. It was there that the philosophers and mathematicians of these times could avail themselves of the advantage of consulting the famous library formed by the Ptolemys from what had been saved out of the wreck of the learning of that part of the

the East which had been overrun by Alexander and his successors—and that they did so there can be no reason to doubt. That this treasure of oriental wisdom and learning did afford abundance of materials of which Euclid and other compilers of Elements of Geometry could, and probably did avail themselves seems highly probable at least. And that this library, among its other valuable relics of the knowledge of the East, contained books on the Science of Algebra there is reason to suppose from that part, still extant, of the work of Diophantus of Alexandria, the only known writer of antiquity on that subject, as in it he treats of algebra, or rather of that mode of calculation which is now called algebra, as a science the fundamental principles and rules of which were then too well known and too well established to require his taking any notice of them.—Diophantus's work consisted of 13 books, but only 6, with part of a 7th, have ever been printed. Regiomontanus, in his preface to his Alfraganus, informs us, that in his time the whole of the 13 books were preserved in manuscript in the Vatican library; and Bombelli, in his Algebra, expressly says, that when Antonio Maria Puzzi Regiano, Public Lecturer on Mathematics at Rome, and he were translating some of these books, *they found that in the said work the Indian authors were often cited, by which they learned that this science was known among the Indians before the Arabians had it.*

About eight hundred years ago the arithmetic as well as the algebra of India was introduced into Europe by the Arabians, a circumstance which soon produced in Europe a complete revolution in arithmetical science, the decimal or Indian arithmetic, and the Indian arithmetical notation--- often called the Arabian though the Arabians acknowledge their having got both the notation and the arithmetic from the Indians---being so decidedly superior to the Grecian and Roman arithmetic and notation, as to occasion the arithmetic and notation of these latter to be soon entirely abandoned, and that of the former adopted in its stead; and the Indian arithmetic and notation has ever since in Europe been the arithmetic and arithmetical notation in common use.

The state of astronomical science in India, Siam, China, &c. at present--- though it resembles, as was justly observed by the truly ingenious and eloquent but unfortunate Bailli, the shattered remains rather than the elements of a science, as containing many precepts without explications and

many

many periods of which the advantages are unknown---is such as seems to support and confirm this conjecture (which is not new but has been entertained by several eminently distinguished for learning and discernment) of the sciences having in some remote period of antiquity and in some country now unknown, attained a very high degree of perfection ; and it seems probable that China--- in which the mariner's compass, gun powder, the art of printing, &c. were so long known before they were known in Europe---has not always been inhabited by the same race of human beings it is at present, who seem incapable not only of making any discoveries or improvements in the sciences themselves, but also of adopting and carrying into effect those made by others:---the arts and sciences having remained stationary in that country for many centuries.

But however this may be, it is to be remarked that few discoveries of importance---at least in mathematics, physics, and astronomy---have ever been ascribed to any Grecian who had never travelled into the East or at least into Egypt; and that the sublime truths and profound philosophical knowledge, thus introduced into Greece, were either soon so altered, corrupted, and disguised, by the Grecian philosophers as to be converted into fiction and fable, or were entirely rejected and abandoned by them from the decided preference they gave to hypotheses of their own conceiving, the mere offspring of a too luxuriant fancy, which, though ingenious, and supported by the most refined eloquence, the most artful sophistry, and all the embellishments and allurements of figurative language and a splendid diction approaching in some cases to poetry, as in the philosophy of Plato, had no foundation in the nature of things ; and which having no solid foundation served no other purpose than to amuse the fancy, mislead the judgment, and involve science in obscurity, mystery, and absurdity. The only part of the philosophical knowledge introduced into Greece which the Grecians seem to have retained, adopted, and naturalized, were those portions of it they had received through the vitiated medium of Egyptian hieroglyphics, allegories, and fables, being that from which in a great degree the Grecian mythology derived its origin. The philosophical doctrines of Pythagoras appear to have been much corrupted and altered by his disciples of the Italic school, before they passed over from Græcia Magna into Greece Proper, where they were soon so vitiated that scarcely a vestige of many of the originals was to be found in the writings of those
who

who pretended to develop, describe, and illustrate them; while many of the others were so obscured as to be rendered almost unintelligible.

From the doctrines of Parmenidas, the poetical Pythagorean, Plato borrowed many of those highly embellished but obscure reveries in which his philosophy consists; and in it he seems to have lost all sight of the real Pythagorean doctrines, substituting in their place an ideal system well suited to the purposes of mysticism and superstition, but very ill calculated for enlarging the stock of useful human knowledge and for investigating and discovering the laws of nature. While the doctrines of his pupil, the mighty Stagirite, who so long with unrivalled sway controuled and directed the opinions of Europe and the schools as to philosophical principles, in place of having had any tendency to instruct and enlighten the world, served only to involve it still more in error, in sophistry, and in endless disputes from which no real knowledge could possibly be acquired. The Romans being abject admirers of the Grecian philosophy, adopted it without scruple or reserve, and without adding any thing of importance to it, or forming any new systems of their own. And in the barbarous ages, as they are called, which succeeded the downfal of the Roman empire, as these corrupt systems of philosophy, founded on fallacious principles, transmitted to them from the ancients, were held in such high estimation as to be regarded as models of perfection; and as the highest ambition in the way of science was to understand, elucidate, and enforce them, it was utterly impossible that any foundation could be formed, or any progress made for the acquirement of just principles and sound philosophy.

As the Grecian philosophers nevertheless were undoubtedly men of great ingenuity, of splendid and superior talents, the bad success which attended their philosophical enquiries must in a great degree be attributable to the fallacious mode of philosophizing or manner of conducting the investigations they adopted and pursued and in attempting to spiritualize every thing; to deduce all knowledge from sources purely intellectual, and reversing the order of nature, not from what is known but from what is supposed only; or to use an expression of Thales, the founder of the Ionic sect and father of the Grecian philosophy, who inculcated and practised the doctrine himself, " to make philosophy descend from the heavens to the

" earth,"

" earth," attempts necesarily vain, and which could terminate in nothing but hypotheses, delusion, and error.

Some men of strong mental powers and sound judgment, as Roger Bacon, &c. even in what are called the barbarous ages, deviated so far from the hypothetical mode of philosophizing adopted and inculcated by the ancients, as to have recourse in their philosophical investigations to experiment—the oracle of nature; but these instances were rare; and the great Lord Chancellor Bacon, Viscount of St. Albans, was the first who had a clear and comprehensive view of the errors and absurdities of the ancient system of philosophy and of the deceitfulness and inefficacy of the ancient mode of philosophizing.

Since Lord Bacon pointed out the proper mode of philosophical investigation, the great progress that has been made in the sciences comparatively to all that had been done before is truly astonishing, and those have ever succeeded best in the pursuit, in the acquirement, and the dissemination of useful knowledge, who have had the least regard for the doctrines of the ancients, and have deviated most from their mode of procedure. But, though this is the case, the progress has notwithstanding on the whole been but slow, so difficult is it even by the most direct and surest methods to penetrate into the secrets of nature, and trace science to its first principles; much remains yet to be done, many are the things which seem to be still hid under an impenetrable veil of obscurity; and what is still more to be regretted, there is reason—from that obscurity and even mysticism which pervades some of the sciences; from those differences of opinion which still prevail with regard to them; from the first principles on which they are founded not being in many cases so clear and convincing as first principles ought to be; and from the reasons and conclusions deduced from these principles, even when denominated demonstrations, being sometimes erroneous, sometimes improbable, and sometimes even contradictory, impossible, and absurd—to believe that science is not yet, in every case, founded on so stable a basis as not to admit of being shaken or overturned; on first principles, facts, and, reasonings, so evident, logical, and decisive, as necessarily to preclude all doubt, and, to impress conviction on every mind capable of understanding them.

The

The insufficiency of the evidence with respect to the justness of the first and fundamental principles of metaphysical science in particular, and the improbability and in some cases even impossibility and consequently absurdity of the conclusions deduced from them,. has impressed mankind in general with no very favourable opinion of the soundness of these principles and the justness of the reasonings on which it is establised, and has induced many to suppose that metaphysical investigations, however ingenious, must all necessarily terminate in fiction, sophistry, or paradox. And it is from this supposition, or a despair of subjects and researches so intricate, abstruse, and perplexing as those comprehended in this science, the principal objects of which come not within the cognizance of sense, being ever treated in such a manner as to be productive of any knowledge which may with safety, certainty, and utility be relied upon, that that indifference now so generally manifested for metaphysical speculation has proceeded. There are several other sciences besides that of metaphysics to which unsoundness of principle and erroneous theory is justly imputable; and among others, some perhaps which at present are generally regarded as being established on evidence the most satisfactory, and on reasonings irresistible.

To treat of subjects so recondite as those of the following Essays with perspicuity must be no easy task, and perspicuity is all that is aimed at in the stile, other embellishments being the less requisite, that it is the object of these essays rather to establish than to illustrate. Any pompous display of words full of sound and seeming import but in reality signifying nought has, therefore, throughout studiously been avoided; and the author has also from a dread of being deceived himself—from having no wish to entrench his doctrines in incomprehensibles and obscurity, and of thereby, perhaps, becoming the unintentional cause of deceiving others—cautiously guarded against the admission of sophistry, of all arguments of a dubious nature, and the use of symbols, except where unavoidable; though he well knows how highly acceptable ingenious sophistry, from its apparent acuteness, pompous pretensions, and seeming to mean more than meets the eye, is to many readers, and with how much admiration and applause it is often received by those with whom obscurity and perplexity of thought pass for profundity and discernment; and that there are no errors so egre-

b   gious,

gious, no blunders so gross, but an algebraical form, and the finesse of an abstruse analysis, will with some sanction for truth itself.

The intention of the following Essays is not so much to amuse the fancy, to interest the passions and affections, or to indulge in poetic description and eloquent declamation, as to reason consequentially, closely, and conclusively; to address the understanding, and from obvious and certain principles consonant to nature and right reason, to endeavour to remove from some of the phenomena of nature that veil of obscurity in which their causes have been involved, and which hitherto has been deemed impenetrable, to investigate and ascertain some important truths, to give some greater degree of stability to opinion, to trace science to its first principles, and to a certain extent to establish philosophy on the solid and permanent basis of reason and of nature; the object of these Essays being an attempt to research into and discover the fundamental principles of philosophy by a metaphysical analysis of the human mind, and a physical and metaphysical investigation into the nature of things; and by means of the facts thus ascertained and of rational deductions from them, to endeavour to ascertain that relation which subsists between the human mind and the objects of its knowledge, the foundation of that right it assumes to become a judge of such objects, and consequently the extent and degree of certainty of this knowledge itself, and to establish the facts and fundamental principles thus discovered on evidence as satisfactory, cogent, and convincing, as the nature of things admits.

With this intention it is attempted in Essay I,—First, To investigate the nature, evidence, and necessary consequences of consciousness. Secondly, To point out the distinction between sensation and perception which in metaphysical disquisitions as well as in common conversation are so often confounded together, and to ascertain the difference between them on principles different from any hitherto proposed for that purpose. Thirdly, To investigate and ascertain the fundamental criterion or test of truth with respect to human knowledge, &c. And in this and the two immediately succeeding Essays a refutation of the ideal system of philosophy is attempted, not on assumed instinctive principles and laws of human thought, but on principles founded on and rationally deduced from the nature of things.

In

In Essay II, it is attempted, First, To enumerate the various faculties of the human mind, to distinguish them accurately from each other, and to ascertain the precise province, intention, and use of each; as of memory, judgment, fancy, &c. each of which is separately treated of. Secondly, To ascertain whether or not there actually are in nature any such existences as abstract general ideas, either real or nominal, or as abstract or absolute truths, immutable, necessary, and eternal. Thirdly, If there really is any such thing in nature as any human knowledge acquired by means of pure intellection only, besides what results from the consciousness of the mind with respect to its own sensations, powers, and operations, and thereby of its own existence and identity. Fourthly, If any kind of human knowledge can with propriety and justice be said to have been acquired purely *à priori*. Fifthly, On the facts thus investigated and ascertained, and the reasonings thence deduced, to endeavour to discover and develope principles on which a system of logic founded in nature, or on the *reality of things* in place of on *ideas, fancies, or phantasms*, may be framed and established; to ascertain the source from which all human knowledge is derived, and the means by which it is acquired, and thereby to establish philosophy on the stable and permanent basis of nature and reason.

The objects of Essay III, are First, To attempt a refutation of Mr. Hume's doctrine of Causation and the consequences he deduces from it, and thereby to complete what has been attempted in the preceding Essays, the refutation of the ideal system of philosophy. Secondly, To investigate and discover the characteristic differences, and nature and operation of powers and substances in as far as they can be discovered from their effects. And, Thirdly, from thence to deduce the GENESIS of matter.

The object of Essay IV is, First, An attempt to investigate and ascertain the nature of mechanic power and action. Secondly, To account for the impressions made in the forms of bodies on percussion when there appears to be no expenditure of power or force on that account, the moment or quantity of motion being the same after the percussion as before it. Thirdly, To account for the impressions or cavities made in soft yielding substances being, *ceteris paribus*, as the squares of the velocities of the bodies by whose action on them they are formed. Fourthly, For the loss of motion in the composition of forces, and the generation and gain of it in

certain

certain cases of percussion as that of elastic bodies increasing in geometrical progression. Fifthly, To ascertain what would be the laws of percussion with regard to perfectly hard bodies, if any such there were. Sixthly, To account for the operation of those simple instruments or machines called the mechanic powers. And lastly, To endeavour to decide and terminate that so very warmly and long contested dispute concerning that fundamental principle of mechanics, the ratio of the velocities according to which the forces ought to be estimated and appreciated.

With regard to the remaining Essays, as distinct conceptions of their intentions and scope are to be acquired only by a perusal of the Essays themselves, it may here suffice to observe that originality of thought and comprehensiveness of views are not less conspicuous in them than in those by which they are preceded ; and that the principles of the sciences treated of in them are represented in a very different light at least from that in which they have hitherto been regarded.

Philosophical Essays.

ESSAY VI.

ON CHEMISTRY, ELECTRICITY, AND MAGNETISM,
(Continued.)

CHAP. VI.

OF INCOMBUSTIBLES.

1. THESE substances which experience has proved to be incombustible have been distinguished into the three different genera of SALTS, EARTHS, and CALCES ; and it is the nature of all incombustible substances, however great their generic or specific differences, or of all the individuals of all the three genera under which they are included, to ponderate or gravitate :—no ungravitating incombustible substance being known.

2. These may be severally defined, agreeable to their respective generic differences, as follow, viz.

3. SALTS are material substances which gravitate, are incombustible, are soluble in water, and more or less affect the sense of taste. Some of these substances, however, which are generally regarded as salts, are not, from containing a portion of mona in their respective compositions, altogether incombustible, as certain acids, ammona, &c. While certain other substances, which are highly combustible, from containing avona in their respective compositions, are generally regarded as salts, and as incombustible from substances owing their incombustibility to avona having never hitherto

B been

been ranked among combustibles; as nitric acid, avo-muriatic acid, and compound salts containing these, &c. But though these are more or less combustible, it may be proper, in compliance with common usage and as they possess the other qualities of salts in an eminent degree, still to include them among the salts, though perhaps on this account they may be regarded as less perfect than some other individuals of the genus; and also to include among the salts even such substances as nitrated ammona, and avo-muriated ammona, &c. though combustible in the highest degree from each containing both mona and avona in its composition though not in chemical combination; and further, in compliance with common usage, to include under the designation of combustibles those substances only which owe their combustibilities solely to their containing mona in their compositions.

4. EARTHS differ in nothing from salts, but in being insoluble in water and insipid.

5. CALCES are simple or uncompounded material gravitating substances, which, from being essentially incombustible, remain, after the substances they formed, when in chemical combination with mona, have been deprived of their mona by means of combustion: and of these some seem to be of a saline nature, some of an earthy, and some of an intermediate nature between saline and earthy; though it seems probable that they all would be saline if they could be completely deprived of mona and avona.

It may be proper, however, to treat of each genus separately and more in detail.

GENUS I.

OF SALTS.

1. SALTS have been distinguished into three species, viz. 1st, ACIDS; 2d, ALKALIES; and 3d, COMPOUND SALTS. Of each of these species I shall treat successively in the above order; but it may be proper to premise, 1st, that the several substances which are regarded as salts, even of the same species, differ exceedingly in their saline qualities from each other, some of them possessing these qualities in the highest degree, while in others of them they are hardly perceptible; and 2dly, that this so considerable diminution of saline qualities renders it extremely difficult, if not impossible, to determine with precision the limits which separate not only saline sub-

stances

stances from others that are not saline, but also which separate the different species of salts from each other.

Species i.—*Of Acids.*

2. Acids may be defined to be gravitating material substances, which redden certain vegetable blue colours, which have a strong affinity to alkalies, and which have in general a sour taste, and are corrosive.

The known acids are :—

1. Sulphuric acid.	18. Benzoic acid.
2. Sulphureous.	19. Succinic.
3. Phosphoric.	20. Moroxylic.
4. Phosphorous.	21. Camphoric.
5. Carbonic.	22. Oxalic.
6. Fluoric.	23. Mellitic.
7. Boracic.	24. Tartaric.
8. Nitric.	25. Citric.
9. Nitrous.	26. Sebacic.
10. Oxymuriatic.	27. Saclactic.
11. Hyperoxymuriatic.	28. Laccic.
12. Arsenic.	29. Malic.
13. Tungstic.	30. Suberic.
14. Molybdic.	31. Tormic.
15. Chromic.	32. Prussic.
16. Columbic.	33. Gallic.
17. Acetic.	34. Acid of Tannin.

3. The favourite hypothesis of the philosophical chemists with regard to acidity has for long been that of there being only one acid principle in nature, one substance only truly and essentially acid, which, by the intimate union it is capable of contracting, and does contract, with several other substances, imparts to them acid powers and properties, in different degrees, according to the different natures of these other substances, and thus constitutes by such unions all that variety of different acids which exist in nature. Of this opinion was the celebrated Stahl, who regarded the vitriolic, or what I now call the sulphic acid, as being this acid principle; of this opinion also was Dr. Robert Hook, of London, Dr.

Mayhow,

Mayhow, of Oxford, and of late that great chemist Dr. Scheele, though they differed from Stahl with respect to the substance to which they attributed this essential principle of acidity. According to the suggestions and conjectures of the two former of these it existed in nitre, in nitric acid, and in the air; and Dr. Scheele, in page 157 of his Chemical Observations and Experiments on Air and Fire, English translation, thus expresses himself " Now I am apt to suppose that empyreal air" (the pure air of Priestley and oxygen gas of Lavoisier) " is compounded of a subtle acid united with phlogiston, and that it is probable THAT ALL ACIDS OWE " THEIR ORIGIN TO EMPYREAL AIR."

4. From phenomena rather than from these suggestions Mr. Lavoisier seems to have formed that system of acidity which has been so much admired for its ingenuity, and which has been so generally adopted, of there being but one substance in nature essentially acid, to their combinations with which all those different particular substances denominated acids owe the several degrees of acidity they respectively possess, and that this substance essentially acid is the gravitating base of oxygen gas (empyreal or pure air) by him denominated oxygen. Though this theory of Lavoisier differs in nothing from that of Scheele but in the substitution of the latent heat of Dr. Black, under the name of caloric, for phlogiston, as a constituent part of oxygen gas or of empyreal or pure air, yet he has rendered it interesting and important by ingeniously conferring on it the appearance of novelty; and, by means of many diversified experiments, analogies, and reasonings, so great a degree of credibility and apparent stability as seemingly to render that matter of fact and sound doctrine which before was surmise and conjecture only and therefore of no value or validity in science.

5. Though this opinion, which has been so prevalent among philosophical chemists, of there being but one substance in nature essentially acid is grand and sublime in a great degree, and may possibly be true, as it seems perfectly analogous to the constant plan of nature in producing various effects by the same means and all effects by the simplest possible means, yet the present state of chemical knowledge is not such as to authorise the adoption of such a conclusion as an established certainty, or as a truth ascertained by accurate experiment and just rational deduction; and far less such as to enable us to determine with precision what that particular

cular substance is which is essentially acid, if any such substance there is:— and it must necessarily be admitted, that the gravitating base of oxygen gas cannot possibly be that substance, if the doct rines developed and attempted to be established in the preceding sections of this Essay shall prove to be well founded and just; since according to these that base is water, a substance manifestly destitute of all acidity. But these doctrines, and the facts on which they are established, do not afford the only reasons for rejecting this theory as hypothetical and unfounded, since there are many other facts from which it may be rationally and justly inferred that that hypothetical entity oxygen—supposing it to be a real existence and to be that substance which combines with metallic calces and with acid radicals on combustion whereby they acquire an encrease of weight—neither possesses any acidity nor any acidifying power, or that it is neither acid of itself nor the cause of acidity in any other substance; as the fact of its not only never existing in a separate uncombined state as an acid, but also the fact of its never engendering acidity in any of those substances with which it is supposed to unite; as in caloric and light, when united with them, as is supposed, in oxygen gas which gives no indication of being an acid; as in hydrogen, when combined with it, as is supposed, in ice, in water, and in steam, none of which give any indication of being acid; and as in azotic gas, when in combination with it, light and caloric, forming, as is supposed, atmospheric air, which also is not acid, &c. Besides, the combining of substances essentially acid with oxygen gas in place of encreasing their saline and acid qualities, actually diminishes them: thus on converting muriatic acid by that means into oxy-muriatic acid as it is called, its fixity, missibility with water, and acid powers and properties, are all greatly diminished; though its dissolving powers, for reasons that will be afterwards assigned, with respect to certain substances are augmented by this means; and the same is the case with regard to other acids, some of which as the Prussic are not even supposed to contain any oxygen in their composition.

6. According to the chemical system at present generally adopted, all acids are generated by the combination of oxygen, or the gravitating base of oxygen gas, with certain substances called combustibles—from their being supposed to be the causes of combustion by their combining with
the

the oxygen and thereby liberating the caloric and light of the oxygen gas of the atmosphere, in consequence of their having greater affinity to this base than the other assumed component parts of the gas, caloric and light, have—which substances are supposed to be altered by combustion no otherwise than in having acquired an additional substance, which is different indeed from any of the various substances of which they themselves are severally composed, but which before its combination with them possessed no acidity, whereby they are all, however different their various natures may be from each other, converted into acids.   Thus, phosphorus is in this manner supposed to be converted into phosphoric acid on its combustion, sulphur into sulphuric acid, carbon into carbonic acid, &c. and metals, as iron, into oxydes, or substances not acid indeed, but which it is assumed would be acid if they were combined with a larger portion of oxygen; and all this for no other reasons than those of there being in these cases an efflux of fire and consumption of oxygen gas without any annihilation of gravitating matter resulting from the process.   It seems strange, however, that the fire of combustion produced in the cases of the combustion of sulphur and of carbon, in particular, should be ascribed to a discharge of caloric from a condensation of gas, when it is considered that the gasses generated in these cases are at least equal in volume with the oxygen gas condensed and consumed by the process; and that the gasses thus generated, if they owed their elasticity and gaseous forms, as assumed in this theory, to caloric, would require at least an equal portion of it with that discharged by the oxygen gas for their production; and not less strange that combustion should in any case be attributed to the condensation of gasses, when it is considered that many facts prove that the gasses may not only be condensed even to solidity, by their combining with different substance, without emitting or evolving any fire; as carbic gas with water, and with quick lime, &c. but also that combustions of the most powerful kinds often take place, and can at any time be artificially produced, where no gas is present, by mere encrease of temperature, and in some cases merely by means of a stroke or slight pressure on certain solid substances, even when they are in vacuo, under water, or confined in close vessels having no communication with the air or any substance in a gaseous state.

                                                            7. These

7. These processes, phenomena, and effects, admit, it is presumed, of a more satisfactory explanation on the preceding principles of combustion, as being undoubtedly owing to a play of affinities; and, where the gravitating bases are not different portions of the same substance, as in the combustion of mona-gas with avona-gas, to double affinities from the gravitating base of the combustible having more affinity at the then temperature to the gravitating base of the avona-gas than it has to the mona with which it is combined, and from the avona of the avona-gas having more affinity to the mona of the combustible than to the gravitating base with which it is in union, whereby a combination takes place between the mona and avona producing the fire of combustion, and another between the gravitating bases producing the compound gravitating incombustible that remains after the combustion, or the acid, if it is an acid, that in the particular case is the result of their union.

8. And, if that is the case, it follows as a necessary consequence that the radical or gravitating base of the combustible is essentially acid or of an acid nature, since it has been proved that the gravitating base of avona gas with which it combines is water. And that this acid radical was in combination with mona, when in the state of a combustible, follows as a necessary consequence from its having then admitted of being brought into a state of combustion at pleasure by an increase of temperature when in conjunction with any substance possessing avona as a constituent part. From these facts it also follows as necessary consequences that phosphorus cannot be the gravitating radical of phosphoric acid, sulphur of sulphuric, carbon of carbonic, &c. or metals of their respective calces, or what has been called their oxydes; and hence the reason of my adopting the term phospha to denote the gravitating base both of phosphorus and of phosphic acid, since its combination with mona forms phosphorus and its combination with water phosphic acid; sulpha that of sulphur and sulphic acid; and carbo that of carbon and carbic acid, &c.

9. The proximate principles of the muriatic, fluoric, and of some other acids, and consequently the natures of their respective radicals, are yet unknown. It was happily discovered by that truly philosophical chemist Mr. Cavendish, that nitrous acid could be generated by passing the electric spark through a mixture of cora gas with avona gas in due proportions.

tions, and that these gasses were entirely consumed or disappeared by the process:---a discovery of the utmost importance towards the ascertaining the nature of this acid, and the ascertaining to which of its proximate principles its acidity is owing. For it is manifest, from the principles developed above, that if the combustion has been complete, and the whole of the avona and mona of these gasses, from their perfect chemical combinations, have been dissipated in fire, that nothing can remain after the combustion but the gravitating bases of these gasses, or but water and cora; and as it must necessarily follow that the acid generated by the process must consist in a combination of these, so it must also necessarily follow that it must owe its acidity entirely to the cora which enters into its composition, since its other component ingredient water is well known to be entirely destitute of all acid powers and properties, and since there is sufficient proof of these component ingredients being only in a state of corpuscular combination. But the combustion and dissipation of the pyrogens is perhaps never complete in the generation of this acid, and hence it is that this acid is always in a state of corpuscular combination with portions either of avona gas, or of mona gas, and generally with portions of both; and the water of the acid seems in some cases to be surcharged with cora its acid radical, while that radical is in a state of chemical combination with a surcharge of one or both of the pyrogens:—this is the case with nitrous gas, the nature of which will soon be more fully described.

10. Whether the radicals of certain acids, as the nitric, muriatic, fluoric, &c. ever enter into chemical combinations in a dry and pure state with mona, forming concrete solid combustibles as those of the sulphic, carbic, and phosphic acids do, forming respectively sulphur, carbon, and phosphorus, is not known; and if they ever do, these concrete combustibles are either unknown, or are not known to have derived their origin from these radicals.

Although acids do not owe the whole of their gravity to their respective acid radicals, since water, another gravitating substance, also enters into their compositions, yet this not being the case with the dry solid combustibles generated by chemical combinations of these radicals with mona, into the composition of which no water enters, as sulphur, carbon, and phosphorus, all the gravity such substances may possess must necessarily

be

be owing to and depend upon their respective acid radicals only, since their other constituent principle mona possesses it not: a fact which decisively establishes the gravitating nature of the acid principle. Besides, it is well known that the specific gravity of certain acids much exceeds that of water, and that the purer and more concentrated the acids the greater their specific gravity, and that the greater their specific gravity the greater also their acid powers and properties. And though acids often enter into corpuscular combinations with avona gas and mona gas, severally or conjunctly, in certain proportions, without having their acidity and other saline qualities destroyed by that means, yet it is never without a diminution of these in proportion, *cæteris paribus*, to the quantities with which they may be combined of either or both of these substances, as is manifest from the cases of avo-muriatic acid, and of monated sulphic, nitric, and carbic acids, or what used to be called phlogisticated vitriolic and nitrous acids, or sulphurous acid, nitrogen, and oxide of azot, and of carbon, &c. which are all less fixed, less dense, less missible with water, and less acid, than the same acids when deprived of more or less of these gasses, on being more or less concentrated and purified by means of fire or heat applied to them, &c. Nor is the combination of either of these gasses with an acid or acid radical ever conducive to its acidity, except when the acid or acid radical happens to be in previous combination with one of them, and the introduction of the other also deprives the acid substance in whole or in part of both of them, from their combining chemically together forming fire or ignite, and in that state being dissipated: but though a diminution of acidity and of missibility with water is induced in acids on their combinations with these gasses, yet their dissolving powers, with respect to certain substances, are under certain circumstances augmented by that means, though they are diminished by it with respect to others, for reasons to be afterwards assigned.

11. The preceding facts and observations serve to throw new light not only with regard to the natures of the different acids, but also with respect to the origin, constitutions, and natures of the various different gasses not hitherto treated of in this Essay, and to evince that there are only two original, simple, and pure gasses in nature, namely, mona-gas and avona-gas; that all the other known gasses consist only in these with

other substances of a different nature dissolved and suspended in them; and that it is to these gasses in which these substances are dissolved that these compound gasses are entirely indebted for their gaseous state; as well as to point out the effects which these primary gasses have on certain substances with respect to their saline qualities.

12. Mona and avona gasses possess no saline powers or properties; for neither gives any indication of its being either acid or alkaline, and neither if perfectly pure is soluble in water perfectly pure; from which circumstances it follows as an unavoidable consequence that the saline qualities of such saline substances with which they may severally form corpuscular combinations must, in place of being increased, necessarily be diminished on their forming such combinations in proportion to the quantity of the gas which combines with them. And if the gas contains a surcharge of its proper pyrogen, the saline substance with which it combines may by such combination be deprived of the whole of its saline qualities by the surcharge of pyrogen combining chemically with the saline base or radical of that substance, and by that means completely saturating and neutralizing it:—that substances are deprived of their saline and other qualities, and acquire qualities totally different from those they possessed before, by chemical combination with a pyrogen, will afterwards appear.

13. Though cora is the radical or acid and saline principle of nitric acid, and therefore is of itself essentially acid and saline, yet cora gas, or that gas which is formed by the dissolution and suspension of cora, or of this substance essentially saline and acid, in a mixture of mona and avona gasses, gives no indication of its being either saline or acid, for it is immissible with water, and when in corpuscular combination even with avona-gas it forms not an acid with it, but either atmospheric air or avonated atmospheric air, substances which give no indication of being acid. The cora gas on which experiments have been made has been procured by separating the avona gas from the cora gas of the atmosphere; and it is perhaps impossible to obtain it in this manner perfectly pure, so obstinately do substances retain the last portions of any other substances with which they may have been combined, except when the separation is effected by double affinities; and it is probably owing to this circumstance that it contains a portion of avona gas in its composition; if perfectly pure it
perhaps

perhaps would consist of a combination of cora with mona gas only. That cora gas contains both mona gas and avona gas in its composition is proved by its being diminished by the electric spark, and that it contains a much larger proportion of mona gas than of avona gas is proved by both these gasses being entirely consumed by passing the electric spark through a mixture of them when the avona gas is added to cora gas or to air in such a manner as that the avona gas of the mixture shall be to the cora gas in the proportion of seven parts of the former to three of the latter; and that it contains cora or the acid radical of nitric acid is proved by that acid being the only gravitating residuum of the combustion and consumption of this mixture of these gasses.

14. Carbo seems to be the radical or acid principle of all the animal, as well as of all the vegetable acids, except of those animal acids which have phospha for their radical. Cora abounds in most animal substances, and in some vegetable, but it seems seldom or never to form the basis of an acid in these, from being always in a state of intimate combination in them with other substances preventing that effect.

15. Acid radicals, as cora, carbo, sulpha, phospha, arsena, &c. are not mere hypothetical entities having no existence but in the imagination, like oxygen and hydrogen the actual existence of which neither comes under the cognizance of sense nor can be rationally deduced from facts and phenomena, but are real entities possessing all the essential qualities of gravitating material substances. For though some of them are never palpable to sense but when in a state of combination especially with water, yet that is not the case with others of them, as phospha, arsena, &c. and the combination of the others with water not being *chemical*, but *corpuscular* only, does not prevent the ascertaining of their actual existence, or prevent the manifestation and discovery of the various essential characteristic qualities they severally possess:---*corpuscular* combinations and especially with water affecting the essential and characteristic qualities of substances no otherwise than in rendering those of the compound intermediate, according to its proportions of those of its ingredients; so that the characteristic qualities of each ingredient are still discernible and distinguishable from each other in those of the compound; whereas these imaginary entities, oxygen and hydrogen, being supposed to be always in a state of *chemical* combination,

if they possessed a real existence, their essential and characteristic qualities could not possibly be known, from their being necessarily so neutralized, disguised, and altered, by these combinations, as to be rendered altogether incognizable to sense. There is no substance in nature perhaps, the solar and stellar rays excepted, that is not in some degree in a state of corpuscular combination, at least with fire.

16. Besides mona, avona, the magnetic powers, and water or the gravitating base of water or of ice, there are in the present state of chemical science many other substances in nature, and among these all the acid radicals, which come to be regarded as elements; since, if compounds, their constituent principles are not known, and since they neither can be composed by art of substances more simple nor can by art be resolved into such.

SPECIES 2.—*Of Alkalies.*

1. ALKALIES may be defined to be gravitating material substances soluble in water, which have a strong affinity to acids, which in general change certain vegetable blue colours into green, and which have an acrid taste, and are corrosive.

2. Three different substances only have hitherto been regarded as alkaline, namely, 1st, LIXA—2d, TRONA—and, 3d, AMMONA; but under this denomination and in this species I include also, 4th, LIME—5th, STRONTIAN—6th, BARYTES—and, 7th, MAGNESIA; making seven alkalies in all. The four last of these, though possessing all the essential qualities of salts, have hitherto been classed among the earths. All the seven are soluble in water, and all tinge vegetable blues green. The third is volatile at the common temperature of the atmosphere, and is not so entirely saline as some of the others as being in some degree combustible; the others are incombustible, and are regarded as fixed; the four last are evidently so, and are also infusible *per se.* The saline nature of the seventh is not so conspicuous as that of the others; and it perhaps may be regarded as that intermediate substance which connects and in a manner links together the alkalies and the earths.

3. Of Salts that are compounded of other salts there are two kinds, viz. 1st, those in which the combination is corpuscular—and, 2d, those in which

it

it is chemical. It is to this latter kind exclusively that the appellation *neutral* salts is properly applicable, for it is in these only that the qualities of the constituent principles are *neutralized by reciprocal saturation.*

4. Both of these kinds of compound salts are extremely numerous in nature, forming a wonderful and beautiful variety of different substances. Few of these substances, however, are known as such, and still fewer of them have been subjected to chemical investigation. They are principally generated by combinations of acids with other substances, with alkalies, with earths, and with calces, which also seem either to be salts or to have been generated by a combination of salts. They are, therefore, commonly arranged in tables, in treatises on chemistry, according to the known and supposed combinations of each known acid with all the known substances with which it has been found in combination, and with which it is supposed capable of forming a saline combination, there being in these a table of salts for each particular acid, and from the name of that acid in conjunction with those of the bases with which it combines, or is supposed to combine, the salts of that table derive their several particular denominations.

5. Though a salt thus generated, of which the component salts are severally soluble in water, will be unsoluble in it when the affinity, union, and saturation subsisting between these component salts combined together in its composition in the proper proportions, is so strong, intimate, and complete, that there shall be no excess or surcharge of either in it; yet a salt compounded of the same component salts will be more or less soluble in water when there is any excess of either of the component salts in its composition above what is necessary for the saturation of its other component salt, and in direct proportion to that excess. On this principle, that hitherto unaccounted-for phenomenon (see Bergman's Elective Attractions) of purified tartar being less soluble in water than either of its constituent ingredients, acid of tartar and lixa, and than soluble tartar, or a combination of purified tartar with lixa, admits of an easy explanation; since it is manifest from these results, and from the well established fact of purified tartar, commonly known by the name of cream of tartar, containing a small excess of acid of tartar in its composition, and that if it was not for this excess of acid it would not be soluble in water at all, while the superior solubility of soluble tartar is to be ascribed entirely to the great excess of lixa in its composition.

position. The solubility of many other compounds in water, in alkahol, &c. is justly attributable to the same cause, and admits not of a rational explanation on any other principle. Some of the compounds thus generated are not salts, as not being soluble in water, and many others of them are but imperfectly saline from being either very difficultly or imperfectly soluble in water, or from being in a certain degree combustible, or from being in some degree both imperfectly soluble and partially combustible; these form species of substances of an intermediate nature between salts, and earths, and calces, and between incombustibles and combustibles.

6. Both the insolubility and combustibility of such compounds is sometimes owing to the water of the compound being in chemical combination with a pyrogen, particularly mona, and to the gas thus formed and the other ingredients being in chemical union to saturation, by which means the corpuscular affinity between the compound and water is destroyed, while the salt thus formed is at the same time rendered combustible from the pyrogen it contains. But if there is an excess of either ingredient in it, and that excess is not either saturated or combined with any gas or pyrogen, it will in that case not only be soluble of itself, but, in general, will also communicate a certain degree of solubility to the rest of the compound.

GENUS II.

OF EARTHS.

1. EARTHS are gravitating, material, fixed, insipid substances, which produce no effect upon vegetable blues, and which seem incapable of forming any very intimate, permanent, or chemical union with either pyrogen; which are not corrosive, and which are neither combustible nor soluble in water, and which are either infusible *per se,* or are very difficultly so.

2. The different kinds of earths are at present supposed to be ten in number, viz. 1. lime; 2. barytes; 3. strontian; 4. magnesia; 5. argill; 6. yttria; 7. glutina; 8. zirconia; 9. Augustina; and, 10. Silica. The first three of these, however, are manifestly saline and alkaline; and the fourth is also possessed of these qualities in a certain though not in so great a degree as these others. The diamond as possessing the qualities of stone in an eminent degree, and not being known to be combustible, was regarded

garded

garded as consisting in a kind of earth peculiar to itself, in a state of chrystallization, till lately that its combustibility was discovered.

3. By these means the number of *known* earths are reduced to six exclusive of those to be mentioned below. The different kinds, however, of earths and stones in nature are probably very numerous, and it would seem, from several circumstances, that the whole of them are compound substances, generated by the combination and perfect saturation and neutralization of different incombustible saline substances with each other. The generation of chalk, and of fluor spar, substances insoluble in water, and possessing all the other essential and characteristic qualities of earths and stones, by the combinations of lime, a saline and alkaline substance, with carbo gas and fluo gas saline acid substances, affords from analogy some probability at least of all the other earths being also compound substances generated by means of saline combinations, and therefore that they all are nothing but neutral compounds which are incombustible and insoluble in water, incombustible either from their possessing neither mona nor avona in their compositions, or from their possessing either or both of these in too small a quantity, and in a state of too intimate union with their other principles to admit of their being detached from them; and insoluble in water from that reciprocal saturation and neutralization of their proximate principles, whereby these principles lose their specific saline qualities; and partly also perhaps from their containing a small quantity of mona in their compositions in a state of very intimate combination with their other principles.

4. Though the earths and stones thus generated are insoluble in water, yet they contain some water in their several compositions; some of them no more perhaps than was necessary to the gaseous state of their acid, while others as the stones contain it in larger proportions. When chalk is in a loose, powdery, and friable state it is regarded as an earth; when in a more concrete compact, and somewhat hard state, as an intermediate substance between an earth and a stone; and when in combination with more water, and in a more hard, compact, and chrystallized state as a stone, being then called limestone. Either earth or stone is formed on the combination of the saline principles, according as they are in combination with less or more water at the time of their union; for after their union they can combine chemically with no more of it; thus, if the lime and the carbo

gas

gas contain very little water at the time of their union, a loose, friable powdery earth called chalk is produced; but if it is with lime in combination with much water, or with water saturated with lime that carbo gas unites a stone, or that compact solid hard substance known by the names of calcareous spar and of limestone is produced. Hence it appears, that the insoluble and therefore insipid neutral compounds thus generated owe the qualities of compactness and hardness they possess in a very great degree to the water which enters into their respective compositions. The means by which the water effects this will be shewn when treating of chrystallization, and will furnish a beautiful example of the process employed by nature in many cases for the formation of stones, and at the same time serve in some degree to illustrate and confirm the above new theory of the generation and composition of earths and stones. Many other instances of earths and stones generated by combinations of saline substances, and of those and water, will readily occur to every intelligent chemist.

5. All the earths, except those known to be compounds generated as above described, are, with respect to the present state of chemical knowledge, elements, as never yet having been either artificially decomposed into simpler substances, or artificially generated from these.

GENUS III.

OF CALCES.

1. CALCES or metallic radicals, commonly known by the name of oxides, are, in general, gravitating material substances, of an intermediate nature between salts and earths, and between combustibles and incombustibles. They differ from salts in being, a few excepted, insoluble in water, and they all also, except perhaps those of the perfect metals, differ both from salts and from earths in being combustible at a very high temperature. They likewise differ from earths, and perhaps from all other substances also, except pure acid, and entertain alkaline radicals and water, in being capable of intimate chemical combination with mona in a pure state even to saturation, whereby substances or compounds of qualities essentially different from those of either of their constituent principles are generated, named metals; and each calx

derives

derives its distinguishing appellation from the particular metallic substance that is generated by its combination with mona. This being the principal distinguishing characteristic of metallic radicals, or calces, I shall substitute the name of metalites for that of calces, to denote such metallic radicals as are in a concrete dry state, and are insoluble in water, as being more appropriate than those either of calces or of oxides, and as metalites, according to this application of the term, differ from such metallic radicals, calces, or oxides, as are saline, and are in a liquid state, from being corpuscularly combined with water, as acid of arsenic, &c. It seems probable that they all would be saline and acid, and completely incombustible if they could be completely deprived of the very little mona they contain. Metalites are often combined with gasses, some with mona gas, and some with avona gas, and some with both in an impure state; and hence though pure metallic radicals, in the present state of chemical knowledge, are elements, metallites, in general, are not so. Metalites are not combustible by the greatest heats produced in the common furnaces, forges, &c.

2. In the present state of chemical knowledge, all the pure earths and pure alkalies, except ammona, as well as the pure acid and metallic radicals, come to be regarded as elements; since, if compounds, their constituent principles are not known, and since they neither can be composed by art of substances more simple, nor by art into such be resolved.

CHAP. VII.

OF COMBUSTIBLES.

1. GRAVITATING combustible substances have, in treating of combustion, Chap. V. article 8th, been distinguished into three different kinds or orders, which may be denominated AVONATES, MONATES, and AVO-MONATES, according as they owe their combustibility either to a combination with avona only, or to a combination with mona only, or to a combination with both

mona and avona, not in a state of chemical union with each other. But as the term combustible is in common language applied to no other substances but those that contain mona in their composition, in compliance with this general application of the term, I shall in this chapter regard no other substances as combustible but those that contain mona, and, in it, treat of these exclusively, having, according to common usage, regarded avonates, or those substances which owe their combustibility to their containing avona in their composition, either as gasses, salts, or metalites; and already treated of them in treating of these.

2. Combustibles, as thus particularized and characterized, are distinguishable into the two different classes of those that contain not, and those that contain, water in their composition. The first of these classes is distinguishable into three different genera, viz. Those substances, which, without much propriety, have been denominated sulphurs: those which with no greater propriety have been denominated hæpars; and those denominated metals. Those of the other class are distinguishable into several different orders, genera, and species; as oils, resins, balsams, gums, ardent spirits, &c. Of the several genera and species, comprehended under these two different classes, it will be necessary to treat more particularly.

CLASS I.

Of Monates which contain not Water in their composition.

GENUS I.

OF SULPHURS.

3. Sulphurs are gravitating, dry, solid substances, which, when heated to the temperature of 370°, or under, of Fahrenheit's thermometer, in the open air, take fire spontaneously, and by combustion are converted either into acids or into alkalies. Of this genus there are two species, viz. 1st. sulphurs having an acid radical or base; and 2d, sulphurs having an alkali for their base or radical. Of species 1st. three individuals only are known, viz. sulphur, commonly so called; phosphorus; and carbon.

SPECIES

SPECIES 1.—*Of Sulphurs having an Acid for a base or radical.*

1st. OF COMMON SULPHUR.

4. Sulphur, commonly so called, is a solid substance that has been long and generally well known, of a yellow colour, without smell, and, if perfectly pure, probably without taste, which does not conduct electricity, and of which the specific gravity is 1.990. The presence of the air or of avona gas is necessary to its combustion; and when heated to the temperature of 302°, in the open air, combustion spontaneously ensues, from the double change of affinities which then takes place, the sulpha, or gravitating base or radical of the sulphur, having, under these circumstances, greater affinity to the water, or gravitating base of the avona-gas of the air, than to the mona of the sulphur; and the water of the avona-gas having more affinity for the gravitating base of the sulphur, than for the avona of the gas, whence these different gravitating bases combine together, forming sulphic acid gas, which, afterwards uniting with a larger portion of water and a portion of avona gas, forms, according to circumstances, either sulphous or sulphic acid, while the mona of the sulphur—or at least the greater part of it, for the sulpha still retains a sufficiency of it to give it, in conjunction with the water it derives from the avona gas, a gaseous form in the sulphic acid gas—thus liberated from its gravitating base, combines with the avona of the atmosphere, also thus liberated from its gravitating base, forming fire; and it is in the evolution and dissipation of the fire thus generated, and in the other new combinations which take place as above described, that the combustion in this case consists.

5. That sulphur contains no water in its composition, or that the water which forms a constituent part of the acid gas, or acid produced, formed no part of the sulphur, is proved by the addition of weight, precisely equal to that of the water contained in the acid, acquired by the sulpha, or gravitating base of the sulphur, during the process. The process of combustion described above affords an analytical proof, sufficiently conclusive, of sulphur being a compound of a gravitating base with mona, in place of being a simple substance; and this is a fact that admits of a synthetic proof also, as will appear in treating of carbon, when the loss of weight in the ingredients employed in that process will serve to confirm the conclusion deduced

from

from the gain of weight in the above process, of the sulpha, or gravitating base, being in a dry state in sulphur; and, consequently, of sulphur containing no water, or any other gravitating principle besides sulpha, in its composition.

2d. OF PHOSPHORUS.

6. Phosphorus is a solid gravitating substance, of a clear, transparent, yellowish colour, of which the specific gravity is 1.714. The combustion of phosphorus takes place in air at so low a temperature as 43°, whereas, in avona gas, a temperature of 80° is required for its spontaneous combustion. This combustibility of phosphorus, at a lower temperature in air than in avona gas, indicates a stronger affinity between phospha, or the gravitating base of phosphorus, and cora, or a combination of cora with water, than between phospha and water alone. The combustion of phosphorus is also effected by means of a double affinity, the presence of air or of avona gas being necessary to it, and in the same manner, and on the same principles, that the combustion of sulphur is produced, except that the cora may have some influence in this case, when the combustion takes place in air; and the product of it is also an acid, composed in this case of phospha, or the gravitating radical of phosphorus, in combination with the water derived from the decomposition of the avona gas, and this acid is so far volatile as to be sublimed in flowers, which, absorbing more water from the atmosphere, forms the phosphic acid. This process, for the same reasons that were given when treating of sulphur, affords a most decisive proof of phosphorus not being a simple substance, but a compound, and a compound of phospha with mona, and that water does not enter into its composition.

3d. OF CARBON.

7. When common wood charcoal is freed from its impurities it forms carbon, which is a gravitating solid black substance without taste or smell, not soluble in water at any known temperature and not acted upon by air at the common temperature, and therefore under such circumstances incacapable of putrefaction or decay from age. It likewise cannot be fused, and is inconsumable, in close vessels not containing air, by any known degree of temperature; and it also is a good conductor of electricity. At the temperature

ture of 370° the combustion of carbon takes place. The presence of air or avona gas is as in other cases of combustion necessary for it; and the combustion in this case is also as in others, an effect of double affinities; the carbo or gravitating base of the carbon combining with the water, or gravitating base of the avona gas forming carbic acid, which from its still retaining so large a portion of the mona of the carbon as to render its solubility and missibility with water less perfect than that of most of the other acids, makes it not only assume the state and form of a gas, but also permanently retain that state when not in chemical combination with some other substance, while the mona of the carbon and the avona of the gas liberated from their respective gravitating bases combining together forms the fire of combustion in this case, which is dissipated in diffusing itself around and restoring an equilibrium of temperature. These are facts which afford an analytical proof sufficiently satisfactory of carbon being a compound of carbo and mona in place of being a simple substance, and of its containing no water in its composition.

8. Mr. Lavoisier concludes from his experiments and calculations that 28 grains of charcoal gain by combustion 72 grains of additional weight, making 100 in all---that 100 grains of phosphorus gain by that means 154 grains of additional weight, making 254 grains in all---and that sulphur also gains much additional weight by combustion, though the quantity cannot be exactly ascertained. See Lavoisier's Elements of Chemistry, chapter 8th.

9. That the analysis of the sulphurs and the causes of their combustions, given above, are just, or that the facts actually are as above represented, is proved not only by the phenomena, but also by the natures of the materials or substances subjected to combustion, and of the products or those substances which are the result of it: Thus, in each case, the only products are fire and an acid, and the weight of this acid is found on experiment to be precisely equal to that of the gravitating bases of the materials or substances subjected to the combustion, so that there is no gain or loss of weight by the process, and this acid is also found to be an incombustible whether alone or in conjunction with substances containing either mona or avona in their respective compositions, whence it necessarily follows that the substances whereby the fire of the combustion was

generated

generated were not ponderating; and this being the case that these could only be mona and avona as being ungravitating substances, and the only substances in nature essentially combustible or capable of generating fire. And since it has been proved that one of the materials or substances subjected to the combustion, the avona gas, consists of avona in combination with water as its gravitating base, it follows as a necessary consequence that the other, the sulphur, must consist of mona in combination with the acid radical as its gravitating base.

10. But these are facts which admit of being proved synthetically as well as analytically, or by the artificial generation of sulphurs, from combinations of those substances into which they have been resolved by the preceding processes: thus phosphorus is generated by subjecting a mixture of phosphat of lead with charcoal to a certain degree of temperature under the proper circumstances for producing that effect. In the celebrated experiment of Mr. Tennant for the production of carbon, a mixture of pounded marble with phosphorus is treated in the same manner, and in the no less celebrated one of Stahl, whereby sulphur is artificially generated, a mixture of sulphat of lixa with charcoal is subjected to the same treatment. That all these various results are effects of double decompositions in consequence of double affinities, or that the several sulphurs thus generated are generated by combinations of their respective gravitating radicals in a dry state with mona, while the several other sulphurs decomposed by these processes in parting with their mona to those that are generated by them, are converted into acids or salts from a combination of their respective gravitating radicals first with the water of the salt employed, and next with its alkaline or metallic base whereby different acids and salts are formed according to the different natures of these several radicals or bases, is also proved not only by the phenomena, but likewise by the natures of the substances decomposed and of the substances generated by the processes; the mona of the carbon in the first case quitting, under the then degree of temperature, the carbo to combine with the phospha forming the phosphorus, while the carbo combines with the water and metallic radical of the phosphat of lead forming a carbated metalite of lead;—in the second case, the mona of the phosphorus quits the phospha to combine with the carbo of the marble forming carbon, while the

phospha

phospha combining with the water and lime of the marble forms phosphated lime;---and in the last case the mona of the carbon combines with the sulpha of the sulphated lixa forming sulphur, while the carbo combines with the water and the lixa forming carbated lixa. That these several acid radicals combine in a dry state with mona forming the different sulphurs, is proved in the above cases by the loss of weight, as it was in the former by the gain of weight in the products: the loss in these cases being *ceteris paribus* precisely equal to the gain in the others.

11. The nature and the compositions, as above ascertained, of sulphurs prove in the most convincing manner the truth of what was advanced when treating of salts, namely, of certain substances being deprived of all their saline and other qualities, and acquiring qualities totally different from those they possessed before, by chemical combination with a pyrogen, the acid radicals being, in these cases, deprived of all their acid and saline qualities, &c. by their combination with mona, and the mona itself rendered immissible or uncombinable with water: circumstances which prove that the combinations in these cases are intimate and chemical, the saturation reciprocal and complete, and the compounds generated perfectly neutral.

SPECIES 2.—*Of Sulphurs which have an Alkali for their Base or Radical.*

12. That certain earths and alkalies admit of being formed into pyrophori by being ignited and fused in close vessels in intimate mixture with certain combustibles, or by a process much akin to that employed by MM. Gay and Thenard with the intention of decomposing the fixed alkalies, and of obtaining by that means what have been regarded as NEW METALS and SIMPLE SUBSTANCES and as the elementary bases of these alkalies in a pure state, is a fact that has been long known; and the late well conducted experiments of the ingenious Professor Davy, with the very powerful galvanic apparatus of the Royal Institution of London*, from which the doctrines, now so generally adopted, of the decomposition of alkalies and earths and consequent production of new metals, and of these metals being capable of instantly decomposing water on being applied to it, are derived, and to which the origin of the experi-

* See Professor Davy's papers in the Phil. Trans. of the Royal Society of London, for the years 1807 and 1808.

ments

ments of the French chemists mentioned above are to be ascribed, seem to me to prove in a manner the most clear and satisfactory that the alkalies, including under that term certain of those substances which are known under the name of earths, when in a pure state or when deprived of all moisture with any gas or other impurity it may contain, that is the alkaline radicals, admit, like the acid radicals, of being combined with pure mona, and that they then, like the acid radicals when so combined, form sulphurs or phosphori. That the product of these processes have better pretensions to be ranked amongst, and more justly may be regarded as, sulphurs than as metals, is sufficiently manifest from their natures and qualities. And, indeed, the inferences from these experiments of the alkalies and earths being DECOMPOSED AND ANALYSED by these processes, unless depriving the alkaline base of that moisture or water with which it is in combination when in the state of an alkali with any gas or other impurity that moisture may contain can be regarded as decomposing them; of the substances generated by them being either METALS or SIMPLE SUBSTANCES; and of those substances being capable on mere contact of instantly DECOMPOSING WATER; are such as neither the premises nor the products warrant: and such, it is presumable, as nothing but the too great influence of the prevailing chemical theory of the present times could have induced the judicious chemist who has the merit of having first made these important experiments to have suggested and adopted, since of the decomposition either of the alkali, the earth, or the water, in these cases, or of the products being either metals or simple substances, there is no proof whatever. Nor can the operations of these processes, and the various phenomena attending them, or the natures of their products, be rationally and justly accounted for either on the principles of the ANTIPHLOGISTIC theory of Lavoisier, or on those of the PHLOGISTIC hypothesis of Stahl. For the inflammation produced or fire generated on placing these supposed new metals on water when not excluded from communication with air or avona gas can not be justly explained on the assumed hypothesis of the metals attracting and combining with a sufficiency of oxygen, one of the supposed elements of water, for enabling it to resume its pristine state of an alkali, and of a sufficiency of caloric being in this case disengaged from the oxygen thus attracted for producing the inflammation which in this case

takes

takes place, since the oxygen thus disengaged from the hydrogen of the water was in as condensed and solid a state before this process as it is in after it, and therefore could not possibly by it be deprived of a sufficiency of latent matter of heat or caloric for producing this effect; and since hydrogen, the other supposed constituent of the water decomposed, necessarily disengaged by this process, if this hypothesis is just, is in this case impalpable and unaccounted for, there being neither any appearance of it nor any proof of its having been disengaged by the process. And, in the case of placing these supposed metals in water contained in the exhausted receiver of an air-pump, the generation of mona gas, improperly called hydrogen gas, cannot be owing to a decomposition of the water, and a combination of the caloric disengaged, from the oxygen of that part of the water which is decomposed, with that portion of the hydrogen which on the decomposition of the water is also at the same time necessarily disengaged, since, in that event, in direct contradiction to the hypothesis on which this theory is founded, less caloric would be required for the gaseous than for the solid state; since there is neither any appearance of the oxygen from which this caloric is supposed to be disengaged, nor any proof of its existence in this case; and since there are no facts from which it can justly be inferred that what is called hydrogen gas owes its permanent elasticity or gaseous state to caloric. It is on facts and principles very different from those assumed in these theories that the results and phenomena of these processes admit of a rational and just explanation. It is from the facts of the products of these processes being COMPOUND in place of SIMPLE substances; of these compounds being SULPHURS OR PHOSPHORI in place of METALS; of water not being decomposible by their means; and of the substance with which the alkaline bases are in combination in these cases being neither the PHLOGISTON, or pure fire in a fixed insensible state, of Becker and Stahl; nor the CALORIC, or matter of heat without matter of light, of the present chemical theory; nor HYDROGEN, a supposed constituent of water, and the supposed PONDERATING base of what is called hydrogen gas; nor a GAS of any kind; but the UNPONDERATING substance MONA in a pure state, which is not of itself fire, but which in combination with avona forms it, that these results and phenomena admit of a rational and just explanation. For the sulphurs or phosphori thus generated on being moistened produce either inflammation, or mona gas, or in part both, according to differences of circumstances, as whether they communicate with air or not and whether the temperature is high or low, by means of a play of affinities, from the alkaline or earthy base of the sulphur having at the common temperature of the atmosphere a stronger affinity to water than to mona, and from the mona of the sulphur when communicating with the atmosphere having a stronger affinity to the avona of the atmosphere than either to the alkaline base or to water, whereby the alkali is, in this case, disengaged from its mona, and inflammation or fire is produced; though in certain cases of this kind, when the temperature of the atmosphere is low, some part of the mona of the sulphur will often combine with a part of the water, forming a small portion of mona gas :---while, in the case of moistening these sulphurs when placed within the exhausted receiver of an air-pump and having no communication with the atmosphere, the sulphur is decomposed without inflammation or fire being generated, from no atmospheric air or other substance containing avona gas or avona being present in this case, by the alkaline base of the sulphur combining with a portion of the moisture or water in preference to its mona from its stronger affinity for it, while its mona thus disengaged from it combines with another portion of the water generating with it the mona gas which in this case is produced. That it is not the hypothetical ponderating substance hydrogen, nor indeed any ponderating substance whatever, whether in a solid, fluid, or gaseous state, with which the alkaline bases are in a combination in these cases is proved by their acquiring no encrease of weight on being converted into sulphurs by the process.

The particular properties and distinguishing characteristics of the individuals composing this species have not yet been ascertained with sufficient precision and to such an extent as to admit of their being treated of separately ; and, indeed, their great tendency to decomposition from the very weak affinity of the alkalies to mona renders the ascertaining of these a matter of much difficulty.

GENUS

GENUS II.

OF METALS.

13. Metals are dry opaque substances, distinguished from all others by a greater specific gravity and peculiar brilliancy of lustre. Those at present known are twenty-eight in number, viz.

1. Gold.	15. Bismuth.
2. Platina.	16. Antimony.
3. Silver.	17. Tellurium.
4. Mercury.	18. Arsenic.
5. Palladium.	19. Cobalt.
6. Rhodium.	20. Manganese.
7. Iridium.	21. Chromium.
8. Osmium.	22. Uranium.
9. Copper.	23. Molybdena.
10. Iron.	24. Tungsten.
11. Nickel.	25. Titanium.
12. Tin.	26. Columbium.
13. Lead.	27. Tantalum.
14. Zinc.	28. Cerium.

14. None of them are fluid at the common temperature of the atmosphere except mercury. The first fourteen are malleable; the others are brittle; and the last ten of them either difficultly fusible, or altogether refractory. Some of them possess the qualities of tenacity, ductility, and elasticity in an eminent degree; and in others of them some or all of these qualities are wanting. And they are all good conductors of electricity. Gold, platina, and silver, may be regarded as perfect metals, as being incorruptible, or at least as not being destructible by any known natural means, the joint action of air and water having no effect upon them. Mercury, which is acted upon by these but very slowly, unless agitated, seems in that respect to be intermediate between the perfect metals and the others which are soon acted upon and much affected and altered by them. All the metals are combustible, but the highest degree of temperature producible by art is required for the combustion of some of them.

E 2　　　　　　　　　　　　　　　　　15. The

15. The presence of air, or of avona gas, or of avona combined with some other gravitating base having an affinity to the gravitating base of the metal, is necessary to their combustion. The combustions of the different metals take place at very different degrees of temperature. Most of the less perfect metals, when exposed to the air, calcine or corrode and rust, though slowly, at the common temperature of the atmosphere, and their calcination is in general much accelerated by moistening them with water or vapour, and still more so by an increase of temperature, when it is often attended with inflammation ; and, indeed, even for the slow combustion and calcination of some of them a high degree of temperature is required. Mercury, which seems to be intermediate in its qualities between those of the perfect metals and those of the less perfect, boils when heated to 600°, but from its great volatility, and, when heated, explosive power, it is perhaps neither combustible nor calcinable by art, as evaporating or exploding from the heat applied before it acquires a degree of temperature necessary for weakening so far the attraction between its mona and gravitating base, and thereby of disengaging them so much from each other, as to admit of their forming chemical combinations with other substances, whereby their separation from each other may be completed, or as is necessary for combustion and the calcination of the mercury. The metalite which is known by the names of black calx or oxide of mercury, or ethiops *per se*, is formed at the common temperature of the atmosphere by a long and constant agitation of a little mercury in a bottle containing air—that which is known by the names of yellow calx or oxide of mercury, or turbith mineral, by boiling 1 part of mercury with 1½ of sulphic acid almost to dryness, and then pouring hot water upon the mass—that called the white calx or oxide of mercury, by dissolving mercury in nitric acid, and precipitating by an alkali—and that which is known by the names of the red calx or oxide of mercury, and precipitate *per se*, or red precipitate, is formed, either by putting a mattrass, containing a small quantity of mercury, having communication with the air, into a sand bath, and keeping it constantly at the boiling point for a long time, when the black calx of mercury is first formed, and, after several weeks, the whole is converted into a a powder, or rather into small chrystals, of a very deep red colour, which is this precipitate *per se*; or by boiling to dryness, in close vessels, a solution

of

of mercury in nitric acid. The combustions of silver, gold, and platina, are known to us only from the experiments of Van Marum in making electrical sparks, from the very powerful Teylerian machine, pass through wires of these metals, and from those of Mr. Pepys, jun. by means of his very powerful galvanic trough; and the calces of metalites thus obtained have not been examined with sufficient precision for ascertaining their respective natures. Were it not for these experiments, the combustibility of these metals, and their containing mona as a proximate principle in their respective compositions, could only be inferred by analogy from their metallic properties and appearances :—the combustion of gold in mona gas, by the above means, can justly be attributed only to the very powerful electrical machine furnishing a sufficiency of avona in that case for the combustion of the mona both of the metal and of the gas, and to the water, or gravitating base of the gas, combining with the radical or gravitating base of the metal.

16. Metalites, of calciform appearances, may also be obtained from these metals, by precipitating them from their several solutions in acids, by means of other substances, not metallic, having more affinity to these acids; but there is no certainty of these metals being calcined or deprived of their mona in these cases, and the contrary seems presumable from their being recoverable in these cases merely by an increase of temperature, or the application of fire only to these metalites. Metalites which are convertible into metals by the application of fire only to them, necessarily must be either metals in their entire state, not deprived of that mona which is essential to the metallic state, and, therefore, which have not undergone combustion or been calcined, and which owe their partial loss of lustre and appearance of a calx to their being in combination either with water, or with saline substances, or with gasses, or with two or more of these; and their reduction to their former state and appearance by the application of fire only, to their being disengaged from these combinations by its means—or they necessarily must be metallic radicals, in combination with some or all of these substances, which are capable of resolving the fire applied, by which they are revived, into its component parts, whereof the mona, combining with the metallic radical, revives it, and the avona uniting with the water generates avona gas—or metallic radicals, which have greater affinity to the mona of those substances with which they are in combination at that

degree

degree of temperature at which their reduction takes place, than these substances themselves have, and hence the revivification of the metals at that temperature, and their disengagement from the other principles of those substances with which they were in combination: perhaps their reductions may in some cases be owing to one, and in others to others of these causes.

17. The incombustibility of gold, &c. except at a very high temperature, must be owing in part to the very great tenacity of its particles, or the very great attraction of adhesion and aggregation which subsists between them, but more especially to the great affinity of their several radicals with mona. The affinity of the radical of gold to mona is not only much greater than its affinity to water, but also than its affinity to saline substances, since it combines with muriatic acid, the substance with which next to mona it seems to have most affinity, only when that acid is in combination with and assisted by avona, either in detaching and liberating the radical from the mona, or in weakening the mutual attraction between the radical and the mona. That metalites produced by solution and precipitation are often in a state of combination not with water only, but also with part of the acid in which they were in solution, and with part of the precipitating substance likewise, is decidedly proved by the natures of fulminating gold, and of the other fulminating metallic powders; while what has been called yellow oxide of mercury, or turbith mineral, is well known to contain 1-10th of its weight of sulphic acid, and what is called red precipitate of mercury, to contain in its composition a considerable portion of nitric acid : certain metals in their entire state seem capable of combining under certain circumstances with avona gas, but never with avona in a pure and uncombined state.

18. Metallic radicals, like those of acids, are unknown in a pure and uncombined state, as being always either saturated with mona only forming the different metals, or intimately combined with a small portion only of mona, of which they are exceedingly retentive, and with water, and in some cases with several other substances, also forming the different metalites and metallic acids ; and hence though the metallic radicals are according to the present state of chemical knowledge elements, the metalites and metallic acids are not. Mr. Lavoisier found, Elements of Chemistry,

page

page 554, that at a very high degree of temperature all the metalites were combustible, and burned with a flame, which proves that they all contain mona in their composition; and it seems probable that if they could by any means be completely deprived of mona, they would all prove to be acid radicals, since some of them, as those of arsenic, &c. can by art, from depriving them of mona, be reduced to the state of an acid radical in combination with a small portion of water, &c.

19. Metals are converted into metalites either by combustion, or by the action of any substance simple or compound upon them which has either equal or greater affinity under the then circumstances to their two component principles, mona and the metallic radical, than those principles have to each other, from that substance combining in the first case with the metal in its entire state forming one compound substance, and in the second with its two constituent parts severally forming two distinct compound substances, the one consisting in a combination of the mona of the metal with a portion of the added substance, if that substance is simple, and the other in a combination of the radical of the metal with another portion of the same substance; but if the added substance is compound, and has a greater affinity between one of its principles and mona than either between mona and the metallic radical, or between that principle and the other principle of the added substance, at the same time that there is greater affinity between that other principle and the metallic radical, than either between that radical and mona, or between the two principles of the added substance, the one compound substance formed will be a combination of one of the principles of the added substance, with the mona of the metal, and the other substance formed a combination of the other principle of the added substance with the radical of the metal. It is by means of affinities such as those described above that acids, &c. and metals act upon each other, combine together, and decompose each other; and when thus combined the metal is said to be held in solution by the acid from the compound thus formed being in a liquid state, the same as that of the acid before the combination; and from the metal being thus transformed into a liquid, and essentially altered in its properties, it is said to be dissolved by the acid during the process of combination. Metalites more compounded than any of the above are often procured by precipitat-

ing

ing metals, or metallic radicals, from their solutions in acids, by means of substances having greater affinity to those acids, or their radicals, than the metals or metallic radicals have, these metals or metallic radicals carrying down in combination with them not only part of the acid in which they were in solution, but part of the precipitating substance also.

20. All those acids or other substances which dissolve the imperfect metals, and decompose them by depriving them of the greatest part of their mona, and which deprive them of it by generating fire, of which there is an emission during the dissolution in the sensible form of heat, either contain that avona or avona gas as an element or ingredient, or attract it from the atmosphere during the process by the operation of which this effect is produced. If no fire or heat is evolved in the dissolution of a metal by an acid, &c. and nothing besides mona gas, it is an indication of the acid's containing much water in its composition, and of the dissolution being effected by the radical of the metal combining with the acid or acid radical forming a metallic salt, and by the mona of the metal combining with part of the water of the acid forming the mona gas which is evolved during the process. And if it is not mona gas, but an acid gas or vapour, that is evolved, it is an indication of the acid's containing but little water in its composition, and that the radical of the metal combines with the water of the acid forming a metalite in place of a salt, while the mona of the metal combines with part of the acid forming the acid gas or vapour: ---if these dissolutions are accompanied with some degree of heat, a combination more or less of the different pyrogens takes place at the same time, producing that fire by means of which the vapour is evolved. It seems probable that in certain cases of the dissolutions of metals by acids, &c. that the avona which combines with the mona of the metal generating the fire or heat which is evolved during the process is not furnished by and does not form a part of the acid, but is attracted in very large quantities in the form of avona gas, or in combination and accompanied with water, &c. by the joint operation of the fermenting ingredients from the air during the process; and hence the increase of weight in certain cases of this kind notwithstanding the great emission of gas or of vapour which takes place.

21. Muriatic acid evidently derives its superiority of power over the nitric and sulphic acids in dissolving the black metalite of manganese and

other

other metalites containing avona gas, to its possessing more mona gas loosely adhering to its acid radical than they do, since these other acids also readily dissolve these metalites when combined with any substance abounding in mona; the mona of the acid uniting with the avona of the avona gas of the metalite forms fire or ignite, while the acid in combining with the metallic radical thus deprived of every pyrogen dissolves it. Metals in an entire state must either be deprived of a great part of their mona, or have the attraction of the radical to its mona much weakened by a play of affinities, or the operation and counteraction of other attractions, as by the action of acids, &c. containing avona on the metal, before the acid—which must also be either deprived of its avona from its combining with the mona of the metal or have its attraction to it sufficiently weakened by counter attractions—can effectually combine with and dissolve and retain in solution either the metal or the metallic radical, so that by precipitation by the proper means either the one or the other may be obtained in the form of a metalite, the metallic radicals being indissolvable in acids while they are in complete chemical combination with either pyrogen, and in the case of metals till such time at least as the affinity of the mona to the metallic radical is sufficiently weakened by the presence and counteraction of avona. These principles and these facts afford a satisfactory explanation of the seeming paradox advanced in the Chapter upon Salts, viz. That though a diminution of acidity and of missibility with water is induced in acids by their combinations with either mona or avona gasses, yet their dissolving powers with regard to certain substances are under certain circumstances augmented by that means though they are diminished by it with regard to others. This is the case with nitric acid on being combined with mona, which by that means becomes less acid and less missible with water, and a less powerful solvent of metals, but at the same time a more powerful solvent of black metalite of manganese and of other substances which contain avona; and this is the case with muriatic acid on being combined with avona forming avo-muriatic acid, which is less acid and less missible with water, and a less powerful solvent of black metalite of manganese and other substances containing avona than muriatic acid is, at the same time that it is a much more powerful solvent of most metals and other substances abounding in mona.

22. That the mona and the gravitating base of carbon have each some-times greater affinity to different portions of some other gravitating sub-stance than to each other, and severally combine with it, at a certain tem-perature, in preference to their remaining in their then state of chemical union, is proved by that experiment of Dr. Priestley, whereby he con-verted moistened charcoal into carbated mona gas, by the application of concentrated solar rays to it in vacuo, and by the experiment of generating the same product from the same materials, by passing steam through tubes containing charcoal heated to redness ;---in this case a ternary, or triple compound or substance, consisting of three ingredients, is generated from the great affinity of the two products, a combination of one portion of water with mona and a combination of another portion of it with carbo, for each other, at that temperature, whereby they combine in the gaseous state forming carbated mona gas, or the substance formerly known by the name of heavy inflammable air, being a compound of mona and carbo with water. This is not peculiar to carbon ; the same holds with regard to iron, and to many other substances consisting of a combination of mona with a gravitating base, and, with respect to iron, has been proved by the very same experiments as the above, with the difference only of iron being substituted for charcoal, and the only differences in the results are, that when iron is employed in place of charcoal, that the products are mona gas, and the black metalite of iron, and that these products do not, as in the former case, combine together, forming a ternary compound, in a gaseous state, from the great fixity of the metalite and volatility of the gas.

23. That the black metalite of iron is not a combination of iron, either with that hypothetical gravitating entity, oxygen, or with that real ungra-vitating substance, avona, is proved not only by its not inflaming or defla-grating with phosphorus, sulphur, or charcoal, or the most combustible of the metals, when exposed with them to a high temperature, but also from no change being produced upon it by passing mona gas through it when heated to redness on a porcelain tube, which could not be the case if it contained either of these ; since, if it contained avona, it would, in that case, necessarily be deprived of its avona, without being reduced, as having at that high temperature greater affinity to water than to mona, as proved by the above mentioned experiments ; and if it contained oxygen, would
necessarily,

necessarily, according to the presently adopted system, be reduced; for the metalite, being deprived of that oxygen to which it owes its state of an oxide, by its combination with the hydrogen of the gas forming water, would recover or resume its metallic state, and become iron again. On passing mona gas through the brown metalite of iron, which actually contains avona gas, under the same circumstances, the case is very different; here a change soon takes place, the brown being speedily converted into the black metalite of iron, by being deprived of that avona it contained, from that avona's combining with the mona of the mona gas, and with it forming fire or ignite. These are facts which afford a decisive proof of its being with water, and neither with oxygen nor with avona, that the metallic radical is in combination in the black metalite of iron.

24. From the above facts and others, it also appears that iron must not only be deprived of nearly all its mona, but also, that it must be in a state of combination with a portion of water before it will, even at this high temperature, attract and combine with air, and that, when in union with both water and air, it parts with its air before it parts with its water. The same seems to be the case with most or all of the other metals, and also with the acid radicals: they all seem to combine with a portion of water before they combine with air, and when combined with both, they part with the air before they part with the water; and when combined with gasses, as those composing the air, they, or rather perhaps the water they contain, seem to part with cora gas before they part with avona gas. They also in some cases attract and combine with the carbo of the atmosphere, thus lead, copper, and iron, in rusting or calcining, attract much carbic gas from the air, which, combining with the water of their several metalites, form respectively white lead, verdigrease, and the common rust of iron, all of which contain much carbo gas in their compositions. Those metalites which are regarded as oxides in what is called the minimum, or lowest state of oxidation, contain no oxygen, as there is no such existence; and, in general, little or no avona: as the black metalites of mercury and of iron, the brown of copper, the grey of lead, &c. In those cases of minimum oxidation, as they are called, either the metal, or the metallic radical, deprived nearly of all the mona of the metal, seems to be in combination with water only, or at least with but a very small portion of gas, &c. of any

kind;

kind ; and it seems to be owing to this water principally that the metalite attracts carbo, cora, or avona, &c. or carbo, cora, or avona gasses, from the atmosphere, and combines with them, forming what is called oxides in the second or higher stages of oxidation, as the red metalites of mercury and of lead, &c. That mona and avona gasses are capable not only of combining together, but also of combining conjunctly with metals or metalites and other substances, without decomposition or generating fire, when the temperature is not high, will be afterwards proved in treating of explosion and deflagration.

25. That metals are not elements, or even substances so simple as not to be decomposible by art, as assumed in the theory of chemistry at present in vogue, but are compound substances, composed of combinations of those gravitating substances which constitute the several metallic radicals with mona, is proved, not only analytically, by their being combustible, which no simple substances in nature, except the pyrogens, are ; as well as by all the different phenomena and effects attending their dissolutions in acids, &c. but also synthetically, by their being artificially revivable, after having been actually calcined, or deprived of that mona which is essential to their metallic state, by restoring it to them again ; and by this reduction not being practicable otherwise than by means of mona, either in a pure disengaged state, as in those metallic reductions, which are effected by the agency of electricity or galvanism, or in a state of combination with some gravitating substance having less affinity to it than the metallic radical to be revived has under the circumstances proper for accomplishing that purpose ; whether these circumstances are the application of heat to a mixture of the metalite with any monate, in a close vessel, whose gravitating base, at that temperature, has less affinity to mona than the metalite, or the precipitation of the metalite in a metallic state, from any acid in which it may be in solution, by means of some monate, whose gravitating base has less affinity to mona, and more affinity to the acid, than the metalite has. That the several metallic radicals enter into combination with mona in a dry and pure state, constituting the several metals, or that metals contain not water in their compositions, is proved, as in the case of acid radicals in sulphurs, by the gain of weight in metals, on their being calcined, and by their loss of weight precisely equal to that gain on their being revived again.

26. The

26. The disengagement of what is called caloric and light that is of fire in a visible state in vacuo, during the combination of certain metals with sulphur, by means of an increase of temperature in these substances from an artificial application of fire to them, is a phenomenon which has excited much attention and speculation, as being supposed an instance of combustion without the presence, action, or co-operation of oxygen gas, and as being, perhaps, the only one, and therefore as the only anomaly or case of discordance with the prevailing theory of combustion, and many attempts have been made to account rationally for it agreeable to the principles of that theory, but they have all hitherto proved unsuccessful. This phenomenon was first observed by Dr. Scheele, and it has since been examined with much attention by several philosophers, and more particularly by the associated Dutch chemists Von Troostwyk, Dieman, &c. who are of opinion that it is produced by the decomposition of that minute portion of water, which not being excludible by art is always necessarily present: but this explanation has justly been deemed unsatisfactory even according to the principles of the established theory, as the oxygen gas, which may have combined with hydrogen gas in generating the water, must necessarily have parted with its caloric and light on combining with that gas. The real matter of fact, however, is, that no combustion in these cases actually takes place, except an almost insensible degree of it may be produced in a most minute portion of the sulphur by means of any exceedingly small quantity of air that may be contained in the vessel or the water, and that the fire is not produced by a combination of heat which has passed through the receiver with the phlogiston of the mixture as supposed by Dr. Scheele, but that the phenomena and effects produced are merely the result of the discharge of that fire from the substances mixed together, with which they were severally corpuscularly united before mixture, on their combination with each other and consequent condensation. That this is actually the true state of the matter is proved by the results, by no decompositions having taken place except what may have been produced by the agency of the very minute portions of air which may have been present, by no new substances having been engendered, but perhaps some very small quantity of sulphurated mona gas from the action of any very minute quantity of water which may have been present on the sulphur,

sulphur, and by the combination between the metal and the sulphur not being chemical but corpuscular.

The preceding facts decisively prove that it is neither with phlogiston or pure fire in a condensed and fixed state, nor with hydrogen or the supposed gravitating base of what is called hydrogen gas, one of the hypothetical constituents of water, nor with hydrogen gas, but with that ungravitating substance mona, a constituent principle of fire, that the acid and metallic radicals in a pure state combine, forming the different sulphurs and metals; and that the sulphurs and metals thus formed are the more or less perfect, the greater or less the affinity of their radicals with mona, and the greater or less the intimacy of the chemical combinations thence resulting.

GENUS III.

OF HEPARS.

27. Hepars are corpuscular combinations, whether natural or artificial, of sulphurs with alkalies. Several of the corpuscular combinations and even some mixtures not in a state of combination of sulphurs with metals, resemble the alkaline hepars so much in their chemical powers and properties that they may, whether natural or artificial, be included in the same genus, and be denominated metaline hepars. Hepars when exposed to the action of the air undergo a slow combustion, owing to the attraction being weakened between the acid radical of the sulphur and its mona by the presence and counteraction of the alkali, or metal or metallic radical, or to the affinity of the acid radical and alkali, or of the acid and metallic radicals for each other, and to the reciprocal attraction between the water of the avona gas of the air and the acid radical, and between the loosely adhering mona of the hepar and the avona of the avona gas of the air; and thus both the hepar and the air come to be decomposed by means of elective attractions or a play of affinities; and hence the use of hepars for the obtaining of cora gas from air. These effects are much accelerated by the addition of some water to the other ingredients from the great affinity of the alkalies and of the radicals to it, and when this is the case mona gas often holding sulphur or hepar in solution is formed.

28. Phosphori

28. Phosphori and pyrophori are either sulphurs of which the radicals have more affinity to water than to mona at the common temperature of the atmosphere, or they are hepars surcharged with mona from having been charred or exposed to a high temperature in contact with charcoal in a close vessel; but more of this hereafter when treating of avo monates, and of spontaneous combustions and inflammations.

CLASS II.

Of Monates which contain Water in their Composition.

29. Of this class there are many genera, as 1st. oils, 2d. alkahol, 3d. æthers, 4th. sugars, 5th. gums, &c.

GENUS I.

OF OILS.

30. Of this genus there are two species, viz. 1st. fixed oils, 2d. volatile or essential oils. Of the first of these there are two sub species, viz. 1st. fat oils, 2d. drying oils. And of each of these species and sub species there are many varieties.

31. Oil in its purest state may be defined a compound gravitating material substance that is fluid, combustible, and insoluble in water. As it is a proximate principle of all vegetables and animals, and had not been detected of mineral origin, it has been supposed to characterise and distinguish the animal and vegetable kingdoms of nature from the mineral: thus it is said, Art. Kingdoms, Macquer's Chemical Dictionary, " that " though substances are sometimes found in the region of the earth ap- " propriate to minerals, which are evidently oily, such as all bitumens, " yet all the observations on natural history prove, that these oily sub- " stances are only accidentally within the earth, and that they proceed " from the vegetable or animal bodies which have been buried in the " earth by some of those great convulsions which have happened from " time

" time to time upon the surface of our globe." This, however, is a mistake; for the oily principle does not derive its origin from or exclusively appertain to any or either of the three kingdoms of nature, though it is to be found in combination in them all. There is in reality but one oily principle in nature, which principle is identically and essentially the same in all the substances into which it enters, whether animal, vegetable, or mineral; and though there are numerous substances which differ considerably from each other that are denominated oils, yet these differences proceed not from different oily principles in them, but only from extraneous matters combined in different proportions and under different modifications with the oily principle whereby its particular properties are in some degree disguised and seemingly altered. The proximate principles or constituent parts—which principles, indeed, in the present state of human knowledge are elements or primary principles since they cannot be decomposed or further resolved by art—of the oily principle or of oil in a pure and uncombined state are mona and water: for mona gas is not only in reality an oil, though it has never been regarded as such, but the only pure and unmixed oil, and the only oily principle in nature as being that to which all the other substances in it which can with propriety be regarded either as oils or as containing oils in their respective compositions exclusively owe those properties which justly entitle them to be regarded as such. This principle is common to all the three kingdoms of nature, and one of its elements, at least the mona, does not properly appertain to any of them, as not being of terrestrial origin but ultimately derived from the sun. The oily principle burns without smoke and without leaving any soot, coal, or ashes.

32. Though the pure oily principle never has been obtained, and probably is unattainable in a condensed liquid state; yet it always becomes more or less so, and more or less fixed, and sometimes even solid on its being chemically combined with greater or smaller quantities of certain substances as sulphurs, particularly carbon, whereby it acquires, *ceteris paribus*, according to the quantity combined with it different appearances and properties, and burns in air with smoke, with a residuous coal, ashes or acid, and the emission of certain gasses. Thus the different kinds of carbonated mona gas, either as spontaneously produced in hot weather

from

from marshes or stagnate water, or as artificially produced by exposing moistened charcoal in an iron retort to a strong heat, or by passing steam through a tube filled with charcoal in a red heat, or by distilling common pit-coal, or by the process by which that kind of carbonated mona gas is obtained to which the Dutch chemists, by whom it was first discovered, gave the name of olefiant gas, &c. are all more dense, fixed, and less fluid, than pure mona gas; and each *ceteris paribus* more or less so, according to the quantity of carbon, &c. with which the oily principle in it is in chemical combination. That kind of it obtained by distilling pitcoal has been successfully substituted for the oil commonly used in lamps to light up rooms; a use to which it was first applied by Mr. Murdoch, of Birmingham; and a mixture of that kind of it discovered by the Dutch chemists, with a little more than an equal quantity of avomuriatic gas soon condenses into a liquid oil, from the combustion, loss, and dissipation of the more elastic and volatile parts of both on their union: a liquid oil is also generated by means of the carbonated mona gas, produced on exposing iron filings in water to the air for a considerable length of the time, when it is found floating on the surface of the water; the mona of the iron and the water furnishing the mona gas, and the charcoal contained in the iron the carbon with which it is chemically combined in the liquid oil. Oil of this kind naturally produced is often to be seen on the surface of stagnant waters of the chalybeate kind, and it seems probable that petroleum, naphtha, and asphaltum, may in certain cases be thus produced, and that they derive their origin from the same causes. When the fixed sulphurs or substances, which are in chemical combination with the oily principle, are in a large proportion relatively to the quantity of that principle, the fixed oils are produced; and when in a still larger wax, tallow, resins, &c. These oils, &c. differ from each other in their properties according *ceteris paribus* to the quantities of the oily principle which enters into their several compositions, the different modes of combination of the other principles with it, and the differences in the substances with which the fixed oils, &c. thus produced may be mixed or contaminated.

33. Those oils are denominated fixed which do not evaporate at the temperature of boiling water. Fixed oils are insoluble in ether, in alkahol, and in water, from the proximate principles of their constituent parts mona

gas and carbon being in a state of chemical combination and perfect neu-
tralization---there being a reciprocal saturation of the mona and water in
the mona gas and of carbo and mona in the carbon---and from their constituent parts being also in chemical combination though perhaps seldom
or never in a saturated or neutralized state. They are of a specific gravity
a little less than that of water, combine with alkalies forming soap, and all
of them on being long exposed to the open air become gradually more and
more viscid, thick, dense, and fixed, acquiring at last a solid state ; and
from some of them retaining their transparency when in a solid state while
others of them on acquiring that state become opaque and assume the appearance and properties of wax, tallow, or butter, they have been distinguished into the two sub species mentioned above of drying oils and of fat
oils.   Of the first kind or drying oils are linseed, nut, poppy, and hemp-
seed oils ; of the second kind or fat oils are those of ben, olives, sweet al-
monds, walnut, &c. The differences between these different kinds, on their
approaching to and acquiring a solid state, seems to proceed from those
of the first kind containing in their several compositions, intimately mixed
with their other principles, a portion of that mucus which is known to
abound in the seeds from which they are respectively expressed.

34. That this gradual inspissation and increase of fixity whereby they
acquire the solid state is a necessary consequence of their being deprived
of their more elastic volatile or rarer parts by that partial decomposition or
slow combustion which under these circumstances takes place in consequence of the reciprocal action between the avona of the air and the mona
of the oils whereby part of that mona is dissipated in fire or in ignite and
the water which it held in combination is liberated and evaporated, is proved
by these changes taking place only when the oils are exposed to the action
of the air and by that diminution in the quantity of the avona gas of the
portion of the air thus acting and acted upon which always results from it.
This process of nature is often purposely artificially accelerated by an increase of temperature in the case of the drying oils for rendering them the
sooner ready for the uses to which they are applied by the painter, the var-
nish maker, and the preparer of printer's ink. On these oils being boiled
for some time in an iron pot they resemble resins in some respects but differ
                                                                              from

from them in others, and in place of being brittle like them retain a considerable degree of ductility.

35. Fixed oils for the same cause, a slow combustion or fermentation and decomposition, become rancid by long keeping, or acquire a greater consistency, a brown colour, an acrid taste, a disagreeable smell, and the property of converting vegetable blues into red. This is a consequence of part of the carbon as well as part of the mona gas of the oil being in this case decomposed by being deprived of part of its mona, and thereby, in conjunction with the water thus liberated which in this case is not evaporated, forming an acid. It is either from the same cause, or from their attracting avona from the atmosphere which acts upon the mona of the metals, that fixed oils act upon mercury and corrode copper; as they do not produce these effects in close vessels. Those acids which either contain no avona, or which contain it in a state of too intimate combination with their other principles to admit of its affecting other substances, if any such there are, act not upon these oils. But the case is very different with those acids which contain it in a state capable of acting on other substances as the nitric and the sulphic; the latter of which by the combustion and dissipation of the mona of their mona gas decomposes them by resolving them into carbon and water, and the former from the great quantity of avona it contains decomposes the drying oils by the dissipation of the mona of the carbon as well as of the mona gas of their composition, and thereby resolves them into water and carbo gas: on being previously mixed with a small portion of the sulphic acid it produces the same effect on fat oils also. That the constituent principles of these oils are mona, carbo, and water, or mona gas the oily principle, and carbon, is analytically proved not only by the above facts, but also by their being resolvable in a great degree by frequently repeated distillations into mona gas and carbon; and by combustion with avona gas into carbo gas and water: and thus is the synthetical proof of the generation and composition of oils given in the beginning of this article completely confirmed by an analytical proof equally satisfactory and conclusive.

36. Those oils which evaporate at or under the temperature of boiling water are denominated volatile oils, and are those which form the second

species

species of this genus. There are a great many varieties of this species. They are to be found in all the different parts of plants constituting what are called their essential oils except in the substance of the cotyledons, the substance in which the vegetable fixed oils are contained; also in certain animal substances, and the more volatile mineral oils as petroleum and naphtha may also with propriety be included in this species. They are of different colours, and of different consistencies, some of them being liquid, and limpid as water, some thick and rancid, others of them solid as the oils of parsley, fennel, &c. and others crystallized and concrete as oil of thyme, camphor, &c. And notwithstanding their great volatility some of them are of a greater specific gravity than water as those of sassafras, cinnamon, and cloves. They are soluble in alkahol, ether, and fixed oils; and imperfectly with water: mixing them with sugar renders their solution in water more permanent and in some degree more perfect. They are all very combustible, are of an acrid taste, and a strong odour in many highly fragrant and agreeable, but in others extremely fœtid and disagreeable as in those proceeding from putrifying substances, especially animal, and in those which are freed from their combinations by means of a great degree of heat, and are denominated empyreumatic oils. They evaporate from paper without leaving any stain upon it as the fixed oils do.

37. Some of these oils owe their great volatility entirely to the mona gas or oily principle in their composition not being in such intimate combination or mixed and loaded with so large a proportion of fixed substances as either to destroy or counteract its elasticity so much as to prevent its producing in them that degree of volatility which entitles them to the name of volatile oils. Others of them owe their great volatility partly to the above cause, and partly to the fire or ignite and to the water not in chemical union with which they are in combination. The elasticity and aerial form of this latter kind is not permanent, as being affectable by mechanic compression and differences of temperature, and the exhalations thus produced are rather to be regarded as oily vapours than as volatile oils, as not being of their own natures really and essentially volatile.

38. These oils owe their solubility in, and combination with, alkahol, ether, and fixed oils, merely to a similarity of nature; for these combinations are not chemical but corpuscular only. They owe their partial and
                                                                              imperfect

imperfect solubility in water partly to those saline substances which enter into their compositions, and partly to a cause to be mentioned hereafter when treating of alkahol. It is also to their mixture with these saline substances that they owe their acrid taste, corrosive quality, and peculiar flavours. The most common of these substances are the several different vegetable acids, as the acetic, benzoic, oxalic, camphoric, &c. in different states; but the phosphoric, succinic, and probably others, are also to be found in some of them, and ammona in others, besides the carbon, &c. in chemical combination with the oily principle which is to be found in them all. Though cora enters in abundance into the composition of some of them, none of them give any indication of their containing either nitric acid or avona, as none of them seem capable of deflagrating in close vessels, having no communication with air or avona gas: and none of them seem to be in chemical combination with those saline substances they contain, since these acids and other saline substances are manifestly not saturated or neutralized by their combinations with them.

39. Volatile oils alter much on being exposed for some time to the open air, partly by the evaporation of their more volatile constituents, and partly by their undergoing a partial decomposition from that very slow combustion which in those cases takes place in consequence of the mutual action between the mona of the oils and the avona of the atmosphere, whereby the oils are deprived of part of their mona, at the same time that they lose by evaporation that water which was in combination with it, becoming thereby gradually more viscid, dense, and deeper coloured, till they are converted into bituminous oils, if petroleum or naphtha, or if vegetable oils into balsams or resins, when portions of certain of the saline substances they contain separate from them in a crystallized state. It is owing in part to this separation of the saline substances from them in these cases, and in part to the decomposition of portions of some of these saline substances by the process, that the volatile oils obtained again from these resins, &c. on separating the more volatile parts of them from the more fixed by distillation, possess not their pristine odours in such perfection as formerly, and are much less in quantity than the oils from which the resins were produced.

40. The fixed alkalis, and the muriatic acid, appear to have but little action on the volatile oils. But nitric acid, when concentrated, acts upon
them

them with so much energy as to produce a combustion with them, whereby they are entirely decomposed; but, when sufficiently diluted with water, it converts them into resins: avo-muriated acid produces the same effect. Sulphic acid first converts them into resins, and then into charcoal or carbon. It produces this last effect of reducing the resins to a coal or a sulphur, not by depriving them of mona, but by abstracting from them that water with which the mona was in combination in the oils and resins: a resinous being an intermediate state between that of a volatile oil and that of a sulphur, as containing less water than the former, and more than the latter. The solid bitumens and bituminous mineral coal consist of a large proportion of carbon or charcoal---produced perhaps by the action of acids on petroleum, naphtha, &c.—combined with a portion of mineral oil in a more or less pure state.

41. All the volatile oils, like the fixed, are resolvable by combustion with avona gas into carbic acid and water only, except those that contain ammona, phosphic acid, &c. which, besides the water and carbic acid, yield also on combustion, cora, phosphic acid, &c. And all the preceding facts and observations serve to prove that the volatile oils differ from the fixed not from any difference in that principle to which each owes its character as an oil, but only to that principle in the volatile oils being combined with certain saline substances which the fixed possess not, and with little or none of that mucilaginous matter which some of the fixed possess, and more particularly by their containing a much smaller proportion of sulphurs or carbon, and perhaps a greater, *ceteris paribus*, of mona in their compositions than the fixed oils.

GENUS II.——*OF ALKAHOL.*

AND

GENUS III.——*OF ETHERS.*

42. As there is only one substance in nature that is essentially oily; so there is likewise only one substance in nature that is essentially spiritous.
This

This substance is a product of that fermentation and decomposition which certain vegetable substances, under certain circumstances, undergo, which on account of this production, have been distinguished from others by the name of the vinous or spiritous fermentation. This spiritous principle, when in the purest state it can be obtained by art, is denominated alkahol, or rectified spirit of wine. It is a liquid, limpid, gravitating substance of the specific gravity of 0.792, at the temperature of 68°,.when that of water is 1.000. Its smell is pleasant and pungent, its taste hot, penetrating, and agreeable, and, when drunk in considerable quantity, it produces intoxication. No degree of natural cold that has been experienced, and no degree of cold that has been artificially produced, has been capable of freezing it : Mr. Walker sunk a spirit thermometer to—91° without there being any appearance of congelation. It boils, and assumes an aerial form at a very low temperature, in a vacuum at 56°, and, therefore, were it not for the pressure of the atmosphere, it would always remain in that form. Though highly inflammable it is always missible with water in every proportion, and what seems very strange, the more inflammable the purer it is, and the more missible with water. On their mixing, the specific gravity is greater than the mean of the two liquids mixed, though the combination is evidently corpuscular only, the other qualities of the compound being always intermediate of those of the ingredients in proportion to their respective quantities, an effect which therefore can only be the consequence of condensation and an emission of fire not in chemical combination. At moderate temperatures it is not affected by the air. It is entirely to their containing this substance in mixture, or in corpuscular combination, that all wines, and other intoxicating liquors, owe their intoxicating, and other spiritous qualities ; these qualities being always *ceteris paribus* in direct proportion to the quantities of alkahol they severally contain.

43. As the processes whereby ethers are obtained from alkahol, and the phenomena attending them, are not only exceedingly curious, interesting, and instructive, in many respects, but also furnish data from which, by rational deduction, the constituent principles both of alkahol, and of ethers, seem to be discoverable, I have been induced to treat of both at the same time, though of different genera, with the view of being thereby enabled to treat of subjects, so obscure and so little understood, as the nature of these

substances

substances confessedly are, in a manner more perspicuous, and more conducive to successful investigation, than I otherwise could have done.

44. Ether is a transparent, colourless liquor, of a pungent taste, and fragrant, penetrating, and peculiar odour; so volatile that when exposed to the open air it quickly assumes the aerial form. It does not, like alkahol, mix with water in all proportions, but ten parts of water are required for the solution of one part of ether. It acts upon all oily and fat substances, but does not act upon gums. When exposed to a cold of—46° it freezes and crystallizes. At moderate temperatures, neither common air nor avona gas produce any effect upon it, though it is extremely combustible.

45. Ether is obtained by the action of certain acids on alkahol; and there are different species of it, differing in properties from each other according to the differences in the properties of the several acids employed for obtaining them. On this account, and from their always retaining, however well rectified, traces of the particular acid by the action of which they were respectively obtained, it is usual to distinguish each particular species by the acid used in its preparation; thus that obtained by means of the sulphic acid, is called sulphuric ether, that by means of the nitric acid, nitric ether, &c.

46. Sulphuric, or, more properly, sulphic ether, is usually prepared by putting a mixture of equal parts of alkahol and sulphic acid into a retort, to which a large receiver, surrounded with ice, or cold water, is luted; heat is then applied, and, as soon as the mixture boils, the ether comes over, and is condensed, and when it amounts to one half of the alkahol employed, the process is stopped. The ether thus obtained requires to be rectified by repeated distillations, in conjunction with dry salt of tartar, &c. There passes over into the receiver, in this process, along with the ether, a portion of the alkahol, of a sweet penetrating taste, a small quantity of oil, and some monated sulphous acid. Scheele obtained acetous acid also, but no carbic acid by this process; and on mixing a certain proportion of manganese with the other ingredients, he obtained acetous acid as before; the air in the receiver was mixed with carbic acid, and there remained in the retort a residuum of sulphated manganese, but he obtained no monated sulphous acid by the process. When the distillation of the mixture of equal parts of alkahol and sulphic acid is continued after the ether is passed

over,

over, the sulphic acid still acting upon the alkahol remaining in the retort, and already altered by the process, converts it into an oil not missible with water in any proportion, which also passes over into the receiver, and which, on being burned, leaves a residuous coal : to this oil the celebrated Macquer gives the name of sweet oil of vitriol. Sulphic acid is said to be capable of converting ether into a peculiar kind of oil called the sweet oil of wine.

47. Nitric ether is prepared merely by mixing together alkahol and nitric acid in the proper proportions, when they act upon each other without the application of heat, so vividly, and often so violently, as to make it necessary to employ precautions for preventing their exploding and breaking the vessels. Thus then an ether is produced without distillation, which, however, like others, requires to be rectified. The taste and the odour of the ether thus obtained is not quite so pleasant as those of sulphic ether, and it is of a greater specific gravity.

48. All attempts to prepare ether from alkahol by means of muriatic acid alone have failed of success; it has been found impossible to obtain it by that means. But on combining muriatic acid with any substance containing avona as black metalite of manganese, sulphic acid, and no doubt nitric acid also, though it seems never to have been tried; or by employing the avo-muriates of certain metals, as of tin, antimony, &c. in place of muriatic acid, and proceeding by distillation, &c. according to the usual methods in processes of this kind, ether is always obtained. Scheele prepared it by distilling a mixture of alkahol, black metalite of manganese, and muriatic acid; but the quantity of ether obtained by this process is often very small, and is sometimes exceeded in quantity by an oil of greater specific gravity than water, which is generated at the same time. Muriatic ether differs from sulphic ether in having an astringent taste, and in exhaling an acrid odour when burning.

49. It is also impossible to prepare ether by the action of fluoric acid alone on alkahol, as Scheele found upon trying. But by pouring a mixture of that acid with alkahol on black metalite of manganese, and distilling, he obtained ether.

50. That an ether can be produced by distilling a mixture of acetic acid and alkahol, was first discovered by the Count de Lauraguais; and others,

it is said, have since prepared it by the same process he employed, though owing to some unknown cause, Scheele, the most expert and accurate perhaps of all chemists, did not succeed in obtaining it by the same means. He discovered, however, that, by mixing acetic acid with a small proportion of any of the mineral acids, even of muriatic or fluoric, either of which alone are incapable of generating ether from alkahol, and then adding alkahol and distilling, ether is obtained, and in much larger proportion, than by any other means. This ether, even after being rectified, has an odour of acetic acid.

51. Scheele also discovered, that, by distilling one part of benzoic acid with three parts of alkahol and one half part of muriatic acid, an ether is obtained.

52. Such are the various processes by means of which the different ethers have been obtained, and such the phenomena attending them. Ether, of whatever kind, or in whatever manner prepared, is, like alkahol, converted into carbic gas and water, on combustion with avona gas; and, if passed through a red hot porcelaine tube, it would probably yield the same products that alkahol does when treated in that manner, viz. water, carbonated mona gas, carbic gas, carbon, and a very small portion of oil.

53. Many different opinions have been entertained respecting the natures of alkahol, and of ether. According to Stahl, alkahol is a very light oil united to a quantity of water by means of an acid; or a combination of oil, acid, and water. To Junker, it is phlogiston combined with water by means of an acid. While, according to Cartheuser, it is composed of pure phlogiston and water only. The present prevailing hypothesis is, that it contains no water in its composition, and consists of oxygen, carbon, and hydrogen, only; the constituents, it is supposed, of that water, found on its decomposition having existed in it before its combustion, but not the water itself. According to Macquer, ether is alkahol deprived of all its water by the acid employed in its preparation, and combined with a small portion of that acid. Scheele concludes his Essay on Ether, published in 1782, with observing, that he is unwilling to attempt an explanation of the generation of ether from his experiments on it; for though some of them seem to indicate that a substance capable of extracting phlogiston from alkahol is always required, yet others of them prove that this is not the case, as the

acetic

acetic and benzoic acids, by means of which ethers may be generated, have as little affinity for, and are as incapable of, attracting phlogiston from alkahol, as muriatic and fluoric acids, by means of which alone ether cannot be generated: and, though it should be admitted that these acids also attract phlogiston from alkahol, and that it is by depriving alkahol of part of its phlogiston that ethers are generated, yet the separation of ether from the water, with which it was so intimately united in the alkahol, cannot be accounted for on that principle; or that ether should be converted into alkahol, and thereby rendered missible with water, in any proportion, by being combined with phlogiston, and that alkahol should be converted into ether, and be rendered in a great degree immissible with water, by being deprived of phlogiston, that principle which renders all the substances with which it combines less missible with water, and certain liquids, as acids, altogether immissible, in place of more missible with water, on its combining with them, and converting them into sulphurs; and, he adds, it cannot be accounted for thus unless it can be supposed that it is to matter of heat and not to phlogiston, that the alkahol owes its solubility in water, and that it is deprived of this matter of heat on being converted into ether. Pelletier first suggested that theory, which has been most generally adopted, of ether being a combination of alkahol with oxygen. According to those celebrated chemists, Fourcroy and Vauquelin, ether differs from alkahol only in containing a greater proportion of hydrogen and oxygen, and a smaller of carbon; while Dabit is of opinion that ether contains a smaller proportion of hydrogen and a greater proportion of oxygen and carbon than alkahol.

53. It is manifest, from the products of the combustions and decompositions of alkahol and of ethers being of the same kinds or substances, that the constituent parts are the same; and, consequently, that they can differ from each other only by the differences in the modifications and in the proportions of these parts to each other, in each respectively. According to the principles developed in this Essay, these parts, exclusive of any extraneous substances the alkahol or ether may contain, are water, carbon, and mona; and, according to the same principles as applied to the preceding processes for the generation of ether from alkahol, by means of mineral acids, or of these in combination with other substances, the effects produced by these processes must result principally, if not entirely, from that mutual

action

action in consequence of their mutual affinity which necessarily takes place between the avona of the acid, or acid compound, and the mona of the alkahol, whereby they gradually unite together, forming fire, and in that state are dissipated, producing by that means that heat, ebullition, &c. so conspicuous at the commencement of the process, for obtaining sulphic ether, and which is so violent in that for preparing nitric ether, from the very large proportion of avona contained in nitric acid, as to terminate in inflammation, explosion, and a complete decomposition of the alkahol into water and carbic gas, by being thus deprived of the whole, or nearly the whole, of its mona, if the proper precautions have not been taken for preventing the combustion thus produced from proceeding to such extremity.

54. But if this is the case, or if the action whereby the different effects progressively produced from the commencement of the processes is owing principally or entirely to a gradual dissipation of the mona and avona of the different substances subjected to it, it follows as necessary consequences, that the conversion of alkahol into ether must be owing to its being deprived of part of its mona, its conversion into oil to its being deprived of a still larger proportion of it—so that ether likewise must become oil, on its being deprived of a portion of its mona—and that oil, by being deprived of the remaining mona, or the far greater part of it, must be decomposed in the manner already described in treating of oils. And that this actually is the case is proved both by the impossibility of converting alkahol into ether by means of a mineral acid, either containing no avona in its composition, or containing it in a state of too intimate combination with its other principles to admit of its acting on other substances, as the muriatic and fluic acids, and by these acids being rendered capable of acting on alkahol, and of acting on it in such a manner as to convert it into ether, oil, &c. when mixed with any substance containing avona in the proper state for combining with them.

55. From the preceding facts it also necessarily follows that the proximate principles or constituent parts of ether must be a vegetable volatile oil surcharged or supersaturated in a certain degree with mona, and that those of alkahol must be ether combined with a still greater surcharge of mona; or that a vegetable volatile oil combined with a certain surcharge of mona, and not of mona gas, forms ether; and with a still greater proportion of it with a small addition perhaps of water and carbon alkahol. So that
the

the proximate principles of both are the same, and the only difference between them besides that in their surcharges of mona is that the oil in the ether contains a smaller proportion of gravitating matter or of water and carbon than in alkahol, as appears from the differences in their specific gravities, and hence that the oil in the ether approximates more to the nature of a gas. And from this analysis and discovery of the natures of these substances the very important fact, hitherto unknown, that certain substances which are insoluble in water from being saturated with mona become soluble in water in all proportions on receiving a considerable addition or surcharge of it, is justly deducible; for hence it is that ether is more soluble in it than oil, and that alkahol is soluble in it all proportions, and that without being decomposed from the very intimate union between its oil and its mona. A fact which accounts for the hitherto inexplicable phenomena of certain substances which are highly combustible being soluble in water, and for alkahol not being congelible into ice; and it also shews that though the solubility in water of any substance is diminished by combination with mona in quantities not sufficient to saturate it and in proportion to these quantities, and is completely destroyed by perfect saturation with it, yet that this missibility is restored to it again on its being supersaturated or receiving a surcharge of it. It is long since I drew this conclusion with respect to the cause of the different degrees of solubility of these substances in water. It occurred to me first on reading Scheele's very excellent Essay on Ether not long after the publication of the English translation of it; and when the very important discoveries of Messrs. Nicholson and Carlisle and of Dr. Wolaston were publicly announced---not of the decomposition of water indeed---but of the formation of gasses by the combinations of the different pyrogens with water, whether the pyrogens are obtained by what are called galvanical or by electrical means, I could entertain no doubt of its truth, the great affinity of mona to water being incontestibly proved by these discoveries.

It seems probable that certain of the essences, spiritus rectors, and volatile oils, and also sulphurated mona gas, may in part owe their partial and imperfect solubility in water to a surcharge of mona; and this was the cause of solubility alluded to, which it was said would be mentioned hereafter, when treating of volatile oils. What are called spiritus rectors, and

essences,

essences, are only mixtures of the more soluble parts of volatile oils and of ethers in waters.

56. The ethers prepared by the action of vegetable acids on alkahol---in as far as they are ethers, for they approximate much in their natures to those of the acids employed for their preparation---are the result of chemical affinities and combinations very different from those by which the ethers obtained by means of the mineral acids are produced, and indeed are in some respects the very reverse of these. For it is not by the destruction or dissipation of any portion of the surcharge of mona in the alkahol that these acids act in generating ether, nor is that effect produced in any degree in any of the processes for obtaining ether by their agency, except in that by frequently repeated distillations in consequence of the action in that case of the avona of the air on the mona of the alkahol, but on the contrary by their forming a chemical union in whole or in part not only with the surcharge of mona but also with the other principles of the alkahol composing a substance which perhaps may with as much propriety be regarded as a combination of a volatile oil, and perhaps a small portion of alkahol but little altered, with a vegetable acid, not in a state of perfect saturation and chemical union, than an ether; and hence the reason of the products being so very much more abundant in these processes than they are in the other processes for obtaining ethers. When the vegetable acids employed are mixed with a small proportion of mineral acid not containing avona, as of muriatic, or fluic acids, the operation and effect is accelerated without altering the nature of the product which is still the same with that mentioned above; but when they are combined with substances containing avona, a sulphic acid, especially in any considerable proportion, the nature of the product is then much altered and what is truly etherial in it is the result of other agency than that of the vegetable acids employed.

57. Mr. Thenard obtained acetic ether by mixing together equal parts of alkahol and of acetic acid and by distilling the mixtures which he cohobated twelve times; and he gives the following characters of the acetic ether thus prepared which accord well with what they ought to be agreeable to the theory of the formation of acetic ether given above, viz. " This ether has an agreeable smell of ether and of acetic acid, yet it
                                                                " reddens

" reddens neither the infusion nor the paper of litmus: and it has a
" peculiar taste, not very different from that of alkahol. Neither its spe-
" cific gravity nor degree of elasticity was accurately ascertained: but it is
" lighter than water, and swims on it, and heavier than alkahol. Water
" appears to dissolve much more than it does of sulphuric ether. It burns
" with a yellowish white flame, and produces an acid, which is probably
" the acetic. It does not appear to undergo any alteration by keeping;
" at least it did not in the course of six months."*

58. The substance first obtained by Mr. Gehlen, and afterwards without
his having any knowledge of the previous preparation of it by Gehlen, by
Mr. Thenard by subjecting equal parts of muriatic acid and alkahol to distillation in an appropriate apparatus with a moderate equal heat, and
which appeared to them to be a true ether,† is in reality not an ether but
a dulcified acid; as is proved not only by its saccharine taste, but also by
the very large proportion of acid it contains, the whole or nearly the whole
of the muriatic acid employed for its formation being obtainable again in
its pristine state on the combustion of that substance with which it was
united in its dulcified state.

GENUS IV.

OF SUGAR.

59. Sugar differs essentially in its chemical constitution from oil, from
ether, and from alkahol. Alkahol has been proved to be a light oil highly
surcharged with mona and owing its solubility in water in all proportions to
this surcharge. Ether to be an oil still lighter as containing a smaller proportion of carbon, and which is less surcharged with mona and therefore
less missible with water. And oil to be an intimate combination of two
compound substances together, mona gas and carbon, in each of which
compounds the constituent principles are in chemical combination completely saturated and neutralized whence each compound thus formed possesses qualities essentially different from those of its constituents, and among

---

* Nicholson's Journal, No. 78.
† Annales de Chimie, vol. LXI. Journal de Physique, vol. LXIV.

others

others that of being altogether insoluble in water---the qualities of mona gas differing essentially from those of its constituents water and monà and the qualities of carbon from those of its constituents carbo and mona---and the proximate principles being insoluble in water the compound corpuscularly formed of them, or oil, is necessarily the same: any degree of solubility in water which any volatile oils may possess being owing either to their being in some degree surcharged with mona or to their holding in solution but not in chemical combination some saline substance.

60. That sugar is neither an oil nor an ether is proved by its solubility in water nearly in all proportions, and that it is not a particular species of alkahol is proved by its not owing this solubility in water to a surcharge of mona, there being no proof or probability of its containing such a surcharge, and to its possessing none of the other generic characters of alkahol: nor is it to its holding in solution any acid not in a state of chemical combination that it owes this solubility in water, since it gives no indications of its possessing any such.

61. Acid radicals seem incapable of existing in an uncombined state; at least none are known in such a state unless phosphic acid in a dry state is such which seems not probable. They are always in combination with one, two, or more substances, and these combinations are sometimes chemical, sometimes corpuscular only, and sometimes in part chemical and in part corpuscular. In forming sulphurs or metals they combine with one substance only mona, and the combination is chemical. In forming the different acids they also combine in general with one substance only water, and the combination is only corpuscular: in some cases, however, of this kind they also combine corpuscularly with avona gas, in others with mona gas, in others with both avona gas and mona gas. And in forming neutral salts, &c. the acids, or what is the same thing, the acid radicals, in union with water, combine with one or more substances, and these combinations are often chemical, while that between the acid radical and the water of composition of the acid is corpuscular only ; and it is to this latter circum-stance that the solubility and corpuscular combination not only of the acid itself but also of the compounds formed by its combinations with other substances is owing: a solubility in all proportions when the acid which thus enters into chemical combination is pure; and thus in the composi-

tion

tion of the complicated substances thus generated the combination is in part chemical and in part corpuscular.

62. The particular natures, qualities, and distinguishing characters of compound substances, generated of the same constituent principles, are not less influenced by and dependent upon the different modes of combination of these substances with each other than on their relative proportions; thus an intimate combination of mona gas with carbon forms oil, a substance insoluble in water from both the water and the carbo or acid radical of its proximate principles having severally been in a state of complete chemical combination, saturation, and neutralization, with mona, and thereby insoluble in water previous to their combining together forming oil: but when the mode of combination of the same constituents, acid radical, water, and mona, is different, the combination of the acid radical with water not being chemical but corpuscular, forming an acid, while on the contrary the combination of the acid thus formed with mona is not corpuscular but chemical, the product is neither oil, alkahol, nor ether, but sugar, a substance soluble nearly in all proportions in water, in oil, and in acetic acid; and which serves as an intermedium for combining oils with water, as being corpuscularly combinable with each of these substances; for, in this case of a ternary or triple chemical compound, though the acid is saturated and neutralized with mona, yet the component principles of which the acid is formed, the radical and the water, are not severally so much saturated with it as to be converted into carbon and mona gas, substances insoluble in water, when of consequence the compound formed by their union would also necessarily be an insoluble substance or an oil, as is clearly proved by no such effect taking place, but on the contrary the production of a substance soluble in water in all proportions instead of an insoluble, or oil, being the constant consequence of the chemical combination of the acid with mona in cases of this kind.

63. That sugar contains an acid in its composition is proved not only by an acid being obtainable from it on its decomposition by fermentation, distillation, &c. but also by the processes required for obtaining it from the juice of the sugar-cane and for refining it, one of the principal intentions of these processes being to separate the sugar or dulcified acid contained in the juice from that part of the acid contained in it which is yet—

probably from the juice not having obtained full maturity and ripeness—in an unsaturated and unsaccharine state; a separation which is effected in these processes by mixing the juice with a portion of lime, with which this acid combines, forming a salt, which runs off along with other impurities on the graining of the sugar. That this acid is not only a vegetable acid, but also that it is the acetic, is proved by sugar being ultimately decomposible into carbo, mona, and water, the constituent principles of vegetable acids, and by fermentation, &c. into vinegar. That mona forms a constituent principle of sugar is proved by its combustibility; and that water forms another is proved by its being always obtained on decomposing it. That sugar owes its solubility in water partly to the water of its composition, and partly to the acid radical of its composition not being saturated and neutralized with mona forming a sulphur or coal, is proved, first, by its becoming altogether insoluble in water on depriving it of the whole of the water of its composition, and of part of its acid radical in the form of carbic gas, and saturating the remaining portion of acid radical with mona by charring the sugar either by means of heat or of sulphic acid, and thereby converting it into charcoal or carbon, substances insoluble in water; and, secondly, by its missibility with water not being chemical but corpuscular only, and therefore a consequence either of mere similarity of natures, or of the corpuscular affinity of some of its constituent parts to water as of the acid radical of the compound, from its not being so much impaired by its chemical combination with the other constituent parts of it as to deprive it of that affinity.

64. Since the number of different monates containing water in their composition is indefinite, as comprehending all substances, however complicate in composition, of the mineral, vegetable, and animal kingdoms of nature into which the oily principle enters as a component part or ingredient, it would be in vain to attempt an investigation of the chemical qualities of the whole of them; and since those already treated of are those of the most simple kinds, and those the knowledge of the real natures of which is of the most importance towards the attainment of a rational and just system of chemical science, I shall treat only of one genus more of this class; a substance which, though combustible, has always, and perhaps not improperly, been regarded as a salt.

GENUS

GENUS V.

OF *AMMONA*.

65. AMMONA is an alkaline substance which, when in its greatest purity, is always in a gaseous or a vapourous state, or rather perhaps in a state compounded of both of these, as the part of it essentially gaseous and alkaline seems to be in intimate corpuscular combination with a large proportion of steam or aqueous vapour, from its being condensible to liquidity by mechanical compression, and by a cold of — 45°; by a cold of — 46° it crystallizes or concretes into a solid, and at — 68° it loses its smell and assumes the form of a jelly. It is of less specific gravity than air. To breathe it proves fatal to animal life, and it extinguishes combustion in combustibles, from being itself a combustible as is proved by its deflagrating with nitre, and by that combustion and decomposition in it which takes place on passing a mixture of it with avona gas through a red-hot porcelaine tube. Ammona gas is soluble in water, even when combined with carbic gas, which absorbs it with rapidity, and condenses more than a third of its weight when not so combined, whereby heat is evolved and the specific gravity of the water diminished; it also speedily melts ice brought into contact with it. On passing it through red-hot charcoal prussic acid is produced.

66. Dr. Black first discovered the difference between ammona and ammona combined with carbic gas, and Dr. Priestley a method of obtaining it in a state of purity. Dr. Scheele first discovered that ammona is decomposed by means of the metalites of manganese, arsenic, or gold; the ammona disappearing at the same time that the metalites are reduced, and cora gas (by him called foul air) produced; from which he concluded that it consisted in a combination of cora with phlogiston. And Dr. Priestley first discovered that when heat was applied to the red metalites of mercury or of lead confined in ammona gas, the ammona gas vanished, water was evolved, the metalites reduced, and cora gas generated; and also that by taking the electric spark in ammona gas its bulk is gradually augmented to thrice its original volume, and a quantity of inflammable gas is pro-

I 2

duced.

duced. On the application of the Lavoisierian theory to these discoveries of Priestley and Scheele, it was concluded that the constituent principles of ammona are azot and hydrogen; meaning no doubt by these azotic and hydrogen gasses, or the phlogisticated and inflammable airs of Dr. Priestley. And that both these airs actually enter into its composition, and form the principal part, if not the whole of it, is a fact that has been fully proved, both analytically and synthetically, by those eminent chemists Mr. Berthollet, Mr. Davy, and Dr. Austin: analytically, 1st, by converting ammona gas into cora gas and mona gas by taking the electric spark in it; 2dly, by converting a mixture of it with avona gas either into water and cora gas, by passing the mixture through a red-hot porcelaine tube, from the avona of the avona gas combining chemically with the mona of the mona gas forming fire, which is dissipated, and the different portions of water forming the gravitating bases of these gasses combining together in a liquid state, while the cora gas of the ammona remains; or into nitric acid and water when the proportion of avona gas in the mixture is sufficiently great to decompose the cora gas also: and, 3dly, by mixing ammona gas with avo-muriatic acid, when a double decomposition takes place, of which the products are fire or ignite, water, cora gas, and common muriatic acid. And synthetically in generating ammona gas by digesting for a minute or two tin moistened with nitrous acid, and then adding to it a little lixa or lime; the mona of the metal combining with the water and the cora gas of the acid forming it. It had been generated by Dr. Priestley and by Mr. Kirwan before its composition was known. Dr. Austin also succeeded in generating it by different methods, and particularly by introducing into a glass tube filled with mercury a little cora gas and some iron filings moistened with water; the quantity, however, produced in this case was extremely small, for the ammona thus generated was capable only of changing the blue colour of a small piece of paper tinged with radish, suspended in the jar, to a green colour, in two or three days. If neither the cora gas nor the water with which the filings were moistened were mixed with or contained air or avona gas, this experiment would indicate that water alone was capable at certain temperatures of decomposing iron, either by combining with its component parts—the metallic radical and mona—forming the black metalite of iron and mona gas, from the greater affinity of these constituents of iron at that temperature

ture with water than with each other, or from the greater affinity of that radical under the then circumstances to water than to mona, whereby the mona of the metal is disengaged from it, and may combine either with a portion of the water forming mona gas, or with any other substance that may be present in preference to it with which it has more affinity, as with cora gas forming ammona.

67. But though it is fully established by these experiments that both cora gas and mona gas enter into the composition of ammona, yet there are facts which indicate that they are not the only constituent principles of it, and that it is not formed merely by their union. For if formed by a combination of these two gasses only, the compound generated would necessarily be permanently elastic, and not condensible into liquidity by cold or mechanical compression as is the case with ammona gas, so that vapour or steam must also necessarily enter into its composition; besides, Dr. Austin found it impossible for him, by any means he could devise, to combine these two gasses together in such a manner as to form ammona. Nor is there any reason to suppose that two such gasses, each of which is insoluble in water, if combined, would be soluble in water, or capable of uniting with steam. Dr. Austin was of opinion that carbo also enters into its composition; but though that should be the case, it could not account for the solubility of the compound thus formed in water.

68. It appears to me that cora gas, which consists of a combination of mona gas with cora, is converted into ammona gas, or that part of it at least which is essentially gaseous, rather by combining chemically with a surcharge of mona than either with steam or with an additional quantity of mona gas, and that it is to this circumstance that it owes its solubility in water; and, consequently, that ammona in its pure state is cora gas super-saturated with mona, and when less pure in corpuscular combination with a portion of steam. And that this is actually the case is proved not only by the fact of its almost indefinite solubility in water, a fact otherwise inexplicable, but also by the compounds possessing a much greater degree of chemical energy and activity than is usually possessed by substances in which the constituent principles are in a state of mutual saturation and neutralization. This is likewise proved by the fact of ammona gas being converted into a mixture of cora gas with mona gas by passing the electric

spark

spark through it, at the same time that its bulk is augmented to three times its pristine volume; since it is manifest from this, first, that it did not consist of these gasses before the operation, though it contained the constituents of them; and, secondly, that the mona gas generated by the process could not have been generated by it if the ammona subjected to it had not contained in its composition an excess of the constituents of mona gas, mona, and water, above what was necessary for the composition of the cora gas which is essential to it, and which existed in it previous to the process. Nor is it possible on any other principle to account rationally and justly for the result of this process, or to give a satisfactory explanation of this curious and unexpected fact of ammona gas being thus converted into these gasses, and of these gasses being of thrice the volume of the gas operated upon. The surcharge of mona in ammona is in too intimate a chemical combination with the cora gas of the ammona to be separable from it by means of water, or many other substances having great affinity to ammona, but at a very high degree of temperature.

CHAP. VIII.

OF AVO-MONATES.

1. AVO-MONATES are substances which owe their combustibility, as the term employed to characterize and distinguish them from others indicates, to each possessing both of the pyrogens or all the elements of combustion within itself, and these not in chemical combination with each other in a pure disengaged state, but both in chemical combination with gravitating matter of the same or of different kinds; and hence all avo-monates are necessarily compound substances.

2. Nature seems to be very sparing in her productions of these; and never, except in electrical cases, as on the meeting of two clouds differently electrified, or in fiery meteors which are destroyed almost instantly as formed by combustion and explosion, in any considerable quantity but when the

elements

elements of combustion in them are in such intimate chemical combination with gravitating incombustible matter as not to be capable of combining chemically together, and thereby of producing combustion, but at very high degrees of temperature, and even at these but feebly only; as is the case with that immense mass of air which forms the atmosphere of the globe we inhabit, any given quantity of which is at a high temperature combustible and diminished by combustion, as by taking the electric spark in it, though for the reasons given above that combustion is but feeble; and were it not for this wise ordination of the Author of nature, a general conflagration and destruction of all things on the surface of this earth would be the infallible consequence when the degree of temperature happened by any means to be raised very little above that by which the atmosphere was generated.

3. This, however, is very far from being the case with those avo-monates which are formed by art for the purpose of deflagration and explosion; these being formed by combining together artificially those gravitating substances which contain avona in the greatest abundance and but loosely attached to the gravitating matter, as nitre, nitric acid, avo-muriatic acid, &c. with other gravitating substances in which mona abounds and adheres but weakly to the gravitating base, as carbon, sulphur, &c. It is by means of such combinations of monates with avonates that all the deflagrating and exploding powders, as common gunpowder, fulminating powder, fulminating gold, fulminating silver, fulminating mercury, &c. are formed; and it is entirely to each containing both the elements of combustion in itself, but loosely adhering to and easily disengaged from its gravitating fixed matter, that it owes its power of deflagrating and exploding on a certain augmentation of its temperature by whatever means produced, as whether by the immediate application of fire or of a concentrated acid to it, or by friction, pressure, hammering, &c.

4. As the methods of preparing these powders, &c. are well known, I shall not pursue this subject any further. Those explosions which proceed from the generation or disengagement of gasses or of vapour, or the conversion of water into steam, sometimes extremely violent, are not attended with combustion and deflagration, and therefore come not to be included in this Chapter.

CHAP.

CHAP. IX.

OF FERMENTATION.

1. FERMENTATION, in its most limited and proper signification, is that process of nature whereby certain substances are spontaneously and gradually decomposed and converted into other substances differing in their qualities from those of the substances thus decomposed. Chemists, however, often employ this term in a more comprehensive sense, as including under it not only the kinds of fermentations mentioned above, but also all the dissolutions of substances in solvents, natural or artificial, or at least all of them which are attended with any evolution or disengagement of gas or vapour, as those of carbated lime or lixa, in any acid, &c. It is in the first only of these meanings that it is treated of in this Chapter.

2. All substances---vegetable, animal, or mineral---that are combustible are capable of and liable to fermentation; for fermentation is in reality a combustion, though often acting but slowly and feebly. This is a fact that is proved by no substance being capable of fermentation but such as either contain both the elements of combustion in itself, or as contain one of these elements and is in contact with some other substance which contains the others: and it is only in the case of such contact or mixture, or the presence of some substance containing the other element, that a substance possessing one of the elements only is capable of fermentation. Hence it is that no substance---vegetable, animal, or mineral---which contains mona only, however much disposed to ferment under the requisite circumstances, will ferment if perfectly excluded from air or the presence of every substance possessed of avona in the proper state for commencing and promoting combustion. This is also proved by that portion of air which comes into action in these cases being deprived of the whole or nearly the whole of its avona gas by the process, as well as by the sensible heat, evolution, &c. accompanying it.

3. When the mona of any gravitating substance is disengaged from it by means of the mutual attraction between it and the avona of any other

gravitating

gravitating substance, whereby the avona of that substance is also disengaged from it, these elements of combustion thus disengaged from their respective gravitating bases do not always in these cases combine together forming fire or ignite, but often either in whole or in part combine severally with that conducting substance by whose agency they were brought into contact and mutual action, from having more affinity to it under the then circumstances than to each other, as with water forming mona gas and avona gas when water is that conducting substance, &c. and at other times they combine with other substances to which they severally have more affinity than to the conducting substances with which in these cases they combine no further than as a means of conducting them to those other substances with which they have greater affinity. And these are the causes whereby gasses are generated and evolved during fermentations, as the chemical combinations of mona with avona, in as far as they take place, are the cause of that heat, &c. or of that discharge of fire and of vapour with which they are generally attended.

4. The process of fermentation, or that spontaneous and gradual decomposition which certain substances undergo, seems to be the very reverse of that whereby these substances were generated, and they seem to be resolved by it into their several proximate component principles. In these cases, as in others of resolution and composition, whereby any substance is converted into others, it is absolutely necessary towards the production of that effect, that the affinities subsisting between the proximate principles of the substances among themselves, should be weakened in as far as to allow them to mix and combine corpuscularly and chemically with those of other substances to which, under these circumstances, they have more affinity than with each other; and hence the necessity of moistening or diffusing in water any dry substance which it is proposed should undergo a fermenting process, and, at the same time, and with the same intention of attenuating subtilizing and separating the particles from each other by the expansion thus produced and thereby of weakening the affinities between its proximate principles, of raising the temperature at least above that of the freezing point. From these principles and methods of promoting fermentation, the proper methods for preventing the fermentations or spontaneous dissolutions and corruptions of such substances as it is

wished to preserve, are easily deducible; As first, if the substance is a monate, by depriving it of all communication with air or other avonates; and, reciprocally, if an avonate, with all communication with monates; secondly, by freezing the substances wished to be preserved, and retaining them in a frozen state, or at a very low temperature; thirdly, by rendering them dry, or depriving them of too much of their moisture to admit of their fermenting and then retaining them in that state; and, fourthly, by mixing them with incombustible, and therefore unfermentable substances, or with substances of which the proximate principles are in a state of too intimate combination with each other to admit of decomposition except at a very high temperature, &c.

5. In the fermentation of many vegetable substances five stages, or different kinds of it, are evidently conspicuous, viz. 1st. The *saccharine*; 2d. the *vinous*; 3d. the *acetous*; 4th. the *putrefactive*; and 5th. the *saline*. But all of these kinds are not common to all of them; for some vegetable substances being naturally in a saccharine state, the only fermentations they undergo are the vinous, acetous, putrefactive, and saline; others again proceed at first to the acetous, which is succeeded by the putrid and saline, while others of them, as well as most animal substances, and those mineral substances which are liable to spontaneous and gradual corrosion, or corruption, from the action of the air on them, are susceptible of the putrid and saline fermentations only. Of each of these different kinds I shall treat separately and successively in the above order.

6. *Of the Saccharine Fermentation.*—That process which is known by the name of malting, affords a very good specimen of the saccharine fermentation. It consists in first steeping some farinaceous grain, as barley for instance, at least for 40 hours in water, and then spreading it on a malt floor, to the depth of about 16 inches, where it is allowed to remain about 26 hours, when it is turned with wooden shovels twice a day, or oftener, and is gradually diminished in depth, till at last it does not exceed a few inches. When placed on the malt floor, its temperature, at first the same with that of the external air, increases slowly, and in about 10 hours is generally about 10° hotter than the surrounding atmosphere, and then the grain, which had become dry on the surface, becomes moist again, exhaling an agreeable odour, when the grain is frequently turned, with the

intention

intention of preventing the temperature from exceeding that of 60°; during the whole of this process carbic acid is evolved, at first slowly and in small quantity, but afterwards more rapidly and copiously. At the period when the grain becomes moist again vegetation in it commences, and when the roots and part of the rudiments of the future stem are formed, the qualities of the farinaceous part of the grain have undergone a considerable change, part of it having been converted into roots, &c. and the remainder become much more soluble in water, of a white colour, a loose texture, and a saccharine taste; and the grain has lost by the process about a fifth of its weight. The production of this change being the sole object of the malting, the process is stopped when it is attained by drying the malt on a kiln.

7. Perhaps the causes and revolts of this seemingly very involved and intricate chemical process of nature may be thus rationally accounted for. Since the farinaceous matter of grain, while in an unripe state, or at least before its acquiring a solid consistency, is an emulsion, of the nature of milk or chyle; and since emulsions of nearly similar natures can be artificially formed by combining fixed oils with gum and water, it is presumeable that that matter in its solid state consists principally of fixed oil and gum, in a state of intimate combination, so intimate indeed as not to admit of their perfect separation from each other in their respective proper forms of oil and gum by infusion or maceration in water, and as to render the farinaceous matter, or the compound they form, in a great degree insoluble in water, and hence it is that when wheat flour is separated into two different substances by being kneaded under a jet of water, these substances are not fixed oil and gum, but those known by the names of starch, and of gluten, the first of which is by much the most abundant. Gum is a substance which approximates in its nature much to that of sugar, as being like it soluble in water, and from the same cause its containing an acid radical, of the vegetable kind, corpuscularly combined with water, at the same time that both it and this water are in chemical combination with mona, or, in other words, as containing an acid, and not an acid radical, in chemical combination with mona, and that acid of the vegetable kind; and being like it, an intermedium whereby oils may be combined with water: but it differs from sugar in not possessing a saccharine taste, in being insoluble in alkahol, and in containing in its com-

position,

position, besides all the constituents of sugar, cora, lime, iron, and phosphic acid, and sometimes perhaps a little sulphur; and these in greater or
smaller proportions according to the nature of the particular gum, there
being by this means several different species of gums. The starch obtained by the above process from the farina of grain would seem from its
qualities to be a combination of the greatest proportion of the fixed oil
of the farina with the greatest proportion of the monated acid, or saccharine principle of its gum; and the gluten obtained from it by the same
process would seem from its qualities to be a combination of a small part
of the fixed oil of the farina with the whole of the cora, iron, lime, and
phosphic acid, and probably a small part also of the monated acid, of its
gum: and that this is actually the case is proved by the analysis both of
starch and of glutine, for the decomposition of starch, whether by means
of fire or of acid, proves that neither the cora, iron, lime, nor phosphic
acid, of the gum, enter into its composition, none of them being to be
found in it; while the decomposition of gluten affords decisive proof of
their entering into its composition, since they are all to be found in it.
Gluten, from containing these substances in its composition, approximates much to the nature of animal substances, and like mixtures of
animal and vegetable substances, is exceedingly apt to run into the
acetous and putrefactive fermentations. The very small quantity of mucilaginous and saccharine matters which are obtained at the same time
with the starch and gum from the farina by the above process, seem to
consist of part of the gum not in chemical combination with the other
constituents, and in a very small portion of oil or of gum converted into
sugar.

8. These things being premised, little doubt it is imagined can be entertained, first, of great part of the farinaceous matter of the grain in
the above process having been converted into starch and gluten during
the time the grain continued in the steep-water. Secondly, of much of
the mona and the moisture of these substances having been carried off and
dissipated while the grain remained on the malt floor, from the mutual
action and chemical combination, or slow combustion or fermentation which
then took place between the avona of the air and the mona of the grain,
whereby that fire or heat was generated which evaporated the moisture,

and

and proved so conducive to the vegetation which then took place. Thirdly, that the gluten is the substance principally employed in this vegetation, or in the production of the rootlets, &c. since very little of the gluten or of its characteristic constituents are in this case to be found in the residuary product the saccharine matter. And, fourthly, that by the farina being thus freed from the greatest part of its gluten, and of as much of the mona of its carbon as to convert it into one or more of the vegetable acids, and by the chemical combination and neutralization of the acid or acids thus generated with the oily principle, or mona gas of the fixed oil of the farina, and the evaporation of the superfluous moisture, the impure sugar or white crumbly saccharine matter, the object of the process, is produced. The carbic gas, and that vapour having the smell of apples, which is evolved along with the steam during the fermenting of the grain, is owing to the decomposition of the carbon, and the volatilizing of part of the acids thence produced in combination with part of the steam or vapour and part of the mona gas of the oil disengaged from the other principles of the fermenting mass, from a weakened affinity by the increase of temperature. Though it may perhaps seem highly improbable, if not impossible, for the avona of the air to act upon the mona of the carbon, without acting at the same time on the mona of the mona gas, or oily principle of the fixed oil of the farina, or that it should act on the mona of the former in preference to that of the latter, as assumed in the above theory, yet this peculiar mode of operation which the products of the process prove to have actually taken place, however strange and improbable it may appear, admits of a rational and satisfactory explanation; for this effect is a necessary consequence of there being little or no affinity between the gravitating bases of the avona gas of the air, and of the mona gas of the oil, from each being only different portions of the same substance, water, at the same time that there is a great affinity between the gravitating bases of the carbon of the oil, and of the avona gas of the air—carbonic-radical and water.—And thus the above process, by which sugar is generated, proves, synthetically, what in Chapter VII. was proved analytically, that sugar is a neutralized chemical combination of vegetable acids with mona.

9: *Of*

9. *Of the Vinous Fermentation.*—The process of brewing whereby that intoxicating liquor called beer or ale, from which alkahol is procurable by distillation, is produced affords one specimen of vinous fermentation. It consists in infusing the malt or impure sugar obtained by the preceding process, after having been ground in a mill, in somewhat more than its own bulk of water at a temperature between 160° and 180° for two or three hours in a covered vessel, and then drawing off the liquid now called wort by a cock at the bottom of the vessel into another vessel in which it is boiled for some time for the purpose of rendering the mixture the more intimate and of the proper consistency, after which it is cooled down to the temperature of about 52° in very wide flat vessels, from which it is drawn off into a deep round vessel called the fermenting tun. In this situation it soon begins spontaneously to ferment; but from a deficiency of gluten—owing probably in this case to the grain having been deprived of much of its natural quantity of it on the formation, separation, and loss of the rootlets, &c. in the malting and kiln drying, &c. of the grain—the fermentation is but languid and has too great a tendency to run into acidity. To prevent these effects a small quantity of the frothy matter which collects on the surface of beer while fermenting called yeast is mixed with the liquor, a substance which contains a large proportion of gluten in its composition, soon after which the fermentation becomes more vivid, the temperature rises, carbic gas and vinous vapour are disengaged, and the yeast collects upon the top of the liquor now converted into ale from the changes which have been induced in its saccharine matter by this fermenting process.

10. The distillers of ardent spirits in Great Britain prepare their ale for distillation called wash by a process somewhat different. They use raw grain chiefly, which they mix with malt in the proportion of from one third to one tenth of the raw grain employed, and form their wort by infusing this mixture ground into meal for some considerable time in water at a lower temperature than that of the water used by the brewers of malt liquors, and by agitating the mixture much during the time of its infusion. The wort is then drawn off, cooled, and let down into the fermenting tun in the usual manner. The wort thus prepared seems to contain a larger proportion of starch than that procured from malt, the saccharine

charine fermentation not having been carried so far in this case as in malting, and the effect of this process seems to be rather the separation of that part of the grain which is convertible into sugar and alkahol, or the starch, from that portion of it which is not, the gluten, than the conversion of the whole of the starch into saccharine matter. Starch is not convertible into sugar till separated from gluten, and pure sugar is not convertible into wine or an intoxicating liquor till mixed with gluten. The wort being let down into the fermenting tun at a temperature varying from 55° to 70° is mixed with a considerable quantity of yeast, not all at once but successively, and it ferments so strongly in the tun for about ten days that the temperature is generally higher than 90° and sometimes than 100° attended with the usual phenomena of the disengagement of carbic gas, and the lowering of the specific gravity of the liquid, which by this process acquires an intoxicating quality and on distillation affords a large proportion of alkahol. In this case two of the stages or species of fermentation seem for some time to proceed together in the fermenting tun---the saccharine and the vinous--- the saccharine in the conversion of the starchy part of the wort into sugar from the mutual action of the avona of the air and the mona of the carbon of the starch on each other, and the vinous, partly from the same mutual action between the avona of the air and the mona of the sugar, and partly from the action of the yeast or gluten applied on the sugar and from the fire or heat produced by these means.

11. The most perfect specimen, however, of the vinous fermentation is that produced and exhibited by the expressed juice of ripe grapes called must. Must is composed of water, sugar, gluten, jelly, and tartaric acid partly saturated with lixa: the quantity of the sugar in it being very great. On its being put into the temperature of about 70° the fermentation commences spontaneously and continues without the addition of any ferment to the must for some days with increase of temperature and an emission of carbic gas, vapour, and a little cora gas, by the end of which time the thick part of the must having either subsided to the bottom or risen to the surface the liquid becomes clear and is converted into wine.

12. In this last case it is manifest that nothing comes into action, when the natural temperature happens to be 70°, but the must and air to which it is exposed; and in the former cases but the wort, air, and ferment employed;

ployed ; and it is also manifest that no addition of yeast or other ferment being required in this last case is owing to the must containing in itself a sufficiency of gluten, &c. for answering all the purposes for which yeast is employed.

13. This process of nature may be thus accounted for. It having been proved in Chapter VII. that sugar is a compound substance the result of a triple combination which remains unaltered as long as the mutual attractions between its constituent principles continue in equilibrio undisturbed by increase of temperature or the agency of more powerful affinities; and that these constituent principles are carbo, water, and mona; and consequently that sugar contains neither an acid, carbon, mona gas or the oily principle, nor vegetable oil in its composition, though it contains the constituent principles of each and all of these substances; which principles on the dissolution of the equilibrium of this triple union between them from any adequate cause often combine two and two together, while sometimes the compounds thus formed also combine together, so that by one or other of these means all these substances are often generated out of the constituents of saccharine matter. That diminishing the mutual attraction between these principles or constituents of sugar by separating the particles of the sugar in a certain degree from each other by infusion in water and increase of temperature, and then exposing the solution to the influence of the atmosphere is sufficient for disturbing this equilibrium and dissolving this triple combination, is proved by the consequences or by that fermentation or decomposition with which this process is invariably attended. And since in the case of the fermentation of must nothing comes into action, when the must is of the same temperature with the atmosphere at the time, but the atmosphere and the must, it follows as a necessary consequence that the fire or heat engendered by the process can result only from a chemical combination of the pyrogens or elements of combustion contained in these substances---the must and the atmosphere---that is of the mona of the must with the avona of the air to which it is exposed. Part of the mona of the must being gradually consumed by the fermentation or this slow combustion the carbo and the water being thus liberated from a portion of the mona with which they were in union combining together assume the character of an acid, which is in part evolved

in

in the form of carbic gas, and in part retained in the liquid forming that acid principle which experience proves to be contained as a constituent in every species of wine: the acid thus formed, however, is a vegetable acid, and that it is far from being destitute of mona is proved by its being combustible when mixed with avona gas.

14. While a portion of the sugar is thus gradually converting into an acid, another and larger portion of it is gradually converting into a light volatile oil —partly from a combination of a part of the mona with a part of the carbo of that portion of the sugar not immediately affected by the avona of the air forming carbon, in consequence of part of the sugar being deprived of the water of its composition or which is essential to it as sugar, partly from the greater affinity of the acid generated as above described for water, partly from the great evaporation of moisture, and principally from the affinity between the carbo and mona of the sugar being greatly increased while that between these substances and the water of the sugar is much diminished from the great augmentation of temperature produced: causes which are sufficient for producing this effect as is proved by the well known facts of sugar being convertible into charcoal by being deprived of the water of its composition either by means of heat or of acids---and partly from a large portion of the mona of the must, disengaged from that part of the carbo forming a constituent of the acid produced on the equilibrium of attraction between the constituents of the sugar being destroyed by the increased temperature, &c. uniting chemically with a portion of the water forming mona gas or the oily principle which combining with a part of the carbon is converted into a light volatile vegetable oil: many circumstances evince that sugar contains a much larger proportion of mona in its composition, after being deprived of that portion of it which during the process is consumed in combining with avona forming fire, than is barely sufficient to convert the small portion of its carbo which enters into the composition of this volatile oil into carbon.

15. When sugar is decomposed by the action of the air on it a much larger proportion of its mona is disengaged from its carbo in consequence of that action and the rise of temperature consequent of it than that quantity of it which is consumed by combining chemically with the avona of the air forming fire or ignite, as is fully proved in the first place by the fixed or

residuary products of the fermentation being mostly monates and monates containing but a small proportion of carbon in their compositions; and, secondly, by one half of the gas evolved during the process of the vinous fermentation being mona gas, when the wort whether of raw grain or of malt is fermented without any yeast and at the temperature of 80°, in the fermentation of pure malt wort; however, at a temperature lower than this no mona gas is evolved, and none in the fermentation of wort of any kind at this and even higher temperatures when a sufficiency of yeast is used, the whole of the mona which under the former circumstances volatilizes in mona gas being under these circumstances retained by the liquid; and on the proportion of mona thus retained over what is requisite for the generation of the volatile oil of the liquor does the surcharge of mona, and consequently the strength of the liquor and production of alkahol very much depend.

16. Liquors obtained by the vinous fermentation contain little or no alkahol. They consist in a combination of water with oily and saline substances, or at least with the constituents of these, together with a surcharge of mona adhering but weakly to the compound thus formed, and which on a certain increase of temperature, as on distillation, separating from the more fixed principles of the vinous liquor combines chemically with the volatile oil and is sublimed along with it in the state of alkahol. And thus is the analytical proof formerly given of the constituents and composition of alkahol verified and confirmed by a synthetical proof equally satisfactory, convincing, and conclusive.

17. It is entirely owing to loosely adhering mona or to a surcharge of mona that vinous liquors and ardent spirits owe their intoxicating quality, for on depriving them of these they are no longer intoxicating: and thus is ascertained the curious, and in medical science perhaps important fact, so little to be suspected, of intoxication being an effect of the action of one of the electrites or pyrogens on the nervous system of the animal body.

18. *Of the Acetous Fermentation.*—The acetous fermentation consists in the spontaneous and gradual conversion of vinous intoxicating liquors into an acid liquor, not intoxicating, and not nearly so combustible. Pure alkahol, even when diluted with water, is not susceptible of this change.

It

It must be mixed with other substances, which readily ferment, before it will undergo this process, or be converted into vinegar; and it is common to mix even wines which naturally contain such substances with their dregs and tartar when it is intended to convert them into vinegar; from experience having proved such mixture to be highly conducive to the success and acceleration of the process. This process also requires a high degree of temperature for its commencement, approaching nearly to 70°; and in its progress the temperature often spontaneously rises to so great a height as to require being artificially checked, to prevent a too great evaporation from the liquid. But no degree of temperature, however high, is capable of operating upon the liquid so as to make it undergo this process, if it is completely deprived of all communication with the atmosphere, or with avona gas; for the acetous fermentation in reality is nothing more than, first, the disengagement and dissipation in fire or ignite of that surcharge of mona to which the intoxicating quality of the liquor was owing, and then, the disengagement of the acid radical contained in the liquid from the mona with which it is in combination, by that mutual action between the avona of the air, and the mona of the liquid, whereby they combine chemically together, forming fire or ignite, which is dissipated during the process. And hence it is, that as the process advances the different vegetable acids, or those which have carbo for their radical, are gradually developed, from carbic acid, which contains but a very small portion of disengaged carbo in its composition, and is but little soluble in water, according to the gradual diminution of the proportion of mona in combination with the carbo in their respective compositions, till the process terminates in the production of the acetic acid which is indefinitely soluble in water.

19. That these are facts is proved, first by the presnce of avona being absolutely necessary to the process, secondly, by a quantity of that avona being consumed by it; and thirdly, by the results of it, or the natures of the products, that is, by the great quantity of fire generated and evolved during the process; by the wine, a highly combustible liquid, being converted by it into a liquid very difficultly combustible, and which, even in many cases, is capable of extinguishing combustion; and by that liquid being actually an acid containing much carbo and no avona or avona gas, and but very little mona in its composition. No gas is evolved

during

during the process but carbic acid gas, and that only in small quantity, the liquid being capable even of absorbing that gas. It would appear from some experiments that a weak imperfect vinegar may be formed, or other weak vegetable acid, merely by dissolving a small proportion of sugar in water strongly impregnated with carbic acid gas. Acetic acid, or purified and concentrated vinegar, contains a portion of oil and sometimes a little sugar, or at least the proximate principles of these, in its composition, but no alkahol. Vinegar holds in solution, and often deposits a viscid, oily, glutinous, and very putrescent matter.

20. *Of the Putrefactive Fermentation.*—Putrefaction is that spontaneous and gradual decomposition into a liquid or pulpy substance, generally of a very disgustful nature and fœtid odour, to which all organized, animal, and some vegetable substances, when deprived of the vital principle, and also some mineral compounds under the requisite circumstances, are without having undergone any previous fermentation subject; and to which all other vegetable substances, after having gone through some or all of the other fermentations are likewise subjected. The circumstances necessary for the production of this fermentation are as in the others, a certain degree of temperature, and a certain proportion of water; these substances, when either in a very low temperature, or in a very dry state, even though that dryness should be a consequence of a high temperature not being liable to it. The putrefactive fermentation is not always necessarily preceded by the acetous, or the acetous by the vinous and the saccharine, even in the case of those vegetables which are capable of going through all these different fermentations. The progress to putrefaction even in these does not necessarily, and therefore does not always follow that order, as depending on and varying with differences of circumstances, as the different degrees of temperature, the different proportions of water, &c. thus flour merely damp runs into the putrid fermentation at first, without having undergone any of the others—flour made into a paste with water runs at once into the acetous fermentation—while flour diffused in water becomes capable of undergoing the saccharine, vinous, and acetous, &c. fermentations, as in the case of the wash of the distillers of ardent spirits. The order likewise depends much on the natures and proportions of the substances which may be mixed with them as promoters of fermentation; thus mixing must with

the

the lees of wine promotes the vinous fermentation, seemingly by disturbing the equilibrium of combination of its proximate principles, and thereby the disengagement of lees from the must, from the corpuscular affinity necessarily subsisting between the added lees and those separable by the process from the must: and it is such CORPUSCULAR AFFINITIES that seems to be all that is meant by a POWER OF ASSIMILATION—the acetous fermentation is promoted by adding the refuse of vinegar to the wine intended to be converted into vinegar by its producing for the same reason, and by the same means, the disengagement of more refuse—and the putrefactive, by adding to the mass a portion of the same kind of substance in a putrid or putrifying state ; while the cora of the gum, or the gluten, or the animal matter of the fermenting substances, promotes all the different kinds of fermentation, and particularly the putrefactive, by weakening the affinities, and loosening the adhesions, of the proximate principles of the substances submitted to fermentation among themselves.

21. The putrefactive process differs from the other fermenting processes above described in not requiring so a high a degree of temperature, in generating and evolving little fire or heat, and in the presence of a large proportion of air or of avona gas not being absolutely necessary for it, although it is accelerated and rendered more perfect by a free communication with abundance of air or avona gas. And hence it is manifest that this species of fermentation is not so much the effect of combustion as of changes of affinities among the proximate principles of the substances among themselves, and between them and the constituents of the atmosphere, and those new combinations which necessarily result from them. When the particles of the substances are sufficiently attenuated, subtilized, and in a certain degree separated from each other by increase of temperature and mixture of moisture to weaken sufficiently the subsisting affinities and combinations of their proximate principles, the first phenomena they exhibit on incipient putrefaction, if in a liquid state, is becoming turbid and depositing a large quantity of feculent matter, while a considerble number of air bubbles ascend in the liquid, and the emission of an acrid pungent vapour from it is perceptible by the smell, which upon chemical trial proves to be volatile alkali, and which is by degrees succeeded by the emission of other exhalations, not so pungent, but much more nauseous.

seous. And if in a solid state, in swelling, becoming soft, losing the cohesion of their parts, and in being at last reduced to a very disgustful liquor, or pulpy mass, seemingly consisting in part of hepars and soaps; and these successive changes are accompanied with emissions of the same pungent and nauseous exhalations from the putrifying substances as in the former case. In both cases all appearances of acidity vanish.

22. The substances exhaled during the putrefactive process consist principally of mona gas holding different substances in a state of solution, as cora, carbon, sulphur, and phosphorus; or in other words in ammona, carbated mona gas, sulphated mona gas, and phosphated mona gas; the two latter of which have an exceedingly disagreeable odour, that of the sulphated mona gas having a great similarity to the flavour proceeding from rotten eggs, and that of the phosphated mona gas having an equally striking resemblance to the smell of putrid fish.

23. These phenomena and effects are in part owing, especially when the putrid has succeeded the acetous fermentation, to the chemical combination of the acid principle of the putrifying substance with its more fixed alkaline or earthy constituents, whereby part of its remaining mona liberated from its combination with these unites with a portion of the water forming mona gas, which expanding and volatilizing produces the swelling in the substance if solid, and the exhalations from the putrifying substances, whether in a liquid or solid state, as carrying along with it in solution portions of such of the other constituents of these substances as are in combination with or have most affinity to mona: and this combination of the mona gas with the more fixed principles of the compound seems to be much facilitated by the great affinity at that low temperature of mona to water, and of mona gas to monates; and in this case particularly by the great affinity of mona gas to cora, whereby that triple compound ammona is generated, forming the first of these exhalations emitted by the corrupting mass. When the substance or mixture of substances undergoing this process have free communication with the air or with a sufficiency of avona gas the process is much accelerated, and the putrefaction or decomposition is much more complete than when this is not the case. This is owing partly to the reciprocal action of the gravitating bases of the air and of the monates of the mass on each other, and partly to the reciprocal action

of

the avona of the air or avona gas and the mona of the putrifying substance or mass on each other, not so much indeed in this case from the avona and mona combining chemically together forming fire, though they actually do so in a certain degree, as is proved by the light emitted by wood, fish, &c. on putrifying, and by the evolution of some carbic acid gas from the consumption of some of the mona of the carbon by this means, as by that action weakening the affinities of these substances to their respective gravitating bases. A considerable part of the mona gas which is evolved in these cases is generated by the reciprocal affinities of the gravitating bases disengaging part of the mona of the mass or putrifying substance from the several other constituents of that substance or mass with which it was in combinatio, a nd thereby allowing it agreeable to the then predominant affinities to combine chemi cally with a portion of the water. In the preceding different species of fermentation the far greater part however of the mona gas, whether in a pure state or holding carbon or carbo or both, &c. in solution and combination, which is evolved, is not generated by the processes, but is only disengaged from the carbon of the fixed oil of the compound substance undergoing the particular fermentation by the highly increased temperature, &c. and in the putrefactive it is probable that in certain cases a certain quantity of avona gas is also generated when the substances which are subjected to this fermentation contain any avona or substances abounding in it, as nitre, &c. in their composition, part of which sometimes volatilizes or is evolved, and part of it combines with certain of the constituents of the mass, as with the acid principle in it, as is proved by the presence of nitric acid in the putrid mass. It is on the above principles that certain metals when moistened with water and exposed for some time to atmospherical influence spontaneously and gradually calcine, corrode, or corrupt ; and that mona gas and in some cases avona gas also is generated and evolved during the process. The mona gas thus generated sometimes combines with carbon during the process forming an oil, when the metal calcined contains any carbon in its composition; as in the case of chalybeate stagnant waters which from this cause have often an oily pelicle floating on their surface: in some cases the avona gas thus generated volatilizes and in others unites with the metalites, &c.: the avona by which it is generated being in these cases attracted from the atmosphere. Any of these metals is the sooner and the more completely corrupted or calcined in this case for being in contact with any other metal

more

more difficultly calcinable and therefore a better conductor of electricity than itself, from the great facility and promptitude with which the different portions of mona and avona, as they are successively disengaged from their respective gravitating bases the air and the metal by their action on each other, are conducted off in the state of electrites, from the great conducting power of the two metals and the greater affinity of the more perfect or less calcinable metal to mona than to avona, whereby each successive portion is conducted off the very instant it has performed its part in the process giving place to succeeding portions to act over again the same part and then make their exit in the same manner.

24. When the liquid or pulpy mass produced by the putrifying of vegetable or animal substances or of a mixture of these is evaporated to dryness, it entirely loses its odour and is converted into a loose black mouldery substance consisting of a mixture of earths, of salts, and of still remaining carbon and oil, with very small portions of metalites of iron and of manganese.

25. Many substances are known to possess a power of retarding though not of altogether preventing putrefaction in vegetable and animal substances, by means of the proper application of which these substances may be preserved for a considerable time in a sound, entire, and wholesome state. To the experiments of Sir John Pringle we are indebted for our knowledge of several of these, as well as for our knowledge of their comparative powers in this respect. Of these saliva seems to act an important part in the animal œconomy, in preventing in conjunction with the gastric juice or fluid the fermentation or putrefaction of the aliment in the stomach. Many substances are preserved from putrefaction by drying them or depriving them of 'that moisture which is requisite for it; many by covering them or rubbing their surfaces with such substances as the air under the then circumstances has no influence upon from the great affinity of their proximate principles to each other, as alkahol, certain salts, and sugar not diffused in water, &c.; many by freezing, or too low a temperature to admit of putrefaction; and many for a very considerable time by defending them from the action of the air, as by coating them over with wax or other substance proper for producing that effect: thus is it usual to preserve eggs by smearing them with butter or oil, in some countries certain

fruits

fruits are preserved by covering them over with wax, and the human body is sometimes preserved after death for a very long time by the same means, as by covering it closely with cere-cloth in the process of embalming. It is on the same principle that oil, cerate, and other plasters, capable of excluding the air is applied to sores and wounds, it being found that any part of the body, even of a living animal, is extremely liable to corrupt and putrify when exposed to the influence of the air from being deprived by any means of that natural covering the skin by which it was defended from its action; and that it is therefore necessary to apply some substitute for the skin in these cases capable of excluding the air when it is intended to prevent that effect or the corruption of the part of the living body thus deprived of its skin.

26. *Of the Saline Fermentation.*—In the spontaneous and gradual conversion of putrid substances into neutral salts, and earths which are probably nothing but neutralized compounds of saline substances which are insoluble in water, does the saline fermentation consist. When the putrefactive process experiences no check from a deficiency or superfluity of moisture or of temperature, or from any other cause, it does not terminate till the whole of the vegetable and animal oils, acids, and carbon of the putrid mass are entirely consumed and dissipated and nothing of it remains but earths, metalites, and salts, of which part are sometimes in a crystalized state; the whole of the oil and carbon of the putrid mass having volatilized during the process in the states of carbic gas and carbated mona gas. The products of this process give reason to think that during it the mass absorbs not only avona but also cora from the atmosphere; nitrous acid, nitre, nitrate of ammona, nitrate of lime, and muriat of ammona, being all products of this fermentation. Besides these dunghills which have undergone all the different kinds or stages of fermentation contain muriate of lime, carbates of lixa and of lime, phosphates of lixa and of lime, and in some cases small quantities of sulphates of ammona, of lixa, of lime, of iron, and of argil, muriates of lixa and of lime, carbates of magnesia, &c. As most or all of these different salts are also obtainable by chemical processes from vegetables which have not undergone fermentation; some of them from plants of one species and some of them from plants of others, and some of them from certain individuals only of a spe-

cies as depending in certain cases on their being contained in the soil in which the plants vegetated, it is not known with precision and certainty what proportion of them may have been originally contained in the juices of the vegetables subjected to fermentation, and what proportion of them is engendered by or is the product of fermentation. Some of these salts are too deliquescent to be found in a crystalized state in the mass, but others of them under favourable circumstance ares sometimes found in it in that state.

27. Under the article fermentation spontaneous combustions come with propriety to be treated of, as being in reality fermentations or gradual and spontaneous chemical changes of combination whereby certain substances are decomposed and converted into others essentially different. By spontaneous combustions, fermentations which spontaneously take place at a temperature not higher than that of the atmosphere, and which naturally and gradually increases till it terminate at last in combustion and incineration or salts, are in this article exclusively meant, and not those combustions which are a consequence of very high temperatures artificially produced. The presence of air and of water is in most cases if not in all necessary towards the production of spontaneous combustion in substances capable of it under the suitable circumstances.

28. Those spontaneous combustions which take place when vegetables in a damp state are collected together into heaps or stacks are as in other cases of spontaneous combustion effects of that mutual action between the mona of the vegetables thus gathered together, after its affinity and attachment to the gravitating bases with which it is in combination in the vegetables has been weakened and loosened by the intervention and agency of the moisture, and the avona of the atmosphere, whereby the mona and avona gradually combine chemically together forming fire or ignite and thereby raise the temperature; at first slowly, but progressively, each successive augmentation of temperature weakening more the affinity between the mona and the gravitating bases, and thereby occasioning the production of more fire and a still further increase of temperature, till the process terminates in the complete inflammation and incineration of the vegetable mass. To the same causes, the weakening of the affinity of the mona to the gravitating bases with which it is in combination by moisture and gradual

dual

dual increase of temperature and the consequent reciprocal action and chemical combination of the mona of the mass with the avona of the atmosphere forming fire, those spontaneous combustions are owing to which the pale yellow or martial and sulphureous pyrites, pit-coal containing these in large quantities, mixtures of iron filings with flowers of sulphur, and certain other compositions are liable when moistened with water and exposed to the air, whereby their respective natures are entirely changed, the pyrites being by this means converted into sulphate of iron, sulphate of argil, and sulphate of lime, in solution in water; which salts are obtainable in a crystalized state by evaporation of the water. Some chemists have represented a mixture of equal parts of iron filings and flowers of sulphur made into a paste with water as being susceptible of spontaneous combustion even when buried under ground. If this is actually the case as the paste contains no avona in its composition it must necessarily attract the avona requisite to its combustion from other substances containing it by means of moisture or other conductor of electricity in contact with it by an electric or galvanic process. But when this experiment was repeated by Bucqued it did not succeed.*

29. The different elements of combustion when separately combined with gravitating bases unite chemically together, when these different combinations come into contact or mix together, with the greater facility and effect and at a lower temperature the less affinity either or both of these elements have *ceteris paribus* with their gravitating bases, and the greater *ceteris paribus* the affinity of these bases for each other. It is owing to the very great chemical affinity between these elements and water, and to the very little affinity between the gravitating bases of mona gas and avona gas, or between the different portions of water with which they are respectively combined, from that affinity being corpuscular only, that a mixture of these two gasses require so very high a degree of temperature for their combustion and decomposition by the chemical union of these elements forming fire; and that these gasses at lower temperatures mix and combine together without combustion or decomposition, and also admit of their being again conducted separately off and of combining separately in their gaseous

* Fourcroy's Systeme de Connois. Chem. VI. 171.

state without decomposition with other substances with which they have more affinity at the then temperature than they have with each other. And it is owing to the weak affinity of the mona to the acid, or acid radical and water, &c. with which it is in combination, under the then circumstances, and to the affinity of that radical to water, that that very languid combustion takes place in the putrefaction of fish, as of herring, whiting, and mackarel, on the phosphated mona gas which they very slowly and in very small quantities gradually emit mixing with the air, and on mixing with it instantly, at very low temperatures, unites chemically with a proportionally small quantity of its avona producing that feeble combustion which takes place, and that faint, pale, and lambent light which this process exhibits in the dark: this combustion and emission of light, however, is stopped on the temperature becoming so low as to freeze the substances, and on its being so high as to produce too great an evaporation of moisture, &c. in combination with the phosphated mona gas. The same is the case with wood in rotting; it is a slow spontaneous combustion attended with a pale and lambent light and produced by the same causes—the weak affinity of the mona of the compound mona gas emitted by the wood to its gravitating base and its chemical combination with the avona of the atmosphere at very low temperatures. This is also the case with those luminous putrid exhalations which have ever been objects of much wonder and terror to the vulgar, and which are known to them by the names of Will with the wisp and Jack with the lanthorn, which float in the atmosphere in the vicinity of marshes and mosses;—the light they emit being the consequence of their being in a state of slow and feeble combustion from the weak affinity between the mona of the sulphated and phosphated mona gasses of which they principally consist and the gravitating bases with which it is in combination, and from its consequent chemical combinations with the avona of the atmosphere at very low temperatures.

CHAP.

CHAP. X.

OF ANIMAL HEAT AND RESPIRATION.

1. FROM the beginning of the 18th century, when the mechanical philosophy was in such high estimation and repute as to be deemed capable of accounting for all the physical phenomena of nature and mechanical agency of producing all physical effects, till the time that Dr. Black's doctrine of latent heat was known, animal or vital heat, in common with all other kinds of heat or fire, was attributed entirely to motion mechanically produced, either in the minute atoms of matter in general, or in those of one particular kind of matter generally diffused through nature; and in this particular case it was supposed to be generated by attritions mechanically produced either between the particles of the animal body or those of the substances contained in it as aliment, or of both of these: some ascribing it to the attrition between the particles of the solids, some to the attrition between the particles of the fluids, of the animal body; and some to the attrition between the particles of the substances taken into the body as aliments during the act of digestion, which was then regarded as a kind of fermentation. Besides the insufficiency of this theory for accounting for the generation of fire and heat in general, it is particularly objectionable in this case, as inverting the nature and real order of things, and substituting the *effect* for the *cause*, in regarding animal motion and the mechanical attritions thence resulting as the original cause of all animal fire or heat, and consequently of animal life, in place of regarding animal action and motion as originating in and being effects of animal life and of vital heat or fire, and that chemical action whereby they are produced; as well as on account of this animal mechanical action whereby this attrition is produced and maintained being assumed in this theory as an effect without a cause---none being by it assigned for it---and an effect which, contrary to all known mechanical principle and practice, operates mechanically of itself, unsupported by any power, in maintaining this attrition, and without any diminution of force, velocity, or effect, though experiencing a continued resistance to its operation.

2. Certain

2. Certain degrees of heat in animals, in certain cases, may no doubt be owing to a disengagement, discharge, and diffusion of fire from certain substances included in the animal frame combining together and condensing from their greater affinity to each other than to fire, and which consequently may be justly accounted for on the principle of the doctrine of latent heat; but the influence of this principle in the production of animal heat is not nearly so great as was supposed by that distinguished philosopher by whom it was first discovered, or as is supposed by those who have adopted his opinion in this respect, either as given by himself or as somewhat altered and modified by others. For though it is, and, ever since this doctrine was first promulgated by him, has been the prevailing opinion that animal heat is owing to part of the latent heat of the air inspired becoming sensible by being evolved in the lungs and during the course of the circulation of the blood, and though this theory is singularly ingenious and plausible, and the conversion of latent into sensible heat may account for certain changes in the temperature of the animal body in certain circumstances, yet it is by no means sufficient for accounting for vital heat or that heat on which animal life depends, since it is a fact that that part of the air commonly known by the name of oxygen gas, to the condensation of which and consequent evolution of matter of heat this effect is ascribed, actually owes not its elasticity and gaseous state to matter of heat or fire, that it actually possesses it not in its composition, and therefore that it never does, and necessarily is incapable of, evolving any, either in a sensible or insensible state, on condensation, by compression, or any other means. It is to a very different cause that vital or animal heat is owing. This cause I conceive to be, as in other cases of the generation of fire, that chemical combination which spontaneously and gradually takes place between certain portions of mona and avona when they come into contact under the proper circumstances for producing that effect, and that these circumstances take place when the air inspired mixes with the blood in the lungs, and that the mona of the blood of the animal system and the avona of the atmosphere mix, and gradually combine together, in this case in consequence of their mutual affinity and attraction forming fire or ignite, not only in the lungs but during the circulation of the blood through the animal body, and that this mutual affinity and attraction with the
the

the generation of fire and heat, increase of temperature, and the new combinations and excitations consequent of them, are the primary and principal causes not only of vital or animal heat, but also of respiration and the circulation of the blood. And that this is actually the case is proved by the phenomena and effects.

3. It has been known from the earliest times that respiration is necessary for the existence of man and hot blooded animals, that whenever it is by any means suspended even for a very short time the animal dies, and that the fluid respired by animals is atmospheric air. It has also been known for a considerable time that an animal can breathe a certain quantity of air for a limited time only after which it becomes highly noxious producing suffocation. Of late it has been discovered that every kind of aëriform or gaseous substance known except atmospheric air is altogether incapable of supporting animal life; some of them---as carbic acid and ammona gas---being unrespirable from spasmodically closing the epiglottis when applied to it and thereby producing suffocation; some of them---as mona gas and cora gas---proving immediately fatal without affecting the epiglottis partly from the animal being by this means excluded from respiring atmospheric air, and partly from their affecting the blood and the lungs when inspired in a way the very reverse in wh'ch it is affected by air in respiration; while some---as avona gas---though they may be inspired for some short time without much danger yet prove fatal when that time is much prolonged. It has also for some time been known that atmospheric air consists principally and essentially of a combination of cora gas with avona gas---as known by the names of azotic gas and oxygen gas---in the proportion nearly of 0,79 of the former to 0,21 of the latter and that air is diminished by animal respiration as well as by combustion.

4. That animal heat is owing principally to respiration is proved by the temperature of animals that respire being much higher than that of animals which do not respire as fish and certain reptiles; and by the temperature of all animals possessing lungs being *ceteris paribus* in proportion to the quantity of air respired by them in a given time. And that respiration is owing to the cause above assigned is proved by this increase of temperature and by the changes induced both in the state of the air and in that of the blood.

5. The

5. The known effects that are produced by respiration on the air inspired and on the blood in the lungs are, 1st. That the air is diminshed in quantity. 2d. That this diminution in quantity is in consequence of its being deprived of its avona gas, and of a small portion of its cora gas also. 3d. That carbic gas is generated and expired along with the remaining cora gas. 4th. That watery vapour is produced and is likewise expired along with the cora and carbic gasses. 5th. That the blood in the lungs loses a portion of its carbon and of its mona gas. 6th. That by this means it loses its dark red colour acquiring that of a florid red at the same time that the chyle mixed with it disappears. And 7th. That fire is generated or the temperature raised by the reciprocal action of the air and the blood on each other. That these effects or changes are produced by the mutual actions of the avona of the air and the mona of the blood, and of the several gravitating substances with which they are respectively in combination on each other, and that they can be produced by no other cause, or that they are necessary results of a very slow combustion thus produced which continues during the whole time of the circulation of the blood through the arterial system is proved, 1st. by the consumption of the avona of the air, 2d. by the production of carbic gas, 3d. by the florid colour acquired by the blood, 4th. by the disengagement of water from its combinations, and 5th. by the generation of fire and consequent conversion of that water into vapour. For these phenomena and effects prove that a portion of the mona gas of the blood holding a portion of its carbon in solution is liberated and disengaged from its combinations in the blood in consequence of the reciprocal action of the air and the blood on each other, and that this carbated mona gas is converted into carbic gas in consequence of the mutual affinities attractions and combinations of the gravitating base of the carbon of this carbated mona gas with the gravitating base of the avona gas of the air, or of the carbo of the carbated mona gas with the water of the avona gas, and of the avona of the avonas gas with the mona of the carbon whereby fire is also generated. That a portion of the avona gas of the air is absorbed by the blood, and that the avona of another portion of it disengaged from its gravitating base or water is also absorbed by the blood from its greater affinity to it under these circumstances than to water, and that the water thus disengaged from the

the avona gas and also from the blood in consequence of these affinities combines with a large portion of the fire generated forming that aqueous vapour which is expired along with the cora and carbic gasses; and that the avona thus absorbed by the blood spontaneously and gradually combines chemically with the mona of the blood during its passage through the heart and the arteries on its return from the lungs, whereby that fire is gradually generated, emitted, and equally diffused through the whole animal system which produces and supports in a great measure that degree of temperature which is requisite and necessary for animal life and comfort; while the blood at the same time is by these means and the increase of temperature consequent of them freed from superabundant mona, carbo, and moisture; part of which pass off by perspiration as well as by respiration during the progress of the process as the blood circulates through the animal body. It seems probable indeed, though there is as yet no direct proof of it, that animal heat and the perspiration of moisture and carbic gas by the skin is also in part owing to the absorption of avona or avona gas by it from the atmosphere.

6. These facts are corroborated and confirmed by the experiments and discoveries of Dr. Priestley; for that celebrated philosopher found that on exposing venous blood to avona gas it acquired the florid red colour and other properties of arterial blood, and that in exposing arterial blood to mona gas it acquired the dark red colour and other properties of venous blood, and that one fourth only of the avona gas inspired goes towards the formation of carbic gas.*

7. Though the mona gas disengaged from the blood which holds the carbo in solution forming the carbic gas expired may in some cases be equal or nearly equal in volume with the avona gas which disappears by the process of respiration, yet this equality of volume affords no proof of the avona gas having been converted into carbic gas or of none of the gasses inspired having been absorbed or consumed by the process; for carbic gas contains little or no avona in its composition and the volume of mona gas *ceteris paribus* far exceeds that of avona gas from their respective volumes being *ceteris paribus* necessarily in proportion to the expansive or elastic powers of their respective electrites or pyrogens, and

---

* Priestley on Air, vol. III. p. 379.

from the expansive or elastic power of mona being much greater than that of avona, as is proved by the difference of the specific gravities of equal volumes of mona gas and avona gas. The cora of that portion of the cora gas of the inspired air which is absorbed by the blood probably combines with some of the proximate principles of the blood forming that febrin which is known to be generated in it after its passage through the lungs, and which contains a larger proportion of cora in its composition than any of the other constituents of the blood.

8. Inspiration seems to depend primarily and principally if not entirely on those chemical affinities and mutual attractions which at certain temperatures or under the proper circumstances subsist between the blood in the lungs and the air of the atmosphere, whereby the thorax becomes gradually inflated and the lungs turgid with blood till the new combinations in consequence of these affinities have taken place, when expiration succeeds partly from the temporary suspension or cessation by this means of that attraction which was the cause of the inspiration, and partly from spasmodic affections and muscular action excited by irritability produced in the thorax by the agency of the new products thus generated fire and carbic gas on it, whereby the gasses and vapour contained in the thorax are expelled from it and the blood in the lungs returned to the heart. The lungs and thorax in consequence of this expiration collapse in a certain degree, and in a certain degree a vacuum is thereby formed in the thorax into which the external air is impelled partly by the pressure of the superincumbent atmosphere, partly by the reciprocal attraction between it and the blood, and partly by muscular action excited by irritability produced by an excess of mona, &c. in the blood flowing into the lungs from the heart now put into action, whereby inspiration again takes place; and these processes naturally and necessarily under the proper circumstances succeeding each other without interruption the same parts are always acted over again; and thus is respiration produced, continued, and maintained. The irritability which produces the spasmodical action of the heart and arteries whereby the blood is propelled in circulating through the system seems to be owing to the gradual production of fire and of saline products capable of excitation from the chemical action of the different elements or principles of the blood on each other during its circulation through the heart and arteries.

9. The

9. The above stated facts prove that RESPIRATION, and the CIRCULATION OF THE BLOOD, are effects of that chemical process described above, which takes place between the blood and the air; and, consequently, that this process is the immediate physical cause of life and sensation, and the *primum mobile* of all action in animals formed with lungs: and hence the following very curious, and perhaps, in medical science, important facts, hitherto unknown, and so little to be suspected, are discovered and ascertained, viz. 1st. THAT ANIMAL LIFE CONSISTS IN A SLOW COMBUSTION. 2d. THAT THE AIR AND THE ALIMENT SUPPLY THE PABULUM, FUEL, OR COMBUSTIBLE MATTER. 3d. THAT IT IS ONLY BY SUPPORTING AND MAINTAINING THIS SLOW COMBUSTION THAT ANIMAL LIFE IS SUPPORTED AND MAINTAINED. 4thly. THAT THIS COMBUSTION IS EXTINGUISHABLE BY MEANS OF THE SAME SUBSTANCES BY WHICH THE COMBUSTIONS OF INANIMATED SUBSTANCES ARE EXTINGUISHED: and 5thly. THAT IT IS BY ITS PROMOTING AND SUPPORTING THIS COMBUSTION THAT THE PRESENCE OF AIR IS NECESSARY FOR, AND PROMOTES AND SUPPORTS ANIMAL LIFE.

CHAP. XI.

OF VEGETATION.

1. THE means which nature employs for the decomposition of fire and the production of the different pyrogens seem to be many and various. For it is not only decomposed by the means and in the manners already described, but also by means of the particular arrangements and organizations of the parts of certain single substances or bodies; thus fire both in a pure state and in the state of ignite is decomposed into the different electrites by the *tourmalin,* and certain other stones; by the *torpedo, gymnotus electricus, silurus electricus,* and perhaps by some other animals; and it seems probable that leeches and such fish and other animals as are supposed capable of subsisting on water and air alone from their continuing for many years in life and health and becoming fat when confined in vessels containing water only having communication with the atmosphere, and whose blood and

juices

juices are cold, possess also a power of decomposing that fire or ignite contained in the water to which it owes its temperature, into the different pyrogens, mona and avona, and that they derive the principal part of their nourishment and of their substance, particularly their fat, from the oily principle engendered by chemical combinations of portions of the mona thus produced with portions of the water. But whether this is the case or not facts and phenomena induce me to believe, though it has never been suspected from its never having been supposed that fire is decomposible, that plants are possessed of a power of decomposing fire, when it is in a state of light at least, into the different pyrogens; and that this decomposition is one of the principal supports of vegetation, as being one of the principal sources of vegetable nourishment and growth: and indeed these facts and phenomena are such as appear to me to prove in the clearest manner that this is really the case.

2. That plants absorb and acquire by their roots not only moisture but a large proportion also of those other substances dissolved in it which are essential to their nourishment and growth, and which on digestion, &c. assimilating with their several natures become constituent parts of their respective substances, are facts well known; and facts that are proved, 1st. by the large quantities of sap that are contained in trees and shrubs in the spring of the year before the leaves expand and unfold; 2d. by the great quantity of moisture, &c. transpired by them after the expansion and unfolding of their leaves during the day or while it is light; and 3d. by the luxuriancy of plants being always *ceteris paribus* directly as the richness of the soil in which they grow, or as the quantity of the substances proper for their nourishment which it contains. That the substances contained in the soil in which they grow is the source from which by means of this absorption of them by the roots they derive the greater part or the whole of their carbo, their ammona, lixa, trona, lime, earths, and salts, and a part of their mona, with much of their moisture, is proved by the natures of their saps, which in general are found to consist of water, sugar, acetic acid, with the vegetable extractive principle, and mucus; and which on chemical analysis yields the above mentioned salts and earths, &c. That the sap ascends to the leaves and there undergoes certain alterations whereby it is converted into the peculiar juices of each particular plant is proved by the great evaporation of moisture, &c. by the leaves, and the formation

of

of these juices being stopt on depriving a plant of its leaves till such time as new leaves are again formed. That the presence of air, a certain temperature, and a certain degree of moisture, are necessary for vegetation, are facts that have been long known, and of late it has been discovered that all individual gasses except avona gas and all mixtures of them that do not contain avona gas as an ingredient prove fatal to vegetable life, as never failing to destroy any plant placed in them, and excluded from any communication with atmospheric air or avona gas. That light is likewise necessary for vegetation is a fact that has also been long known, and which is proved, 1st. by plants which vegetate in the dark, though otherwise under circumstances the most favourable, being destitute of the green colour of plants, and containing little or no oily or resinous matter; 2d. by these plants on being exposed for some time to the light acquiring oily or resinous matter, and changing their colour from white to green; and 3d. that it is by the action of the smooth or upper surface, or that surface of the leaves which is usually exposed to the light, on the light that these effects are produced is proved by the growth being frequently stopped on turning the other side of them to the light, by altering the position of a branch until the leaves turn their smooth surfaces to it again: in many plants the leaves fold themselves up during the night or the absence of light so as to cover and protect their smooth sides from injuries while their exposure is not necessary, and unfold themselves again at the approach of morning, that their smooth sides may again be exposed to the light of day.

3. That plants owe their green colour, their oily or resinous matter, and the formation of their peculiar juices, to the decomposition of the solar rays, or of fire in the state of light, into the two different pyrogens, mona and avona, by some unknown process in consequence of the action of the smooth side of the leaves on it, is proved, 1st. by the leaves of growing plants emitting avona gas; 2d. by this emission of avona gas from the leaves taking place only when they are exposed to light and never in the dark, and in much larger quantities than could be furnished by any avona gas that may be combined, if any such there is, with the moisture they contain.—There is however neither any proof nor any reason for supposing that the sap or juices of plants holds any avona gas in solution, for water holding avona gas in solution gives out that gas not only on placing plants in it but also on

plunging

plunging dried leaves, black poplar, and even fibres of silk, and of glass, in it, and then exposing it to the light of the sun, as was discovered by Count Rumford, or by plunging filaments of asbestos, baked horse hair, cotton, &c. and exposing it to the solar rays, as discovered by Dr. Woodhouse, or by placing green leaves detached from the plants on which they grew in it, and then exposing it to the rays of the sun, as discovered by Dr. Ingenhousz, who found that none could be obtained by this process from water which had been previously deprived of any avona gas it held in solution by boiling: from which it would appear that water holding it in solution may be deprived of it by light alone, and by increase of temperature, and that none of these substances are capable of resolving light into mona and avona, and thereby of generating avona gas by the combination of the avona thus produced with a portion of the water, so that the avona gas emitted in these cases is obtained by a very different process from that emitted by plants in vegetation, as being emitted in very small quantities only in these cases without being accompanied with the production or emission of either mona gas or carbo gas, and from none being obtainable by these means from water previously deprived of the avona gas it held in solution---3d. by the generation of that mona gas to the combination of which with the principles of the sap plants growing in the light owe those oily and resinous matters, and that green colour, which is known to depend upon resinous matter, of which plants vegetating in the dark are destitute, and which those which have grown in the dark acquire after having vegetated for some time in the light, or when exposed to the solar rays.

4. These facts appear to me to prove in the most satisfactory manner that growing plants---but not detached leaves, &c. as there is no generation either of avona or of mona gas by their means---decompose the solar rays, or fire in the state of light, into mona and avona; which, severally combining with different portions of the moisture or water of the plant form respectively mona gas and avona gas, the former of which enters into the composition of plants, while the latter is emitted by them:---facts which are supported and corroborated by those experiments of Priestley which proved that plants under certain circumstances emitted avona gas, and those of Ingenhousz, which prove that this gas is emitted by plants only when their leaves are exposed to the bright light of day; by those of

Priestley,

Priestley, which prove that air vitiated or deprived of the greatest part of its avona gas by the burning of a candle in it, so that the candle will no longer burn in it, may again be rendered capable of supporting combustion by making a plant vegetate in it in the light for several days; a consequence evidently of the avona gas emitted by the plant during that time, and mixed with the vitiated air in the containing vessel; and by those of Sennebier, which prove that the etiolation of plants which vegetate in the dark is much diminished by mixing the air that surrounds them with a little mona gas, and those of Ingenhousz, which prove that plants vegetating even in the light acquire a much deeper verdure when a little mona gas is added to the air in which they vegetate; an effect which he justly ascribes to an absorption of a portion of the gas by the plants. But though the smooth surface of the leaves of plants possess a power by some unknown means of decomposing those solar rays which are incident upon them, there are no phenomena or facts which give any indication or furnish any reasons for supposing that the leaves of plants are capable of decomposing fire when in any other state than that of light.

5. Since this process of vegetation is the very reverse of the animal process of respiration and of the other processes of combustion---fire being generated in these by a chemical combination of its elements, whereas in this fire is decomposed by being resolved into them---the temperature should by this process rather be lowered than be raised, as it is in these other processes, or at least the increase of it should in some degree be prevented by it; and this in fact seems to be the case, the heat of the day seeming to be moderated in summer, and in hot climates, by this means. But though plants emit avona gas and moisture when exposed to the solar rays, or the bright light of day, yet there are facts and phenomena which evince that on the contrary they absorb avona gas and moisture, and emit carbic gas during the night; and that it is the rough or under surface of the leaves of trees and shrubs and of most other plants that are possessed of the power of absorbing moisture in this case. These facts were ascertained principally by Hales, Bonnet, Ingenhousz, and Saussure. It is to supply this absorption of avona gas during the night which vegetating plants require that the presence of avona gas in the atmospheres in which they vegetate becomes necessary.

6. This

6. This absorption and the consequent formation of carbic gas are necessary effects of those affinities and mutual attractions subsisting under the then circumstances between the principles of certain portions of the carbon of the plants and those of the avona gas of the atmosphere, whereby the gravitating base or water of the gas combines with the carbo or gravitating base of the carbon and a small part of its mona, or a portion of the carbonated mona gas of the plant forming carbic gas, while the avona of the avona gas combining chemically with the mona of that portion of the carbon which is thus decomposed, forms fire; and thus are plants freed from any superfluous and excrementitious carbo and mona they may contain, at the same time that the temperature of the plant is prevented from falling so low during the night time as it otherwise would be by this spontaneous gradual and continued equal production of fire, whereby the pernicious effects of the cold damps and frosts of the night are in some degree prevented and counteracted; and thus the plants are retained by these means in a more equal degree of temperature both during the night and the day than they otherwise would be, partly by the increase of temperature during the night thus produced, and partly by the decrease of it during the day, in consequence of the process formerly described, whereby the solar rays incident on the leaves are decomposed. That the avona gas thus absorbed is not retained in the plants is proved by none being separable from them by putting them into the exhausted receiver of an air pump, by none being extricable from them by the greatest heat they are capable of sustaining without being destroyed, and by their being combustible only when in contact or conjunction with some avonate; and that it is not by the leaf but by the root that plants are supplied with that carbo which enters so copiously into their composition, is proved by the experiments of Mr. Hassenfratz, who found that plants which had vegetated from the bulb or from the seed in pure water, and whether placed within doors or in the open air, flowered but produced no seed, and when chemically analysed yielded a somewhat less quantity of carbon than was contained in the bulb or the seed from which they spring: the quantity of which contained in these he had ascertained by other experiments.*

* Ann. de Chem. xiii, 189.

7. A very

7. A very extraordinary increase of temperature in consequence of a natural vegetable process is related by Bory de St. Vincent, on the authority of Hubert. The stamina of the *aurum cardifolium* at the moment of bursting produced so great a heat that twelve of them placed round the bulb of a thermometer raised it from 70° to 143°*. It would appear from this that the stamina of this plant contained either phosphated mona gas or other substance abounding in mona in a loose and disengaged state, which combining with the avona of the air suddenly generates the fire by which the temperature is raised and the explosion produced, or that they contained some avo-monate or fulminating substance capable when excited by slight friction, compression, or increase of temperature of producing these effects.

8. It seems probable that the petals of flowers may also possess a power of decomposing those solar rays which are incident on them; and that there are various other ways, not so much as suspected, besides those mentioned in this Essay, in which fire is decomposed for answering various different purposes in the great process of nature.

CHAP. XII.

OF THE PHYSICAL CAUSES OF CERTAIN ELECTRICAL PHENOMENA AND EFFECTS.

1. However numerous and various the means employed by nature for the decomposition of fire into the different pyrogens may be, it is not by the immediate decomposition of fire that electricity is produced by means of the common electrical machine, when amalgam is used, but by disengaging the electrites from certain of the various different gravitating substances with which they severally may be in chemical combination. Thus the electricity produced, when amalgam is used, by the excitation of the

* Jour. de Phys. lix, 281.

common electrical machine in place of being furnished either by the glass cylinder, the rubber, or the earth, as is supposed, is principally if not entirely furnished by the atmosphere and the amalgam, from the first of these containing and in this case parting with the one electrite, and the other the other, the glass cylinder and rubber being no otherways instrumental in obtaining them than as means whereby differences of affinities may be induced from the differences of temperature produced by their action on each other in working or exciting the machine, and as operating as conductors of different conducting powers when the temperature is by this means augmented: the gravitating bases of the avona gas of the atmosphere and of the amalgam acquiring by these means greater affinity for each other than each has for its respective electrite, whereby these bases combine together, and their electrites are thus so far liberated and disengaged from them as to admit of their being conducted off separately by means of other gravitating substances of different attractive and conducting powers with which they have respectively more affinity under the then circumstances than they have with each other; the mona being generally carried off by the best conductor whether, according to circumstances, it happens in these cases to be the cylinder or the rubber. The use of the conducting communication between the electrical machine and the earth is not in this case to attract and convey electrical matter from the earth to the machine, as has been supposed, and is assumed in the Franklean hypothesis, but on the contrary to carry off and convey electrical matter to it, as affording a proper vent and discharge for one of the electrites thus disengaged and liberated, the other being carried off and discharged by the prime conductor of the machine.

2. The electricity produced by galvanical processes, as by means of the pile of Volta, is likewise the effect of differences of affinities from differences in the attractive and conducting powers of the substances employed; and the electrites thus produced are obtained by being disengaged and liberated by these means from the gravitating bases with which they were severally in chemical combination: and the electrites are furnished in this case also, when pure water only is employed for moistening the pasteboards between the metallic discs of the pile, by the atmosphere and the metals; the one electrite, the avona, being furnished by the avona gas of the atmosphere, and the other, the mona, by the metals. As it is not peculiar to water, or

to

to the imperfect metals moistened with water, either singly or when two of more of them are in contact, to attract avona or avona gas from the atmosphere, they possessing this power in common only with many other substances particularly saline ones; so there are many cases besides the above, in which pure water only is employed to moisten the pasteboards, in which one of the electrites, the avona, is furnished by the atmosphere. And hence the action of such saline liquids as contain not avona in their compositions, as solutions of the alkalis in water, in producing electricity when applied to the galvanic apparatus either by soaking pasteboards or pieces of cloth with them, or by filling the vacuities of the trough with them, when a trough is employed, admits of an easy and satisfactory explanation:---the highly and justly celebrated Torbern Bergmann has clearly proved that the presence of atmospheric air is absolutely necessary to the corrosion or calcination of copper by volatile alkali.* Whence it is manifest that the saline solution in this case attracts, and there can be no doubt of the same taking place in other cases when other alkalis are employed and the same effects are produced, that avona or avona gas from the air so instrumental to the disengagement of the mona of the metal, and which in these cases furnishes or forms the one electrite produced by the process, while the mona disengaged from the metal forms the other. When the saline substance or mixture employed is an avonate or contains avona in its composition, as certain acids or neutral salts, &c. diluted or dissolved in water, the presence of air or of avona gas is not necessary to the production of electricity by galvanic processes; as in these cases the avonate furnishes the avona, and the metal or other monate employed the mona, in consequence of that reciprocal chemical action which takes place between these substances from the different affinities of their respective component principles, whereby on their coming into contact they decompose each other, and their electrites are so far liberated and disengaged as to admit of their being conducted off separately in a pure state; the one at the one pole or extremity of the pile or trough and the other at the other, the mona being in these cases as in others generally conducted off by the substances that are the best conductors of electricity; and hence it is manifest that

* Bergmann's Dissertation on Electric Attractions, § 39, p. 176.

electricity

electricity may be produced by galvanic processes in cora gas, in carbo gas, &c. or even in vacuo, when avonates such as the above are employed in them.

3. That electricity is produced, and that the different electrites are furnished in the above cases, by the means and in the manners above described, is proved by no electricity being produced either in vacuo, or in gas or mixture of gasses not containing avona, either by means of the common electrical machine when amalgam is used or by means of the galvanic apparatus when no avonate is employed—by the air or other avonate present being in these processes when electricity is produced more or less deprived of its avona, and the metal or other monate employed more or less of its mona by the process—by the gravitating base of the monates employed when the avona is furnished by air or avona gas gaining in weight by the process precisely as much as the air or gas loses by it—and by the quantities of electricity thus produced being *ceteris paribus* precisely in proportion to the combinations which take place between the gravitating bases of the different substances furnishing the electrites.

4. It appears from the above facts that water has more affinity at the temperatures at which these decompositions take place to the radical of the metal or other monate than to avona, and that that radical has more affinity to water than to mona; that these decompositions are more owing in these cases to these affinities than to the affinity between the electrites themselves, since the electrites in place of combining chemically together, severally attach themselves and adhere to gravitating conducting substances; that the electrites have more affinity to metals and certain other monates than to water, and most to those metals which are most retentive of their mona as gold, &c. and that the metals and monates *ceteris paribus* conduct mona in preference to avona. The result, however, is very different when the temperature is high and the electrites in a condensed state, the affinity between the different electrites being then so much stronger than their affinity to gravitating conducting substances that even when in chemical combination with these they separate from them to combine chemically together; and when not in chemical union with them and only adhering to them and when even at a distance from each other if that distance

is

is not too great, if in sufficient quantity and in a very condensed state, they combine together even at a low temperature and under water.

5. In all the above cases it is by the immediate decomposition of gravitating substances and not by the immediate decomposition of fire that electricity is produced, though all electricity is necessarily ultimately the result of the decomposition of fire. But by whatever means electricity is produced, whether by immediate decomposition of fire, or by the decomposition of those gravitating substances of which electrites form proximate principles, the phenomena and effects resulting from it are *ceteris paribus* precisely the same provided the electrites obtained are in a state sufficiently disengaged from gravitating matter or in a state of sufficient purity for producing these effects. For in that case they are subject to all those laws of attraction and repulsion on which electrical phenomena and effects depend, and admit of being transferred from one gravitating substance to another whereby electricity can be induced in gravitating substances merely by *communication* without any chemical decompositions or combinations whatever taking place, in such a manner as that insulated conductors may be charged or surcharged with either electrite, and electrics be charged with both at once. Electricity may likewise be induced in gravitating substances by means of the charges or surcharges thus produced by mere approach without communication or transference. The electricity thus produced has nevertheless hitherto very improperly, a distinction between the method by communication and the method by approach never before having been made, been denominated either electricity by communication, or electricity by induction as if electricity could be induced in gravitating substances by no other means. The process whereby electricity is produced by the method of *approach* differs essentially from that whereby it is produced by *communication;* as it is always the result of chemical agency and immediate decomposition in the former case and never the result of these in the latter.

6. It is manifest that electricity could not be induced by the method of approach in perfect electrics or non-conductors, if any such there were, as the electrites generated in the electric could not be separated from each other, or could not be conducted off separately to different parts of it according as they are severally attracted and repelled. But as there are no perfect
electrics

electrics known, the best of those we are acquainted with as glass being in some degree pervious to the electric fluid, as is evident from many experiments as those of the Leyden vaccuum, of charging a plate of glass included between two other plates of glass, of producing electricity by approach through the intervention of a thin plate of glass, &c. so electricity in some small degree may be produced by the method of approach even in the best electrics when at the common temperature of the atmosphere. And in less perfect electrics this effect is more perceptible and considerable, and in some cases seems to extend much further from successive alternate zones of the different electrites being generated in the electric; each successive zone repelling the electricity of the same kind with its own to some distance from it till it accumulate into another zone of the same kind of electricity in a state of too much condensation to be capable of penetrating further into the electric, which successive zones always become weaker and weaker in power as they recede further from the charged body approached to the imperfect electric by whose immediate agency the first and principal zone from which all the others are derived is generated till at last they entirely vanish.

7. Were not glass and other electrics permeable in a certain degree to the electrites even at the common temperature of the atmosphere they could not possibly be charged with them by the common methods of coating the electric, as a plate of glass, on both sides, with some conducting substance, that an electrite applied to any point of its surface may be quickly and equally diffused over the whole of it, and then presenting a body highly charged with one kind of electricity or with one electrite at the proper distance to one side of it while a conductor communicating with the earth is applied to the other side of it, since if perfectly impervious to the electric fluid or power that fluid or power could not possibly act upon or affect substances on the opposite side of it to that to which it is presented, or act upon and affect them through the intervention of the plate of glass: and if they were perfectly impermeable and yet could be charged they would necessarily retain the charge for ever after without diminution provided there was no conducting communication between their opposite surfaces, and their not being thus retentive of their respective charges affords a proof of their not being altogether impervious to the electrites, or to that with which
                                                                        they

they are charged. They, however, retain their respective charges for a considerable length of time, and the slowness of their spontaneous discharge furnishes one proof among many others of electrics being but very imperfectly permeable to the electrites, and that it is only when electrites are in a state of great exility that they are capable of pervading glass and other electrics; these being impermeable to them when they are in a dense or condensed state otherwise than very slowly as they may gradually acquire a state of greater rarity. In charging of a plate of glass or other electric in the manner above described the use of the conducting communication between one side of the glass plate and the earth, and without which the plate could not be charged, is not as supposed and assumed in the Franklean or prevailing hypothesis to convey the electrical fluid from that side of the plate to the earth so as to reduce that side of it to a minus state of electricity by depriving it of part or the whole of its electrical fluid, but on the contrary to afford a medium or means whereby the body highly charged with the one kind of electricity or with one electrite presented to the other side of the plate may attract from the earth to the opposite side of the plate the contrary kind of electricity or the other electrite; and the fact is that no electricity is in these cases conveyed from the plate to the earth, but that an electrite of a contrary kind to that with which the body presented to the other side of the plate is charged is conveyed from the earth to that side of the plate having a conducting communication with it, and it is by the different electrics being thus accumulated and retained, partly from their attraction to the glass and partly from their mutually attracting each other, in a condensed state actually in the glass, whether in its substance or pores, though not chemically combined together from the glass plate being so far impervious to them as to prevent their combining together in and through its substance in a state sufficiently dense and in a manner sufficiently intimate to saturate and neutralize each other, that the plate becomes charged. And the glass plate *ceteris paribus* acquires a higher charge the thinner it is, because the thinner the different electrites condensed in it being opposed by a less thicknes of glass combine the more intimately together, and the more intimate the combination the more powerful their mutual attractions. That the plate is thus charged and each side of it principally with a different electrite from

that

that of the other is clearly proved by these electrites combining together in consequence of their mutual attraction when a conducting communication is afforded them; and that they are incapable in consequence of their mutual attraction of penetrating the glass in a state of sufficient density and in a state sufficiently disengaged and with sufficient rapidity for their combining chemically together is proved by no such effect being ever produced, though they sometimes when the charge is very high and the glass plate very thin and weak combine thus together from breaking or perforating the glass.

8. A body as a glass plate or jar coated on both sides, or two bodies as two plates of glass each coated on one side only and with their uncoated sides in contact, or the metallic cup and sulphur formerly mentioned, &c. may be highly charged with electricity without their having any electrical action or effect on any contiguous bodies or substances, as on the immediately surrounding air, &c. if the different electrites with which each is charged are in each in exact equilibrium, from their expending in these cases all their action that is not employed in attracting the particular bodies to which they respectively attach in attracting each other. It is owing to these attractions that the electrites adhere so firmly to the electrics as not to be detachible from them by the removing of the conducting substances with which they are coated, &c. or the surrounding air or other immediately contiguous substances from them—a sufficient proof of the charge not being contained in these—or by any other means except that of a conducting communication between their opposite sides, and it is owing to their being contained within the limits of the electric that in these cases they seem to occupy no perceptible space. Bodies in this state exhibit no phenomena and produce no effects from which it can be inferred or which indicate that they are in an electrical state or are charged with electrites till they are either discharged by means of a conducting communication between their opposite sides or till the plates, &c. are separated from each other. That electrites become perfectly insensible and ineffective as electrites on their combining chemically with gravitating substances, as in combining with metallic radicals forming metals, &c. has already been shewn: this, however, is far from being the case with bodies charged with one electrite only or with bodies charged with both

electrites

electrites when they are not in equilibrium so that there is a surcharge of one of them and when the electrites in these cases are not in chemical combination with the bodies but only adhere to them in a less perfect and complete manner; for these bodies exhibit phenomena and produce effects which afford the most unequivocal evidence not only of their being possessed of electrical powers and properties but also of the agency of these powers not being confined to the precise limits of the bodies but of their extending considerably beyond them; and it is not merely from the extension of the agency of these powers beyond the limits of the bodies as justly inferred from the extent of their influence and effects that it may be concluded that these bodies are enveloped in electrical auras or atmospheres, for it also follows from the repulsive nature of the electrites and from their imperfect adhesion to the bodies in these instances that this necessarily must be the case. And that it is so or that there are actually such atmospheres is proved by the experiments of the electrified pith-balls, the electrical shuttle-cock, and many others familiar to every electrician. On exciting the very powerful electrical machine in the museum of Teylar at Haarlem the sensation which resembles that of a cool wind, or of a spider's web passing over the skin, a sensation which seems to be superficial only, is felt at the distance of eight feet from the machine—a pointed wire presented to the conductor appeared luminous at the distance of 28 feet from it—and a thread six feet long suspended perpendicularly was sensibly attracted by it at the distance of 38 feet from it. In thunder storms when a large portion of the terrestrial atmosphere is strongly electrified the bodies it surrounds seem not to be much affected by its electrical state, owing probably to the air which forms it and the electrites with which it is charged being in a state of very intimate combination, as there appears no extraordinary attractions or repulsions between these bodies or any extraordinary expansion of their parts on that account, and as human sensations seem to little affected by it except that some few persons of particular constitutions are liable to become sick in these cases. Electrites when in a state of atmospheres to gravitating bodies seem not in every case to be in a state of perfect purity, but in many cases to be combined and contaminated with gravitating matter from their great affinity to it, as the smell emitted on discharging them by taking the electrical spark seems to evince; it is, however, electrites obtained by means of excitation from friction that principally or only emit a smell in this case.

9. It having been observed that material bodies, as magnets, are under certain circumstances attracted towards and under others repelled from each other, even when there is a considerable distance between the bodies thus affected, and that the same is the case with bodies of any kind that are in an electrical state, those possessing the same kind of electricity being mutually repulsive and those possessing different kinds mutually attractive though at a considerable distance from each other; and it having likewise been observed that the earth and small bodies near its surface are mutually attracted towards each other, and that the same is the case with regard to the planets amongst themselves though at a very great distance from each other—it has been concluded that certain bodies, and perhaps all bodies, are capable of acting upon and affecting one another though at a distance from each other; or, in other words, of acting where they are not: and, however strange and paradoxical this conclusion may seem, it apparently accords so well with phenomena, and is rationally deduced from facts so well ascertained, as now to be deemed incontestibly established, though how to account rationally and satisfactorily for the phenomena and facts from which it is deduced or for this capability in bodies of acting where they are not has hitherto been regarded as an effort of ingenuity far beyond the reach of human abilities to accomplish. Some attempts indeed have been made with this intention, and recourse has even been had to the immediate agency of mind in these cases, but these attempts have proved unsuccessful. The fact, however, being deemed fully established and incontrovertibly proved, though the means and manner by which it is effected are unknown and seem to be inconceivable and undiscoverable, the conclusion deduced from it of the *material bodies* thus mutually affected being the causes of these mutual affections, or mutual attractions and repulsions, or of its being in consequence only of their mutually attracting or repelling each other that these effects take place has been universally admitted and adopted.

10. On a mature consideration of all the circumstances however this conclusion must nevertheless, I am convinced, be allowed to be unfounded

and

and erroneous in as far at least as it regards those attractions and repulsions which take place with respect to magnets among themselves, and between bodies that are in an electrical state; and hence by analogy it may reasonably be presumed to be so also with regard to that mutual attraction which seems to take place between the earth and other material bodies, and that whereby the sun and planets attract each other. For in cases of magnetical and electrical attractions and repulsions the bodies actually do not though the phenomena seem to indicate it attract and repel; but, on the contrary, are attracted or repelled. It is not in reality in these cases the MATERIAL BODIES that are supposed and believed to attract and repel, that attract and repel, but that POWER OR SUBSTANCE which adheres and is attached to them at the time, and which is not essential to them as bodies or as distinct material substances since they can exist without them, the iron or steel without being magnetical, and the electrites and conductors of electricity without either being excited or charged with electricity. It is neither the magnetified steel nor the electrified material body that acts in these cases, but the powers or substances attached to them; and these powers, though invisible and impalpable to sense under the then circumstances as extending from these bodies to as great a distance as the effects produced, do not act where they are not or at a distance but where they actually are; or, in other words, their *sphere of extent* being equal to their *sphere of action* they act only where they are.

11. That the attractions and repulsions in these cases is entirely owing to these adventitious and adhering powers or substances, and in no respect to the bodies themselves, is incontestibly proved by there being no tendencies in the bodies either to attract or repel each other when not affected by these substances, or when in their natural states and perfectly devoid of all magnetic and electric powers. Though the state of rest, motion or direction of a body is in these cases often affected and determined by the state of rest, motion, or direction of another body at a distance from it, yet that does not proceed from any immediate direct action of the one body on the other body thus affected, or from that body acting at a distance and where it is not; but on the contrary from that body's acting where it is immediately and directly on the substance or power attached to it, and which extends from it as an atmosphere; from that substance or power

acting,

acting, in consequence of this action of the body upon it, immediately and directly on another substance or power in contact with it which is attached to the other body and extends from it as an atmosphere; and from this other substance or power acting in consequence of thus being acted upon immediately and directly on that particular body to which it is attached and of which it forms the magnetical or electrical atmosphere:—and thus it is that the mechanical action or changes of state as to rest, motion, or direction in the one body is in these cases communicated to and induced in the other, though they are at a distance from each other.

12. It is only from the extension of the electrical effects that we infer the extension of the electrical powers or substances producing them, and from the extension of the electrical powers that we infer the electrical auras or atmospheres: powers when not acting by means of a medium being supposed equal in extent with the effects they produce. Thus from the repulsion which takes place between the balls of an electrified pith-ball electrometer, whereby they diverge and remain separated from each other with a force superior to that of their gravity, we infer that the powers producing this effect extend as far as the effect extends, and that these balls are each surrounded with a substantial atmosphere which interposing between them produces these effects, and with reason; for, if these powers are not as extended as the effects they produce, or if their extent is not equal to that of their action, they must necessarily either act by means of an extended medium or instrument, or they must without such medium act where they are not; but there being no reason to suppose that these powers act by means of any medium or instrument, and since it necessarily must be as impossible for any created thing to act immediately and directly WHERE it is not, as it would have been for that thing to have acted WHEN it was not, we must of necessity conclude that this last case is impossible and that their extent is equal to the extent of their action or of the effects they produce.

13. It is principally from the attraction of gravitation that it has been concluded that matter is capable of acting on matter at a distance, partly from material bodies as the planets seeming to act on each other at the greatest distances, and partly from their seeming to act in this manner without the intervention or instrumentality of any medium from

none being in these cases by any means cognizable to sense, from the means and mode of action whereby mediums impalpable to sense could produce these effects being altogether unknown and inconceivable, and from the general opinion of nothing being capable of acting upon material bodies otherwise than either mechanically or chemically. Electrical and magnetical phenomena and effects however furnish proofs the most direct and decisive of change of state as to rest, motion, or direction being produced in material bodies by the action of mediums on them which are not according to common opinion material, and which seem not to be in motion and therefore must be incapable of acting on them mechanically, and which evidently do not act on them chemically, from no chemical change or result being the consequence of that action; and hence it is manifest that material bodies may be acted upon otherwise than either mechanically or chemically though we are as ignorant of the manner and means whereby powers, substances, or mediums impalpable to sense can thus act upon matter, as how and by what means they act upon each other, and probably ever will remain, it being sufficient for our purposes that we know that such things do actually take place in nature. Though all the physical action in nature, mechanical excepted, depends upon and is the effect of attractions and repulsions, yet the discovery of the proximate causes of attractions and repulsions seems to lie far beyond the reach of our philosophy. It is to be observed, however, that *electrical* attractions become *chemical* when the attracting powers or substances combine together in such a manner as to generate a new substance by their union essentially different from either of the substances of which it is composed.

14. In the above cases by matter and material, matter palpable to sense is exclusively to be understood; and by the term body a material substance of some determinate quantity or shape is meant; but matter that is generally or in most if not in all cases palpable to sense is not the only kind of matter in nature, for there are others known, and perhaps there are many unknown substances in nature which though not commonly palpable to sense are yet material, and material even according to the human standard of materialism. That fire is a substance of this kind was proved in Essay V.; and that the electrites are of the same kind, or at least that the atoms of which they are formed are solid substances, is decisively proved by that

resistance

resistance they experience in attempting to penetrate through or to perforate electrics; and by the effect produced when they do actually perforate them, the fracture in these cases being necessarily a result of mechanic action or impulse, the chemical qualities of the perforated bodies being no way altered or affected by it, and nothing being capable of acting in this manner but that which is itself solid relative to that it acts upon. And that aggregates of these atoms or particles, even when not in a very condensed state, whether in chemical combinations with certain gravitating substances as with water forming gasses or only loosely adhering to them, constituting their electrical atmospheres, are in some degree solid and material, is proved not only by their being extended and therefore occupying space, as is manifest from the great expansion which takes place in the water on combining with them in forming the gasses, &c. but more particularly from the force with which they in these cases resist compression, or with which they oppose the action of gravitating bodies in compressing them; while the case of the electrified pith-ball electrometer proves not only that these electrical atmospheres are not compressible by the gravity or weight of the balls, but also that electrical atmospheres are in certain degrees according to their densities, *ceteris paribus*, solid or material, relatively to each other, and consequently that in such cases the balls or bodies are severally surrounded to a considerable extent with atmospherical orbs which are solid, relatively at least to each other. Experiments prove that electrical atmospheres increase in density *ceteris paribus* as they approach nearer to the electrified or charged body, and hence it may rationally be inferred that they increase in the same degree by the same means in their solidity relatively to each other also: these atmospheres probably extend much further from the bodies than these effects they produce, which are perceptible to human beings, seem to indicate, human senses being by much too imperfect to trace in any case these effects to their utmost extent.

15. Whether or not a perfect vacuum of gravitating matter is a conductor or a non-conductor of electricity, or in other words whether or not it admits of electrical action taking place in it, was for long a subject of controversy among electricians; and the case was regarded as doubtful and undecided till an account of the experiments, first of Mr. Walsh, and then of Mr. Morgan, relative to this subject, made their appearance in

public ;

public;* when it was supposed that this matter was finally determined by the proof these experiments afforded of a perfect vacuum being a non-conductor of electricity. Mr. Walsh "found"—says Dr. Priestley, Experiments on air, Vol. I. page 284—" that the electric spark or shock would " no more pass through it"—a perfect vacuum—" than through a stick of " solid glass." That vacuum cannot conduct electricity or any thing else, and that it possesses neither any conducting nor any non-conducting power, are facts that admit not of dispute, since it necessarily must be devoid of all power; but that it should be impervious to electricity or to any thing else is not only inconceivable but impossible, or that an electrite in motion would be arrested by it and be prevented from exerting its natural powers, and could neither enter it if without it, nor if within it diffuse itself from its native repulsive power if otherwise unrestrained freely in all directions, or could prevent the different electrites from acting upon and attracting each other, is not to be believed: and that they should be incapable of acting or of expanding and diffusing themselves and of attracting each other without the instrumentality of a gravitating medium, seems so improbable at least as naturally to create some doubts with respect to the justness of the conclusions deduced from these experiments, and some suspicion of these very acute and ingenious philosophers having been deceived by appearances which seemed to indicate results different from the real ones. I have not the accounts of these experiments just now lying before me, but if I remember right, Mr. Morgan says the glass, including the vacuum on which the experiments were made, sometimes cracked from the charge being often repeated. An effect which I imagine could in this case be the consequence only of the agency of electrites of different kinds acting in opposite directions on each other through the glass, and if this is the case the glass must necessarily have been in a charged state, but if in a charged state it is manifest that the vacuum within it must be pervious to electricity and electrical action as admitting of its being charged, since it could not possibly be charged if that were not the case.

16. There necessarily must be electrical atmospheres in a perfect vacuum when there are electrified bodies within it, which though at a distance from

---

* Phil. Trans. Vol. 75.

each

each other are mutually affected by electrical action, as otherwise the bodies must act where they are not, and without the intervention of any medium, which, as has already been proved, is in the nature of created things, absolutely impossible. Electrical atmospheres are attached to bodies either by their being surrounded and confined by non-conducting substances as air, or by mutual attraction between the electrite and the body, an attraction often very strong, as is manifested by the metal plate of the electrophorus, &c. or by the body being charged in some degree with both electrites, and containing a superfluity or surcharge of one of them above what is required to balance and retain the other, which surcharge forms an atmosphere to it as extending beyond the limits of the body, from the attraction of the other electrite by the comparatively smallness of its quantity being too weak for retaining it in a more condensed and contracted state: or more or less by two or all of these causes, the first of which cannot obtain in a perfect vacuum of gravitating matter, and the last of which is not applicable to perfect conductors of electricity, if any such there are. It is manifest that those electrical atmospheres and charges which are attached to the bodies either by means of their being surrounded by external non-conducting substances as the air, or by means of the mutual attractions between the different electrites, must necessarily be proportioned rather to the extents of surface than to the mass of the bodies, and often be directly as the surfaces, and inversely as the masses, from the extent of surface of the surrounding non-conducting substances by which the charge is confined and retained in the first case being directly as the extent of surface of the bodies; and from thick non-conducting substances not being chargeable by the application of the different electrites to their opposite sides from their not being penetrable by them, and from the charges of extended thin ones being directly as the extent of their respective surfaces, it must necessarily be the same in the last case also.

17. Though the electrites are material, though not in general palpably so, and under certain circumstances are capable of acting mechanically; and though they are repulsive of their own natures, and are capable of producing a very great degree of expansion in water, yet their expansive power seems not to be so great as to be capable of producing explosion except in consequence of their being when combined with water and in the state of a gas
liberated

liberated from mechanical compression, or when liberated from a chemical combination by increase of temperature, &c. when in the state of a gas condensed even to dryness and solidity by that combination from which it is thus disengaged: there being no other instance of explosion having been produced by the agency of a *single* electrite. That deflagration is a result of a chemical union of the different electrites with each other has already been proved, and hence it necessarily follows that it can never possibly be the production of a single electrite. From these facts it is manifest that those explosions which are regarded as electrical or as produced by the electrical fluid or the ingress of positive electricity into a body in a negative state or devoid of electricity, are in reality results of deflagration, and that these deflagrations are in consequence of chemical combinations between the different electrites. It has already been shewn in Essay V. that fire is capable of producing explosion, and that it is never suddenly liberated from a condensed state in any combination with gravitating matter without producing that effect, even though it should not then be in an entirely pure state but should still be in combination with a small portion of gravitating matter, as with water, forming steam. But that fire in a pure state or without being thus combined is capable, even by electrical processes, of producing explosions is proved by many electrical experiments: thus if an electrical jar or battery is discharged through a slender piece of metal included between two plates of glass, the different electrics combine in a condensed state, which on expanding produces deflagration and explosion, by which the piece of metal is melted and calcined, and the glass plates are shattered to fragments; and if the glass plates including the metal are pressed with weights, these weights though very heavy will by the explosion be lifted up, and the glass plates will be broken into numberless pieces, scattered in all directions, even though the consequence of a very small charge: thick pieces of glass pressed by weights are also reduced to fragments without the interposition of any metal merely by passing the charge over a small part of their surfaces. Though the electrites in an uncombined state are capable of perforating or breaking by means of their mutual attraction, in certain circumstances, electrics opposing their union yet they are incapable of producing explosion.

18. The reason of that surprising fact, first observed by that very intelligent chemist Mr. Fourcroy, hitherto unexplained, of the inflammation and combustion being greater and the shock less when the number of plates of the Voltaic pile are few than when they are many, the extent of surface of metal being in both cases the same, is, that the electrites meeting in more directions from the large plates than from the small, concentrate into a finer point, and are thereby more completely condensed than in the other case, whereby the greater effect is produced: and it is from the same cause that the electrical shock in this case is less, for the shock is not the effect of fire, but of the electrites passing through the human body: fire cannot be made to pass through it in the manner the electrites do in giving the shock, and the different electrites in passing through it are incapable of combining together even when they meet from their attraction to the substances by which they are conducted. In the case of the *Coronne de Tassis* the same effect takes place, the different electrites are too much attached to the respective conductors to combine together on meeting.

CHAP. XIII.

OF MAGNETISM.

1. FROM a paucity of pertinent facts the doctrine of Magnetism does not admit of being treated in so ample and satisfactory a manner as its kindred doctrine of Electricity has been, it being impossible, from a deficiency of data, for the mind by rational deduction to investigate the nature of magnetism, and to ascertain the causes of its various properties and effects, to the same extent, and with the same precision and certainty, that the nature of electricity has been investigated and the causes of certain of its properties and effects ascertained; and by that means to obtain as many just and important conclusions with regard to these, as, with the assistance of apposite chemical facts, were obtained with regard to electricity when treating of that science.

2. MAGNETISM

2. MAGNETISM consists in the agency and operations of that power or powers whereby different ferruginous substances---and perhaps a few others, as Cobalt, Nickel, and Chromium---under certain circumstances, are attracted to or repelled from each other, and which thereby imparts to different bodies or portions of these substances the appearance of these bodies, being according to circumstances either mutually attractive or mutually repulsive of each other :---that these bodies owe this appearance entirely to the magnetic power or powers is proved by their neither repelling nor attracting, and being neither repelled nor attracted---unless in as far as they may be mutually affected by the attraction of gravitation---when they are in their natural state, and not influenced and actuated by the magnetic power or powers.

3. It is only under particular circumstances that ferruginous substances are affectable by the agency of magnetism or magnetic power. Thus the red metalite of iron, which of all the known metalites of it contains the least mona in its composition, is in every case entirely exempted from its influence, and even iron and steel themselves are so when in a white heat--- and also perhaps when in combination with certain substances, and even with too large a proportion of substances which in a smaller proportion would add to the magnetic operation and effect---they being then neither attractible nor repellible by a magnet, nor capable of being rendered magnetical or of becoming magnets themselves; that is, of being combined and invested with magnetic powers and properties. A MAGNET is a gravitating body endowed with the power of affecting magnetically such other bodies as admit of being so affected, and which at the same time admits of being magnetically affected itself, the action in this case as in others being reciprocal and equal. The above mentioned facts prove that ferruginous substances, to be affectable by the magnetic influence, must necessarily be in combination with as large a proportion of mona as to reduce them more or less to a metallic state, and at the same time that they must also necessarily be under or within a certain degree of temperature. The black metalite of iron, cast iron, malleable iron, and steel, are all at the proper temperatures under the magnetic influence, or are capable of being rendered magnetical. From the experiments of Mr. Lavoisier* it appears

* Ann. de Chem. i. 131.

that

that copper alloyed with so small a quantity as 1-16th only of iron is attracted by the magnet:---a circumstance which is apt to create a suspicion of the magnetism of Nickel, Cobalt, and Chromium being owing to the same cause, an alloy of iron in small proportion; more especially as those metals have been but lately discovered, and as it is attended with great difficulty to disengage that iron from them with which they are found naturally combined in the state of ores, and from which it is perhaps impossible to free them entirely by any known means.

4. Phenomena and experiments evince that though malleable iron and soft steel are more susceptible of magnetism than hard steel, yet that they are, after having been rendered magnetical, not nearly so retentive of it as hard steel. From the experiments of that very ingenious and expert chemist Mr. Hatchet it appears* that iron combined with a portion of sulphur becomes susceptible of permanent magnetism, but that saturated with it it is rendered altogether incapable of acquiring or retaining the magnetic virtue; that iron united with a portion of carbon is susceptible of permanent magnetism, but saturated with it becomes altogether insensible to the magnet and incapable of magnetism; and that iron on being combined with a portion of phosphorus is also rendered capable of acquiring permanent magnetism, but whether it is deprived of that quality by increasing the proportion of phosphorus has not been ascertained. The natural magnet is an ore of iron which contains a greater quantity of ferruginous matter either in the state of iron, or of iron not much calcined, than most other iron ores, in combination with a portion of silica and argil, and sometimes with some lime, magnesia, carbic acid, and a very small quantity of sulphur also:---natural magnets are found of different colours and in different countries. The cause of the retentive power iron acquires with regard to magnetism induced in it on its being combined with certain portions of certain substances, as of sulphur, carbon, phosphorus, and silica and argil, or which steel acquires on the hardening of it by immersing it in cold water while ignited; or the means by which the substances thus united with it, and the hardness thus produced, renders the iron and steel, which were not so before, capable of permanent magnetism, is not known, unless it may be owing to the iron or steel becoming by these means less permeable to magnetic power or powers.

* Philosoph. Trans. of Lond. for 1784.

5. It

5. It was from the phenomena exhibited by these natural magnets, or by pieces of iron naturally in a magnetical state, that the knowledge of the existence of magnetism was originally derived. Natural magnets were known to the ancients, who had found them in different parts, particularly in Lydia; and they had observed one at least of the many phenomena they exhibit, namely, that attraction which seems to take place between them and iron, and which is mentioned even by Plato and Euripides:—of the directive power of magnetism they were entirely ignorant, and probably of the repulsive also, and of each magnet being possessed of two magnetic poles, &c. They distinguished magnets into five different species, according to their different colours, and supposed different virtues, and to the different countries they were found in, viz. into the Ethiopic, Magnesian or Lydian, the Bœotic, the Alexandrian, and the Natolian. They imagined they were male and female: and the principal use they made of them was in medicine as a cure for different diseases, and especially for burns and defluxions of the eyes. It was not till the 12th or 13th century that the directive power of the magnet and the use of it in navigation was known in Europe, and probably that artificial magnets and magnetic needles were formed, though there is reason to believe that it had been known, and that such needles had been formed in China and in India many centuries before. The variation, or declination from the pole of the earth, by the magnetic needle, was first observed by Sebastian Cabot, a Venetian, in the year 1500; and the variation of that variation by Mr. Henry Gillibrand, Professor of Astronomy in Gresham College, about the year 1625; and about the year 1576 the dip or inclination of the needle was first discovered by Mr. Robert Norman, another Englishman.

6. After it had been discovered that each magnet, natural or artificial, had two poles, of different natures, to which different names were appropriated; that the poles of different names in different magnets attracted, while those of the same name repelled, each other; and that one and the same pole of each magnetic needle, when at liberty to traverse, always pointed to the north pole of the earth or nearly so; it was naturally and justly inferred and concluded that the one pole of the magnetic needle was attracted by the north pole of the earth, and its other pole by the south pole of the earth; and conversely that these poles of the needle were severally
rally

rally repelled by those poles of the earth which are of a different name from those by which they are respectively attracted, in the same manner as the poles of different names of two magnets attract, and those of the same names repel each other; and, consequently, that the earth itself is possessed of magnetic powers and is actually and in reality a magnet:---and thus were these three most important facts, both with respect to practical utility and theoretical investigation, of the repulsive and the directive powers of magnetism, and of the earth itself being actually a magnet, discovered and established.

7. The magnetic power seems to penetrate with the utmost facility all the other known substances in nature except those which are capable of being rendered magnetical, and even these at a red or white heat;---it also penetrates soft iron, at the common temperature of the atmosphere, though slowly and with difficulty.

8. That magnetism is not, and cannot be, generated in any body susceptible of it, by communication or transference is a fact that is decisively proved by there being no loss or diminution of magnetic power in those bodies by whose agency it is engendered in others, and which are supposed to engender it in these others by communicating it to them, in consequence of their engendering it in them, or of this supposed communication.

9. As Electricity consists, as has been proved in the preceding part of this Essay, in the action and operation of two substances or powers of which the natures are in some respects the very reverse of each other; so Magnetism also, though this has never so much as been suspected, seems to be the result of the action and operation of two substances or powers likewise of natures which are in some respects the reverse of each other, and which, differing also from the electrites, may be denominated MAGNITES. And that this is actually the case, or that there are two different kinds of magnetism or two different magnetic powers or magnites, that each kind is repulsive of itself and attractive of the other, and that each magnet has two poles of different and opposite natures, the action of different magnets on each other affords the most satisfactory, clear, and convincing evidence, by the one pole of each magnet, in these cases, attracting and being attracted by one pole of every other magnet, while it repels and is repelled by the other pole of each of these magnets; at the same
time

time that the other pole of that magnet attracts and is attracted by those very poles of these other magnets that its other pole repelled and was repelled by, and repels and is repelled by those very poles of these other magnets that its other pole attracted and was attracted by; by all those poles of magnets which are attractive or repulsive of any particular pole of any other particular magnet, as of one particular pole of the earth, and which are all consequently of the same kind or nature, being repulsive of each other; by those poles of different magnets which are attracted by some pole of any particular magnet necessarily differing essentially in their nature from those that are repelled by that same pole of that magnet; and by those poles that are of different and opposite natures being attractive of each other. And that magnetism in any gravitating body is the consequence of the DECOMPOSITION of some substance, be it what it may, contained in the body itself, into the different magnites, is decisively proved by various magnetic phenomena and effects, and more especially by the several methods whereby magnetism is generated in bodies and magnets formed.

10. For the purpose of preventing that ambiguity of expression, and that confused conception, which must necessarily result from giving the same name to magnites or magnetic powers, and to magnetic poles, which are of different and even opposite natures---as by giving the name of northern magnetism and of the north magnetic pole both to that magnetism and that magnetic pole which is situated near the geographical north pole of the earth, and also to that magnetism and that magnetic pole of the magnetic needle which points towards it though of a different and even opposite nature---it becomes necessary to distinguish these different kinds of magnites or magnetic powers, and their different poles, from each other by means of appropriate names having no other signification but what they derive from this appropriation of them, the natures of the magnites not being yet sufficiently understood to authorise the adopting of others; and, on this account, I shall employ the terms Autha, and Orautha, to denote the two different magnites or kinds of magnetism, denominating the magnetism and the magnetic pole of the south pole of the earth the Authic, and those of the north pole of the earth the Orauthic, and consequently that pole of the magnetic needle which points towards the north,

as

as being of the same nature with that of the south pole of the earth, the Authic; and that which points to the south, as being of the same nature with that of the north pole of the earth, the Orauthic :—terms which may suffice till such time as they are superseded by terms expressive of the ascertained real natures of the different magnites.

11. Electricity cannot of itself, as is supposed, generate magnetism; neither is magnetism ever the effect of mere heating and cooling or differences of temperature, of hammering, of drilling, of filing, or friction, &c. Magnetism can be no more generated in any body by any or all of these than it can by communication, or than it can be transferred from one body possessing it to another body possessing it not. It is only by means of magnetism that magnetism can be generated. For no other powers or substances but the magnetical are capable of DECOMPOSING that unknown substance of which they form the constituent principles :—and this they effect merely by means of that mutual repulsion which takes place between portions of them of the same kind or of the same magnite, and of that mutual attraction which takes place between portions of them of different kinds or of different magnites, when they approach each other; and, consequently, by that method ONLY which, in treating of Electricity, I have denominated *the method of Approach.* It is thus that when one pole of a magnet approaches a piece of iron the magnite or magnetic power of that pole repels the magnite of the same kind of that unknown substance contained in the iron which is resolvable into the different magnites, and attracts that magnite contained in it of a different kind from that of the pole of the magnet approached and applied; from which repulsions and attractions, and the permeability of the iron to these powers or magnites, the magnites or constituent principles of this substance are separated from each other, the substance thereby decomposed, and magnetism produced. Magnets in thus generating magnetic powers in bodies that possessed them not lose none of their own magnetic power by that means; and hence, as was observed above, it is manifest that the bodies thus rendered magnetical by their means cannot, of consequence, have derived their magnites or magnetic powers from them; and that, as not being derived from them, they cannot be the result of communication or transference; and, not being the result of communication or transference, that they necessarily

must

must have been engendered from the DECOMPOSITION of some substance *contained* in the body itself.

12. As it is magnetism only that can generate magnetism in bodies that possess it not, or that are not naturally and essentially magnetical, the primitive or innate magnetism of the earth must necessarily be the great and original source of all the magnetism of all the numerous and various magnetical bodies or magnets contained in or dispersed over its surface. And that this is actually the case is proved by the different methods whereby magnetism is induced in bodies, and magnets formed by the magnetism of the earth without the aid of other magnets either natural or artificial. Thus, all that is required, in this case, to render a rod or bar of soft iron magnetical is to place the rod or bar in the magnetic line of the earth, that is in the direction of the dipping needle; and to allow it to remain in that position for some time : and the magnetism thus engendered in the bar by that of the earth is *ceteris paribus* more or less permanent, in proportion to the degree of hardness of the iron, and to the time of its remaining in that position : that extremity of the iron bar that points towards the north acquiring the authic magnetism, or that of the south pole of the earth, and that which points towards the south the orauthic, or that of the north pole of the earth. The magnetism, however, thus produced in soft iron continues no longer than while the iron is acted upon by the magnetic powers of the earth under the proper circumstances for producing that effect, so that on removing the bar from that position in which it was placed, or out of the magnetic line, and thereby in as far out of the influence of these magnetic powers by whose action that substance contained in it which is resolvable into the different magnites was decomposed whereby it became magnetical, these magnites instantly, by means of their reciprocal attraction and the facility with which they penetrate soft iron, unite again forming the very same substance they did before. If the bar of iron is hammered, or filed while in the magnetic line, or if it is in a red heat when placed in it and is left in that position till cool, it thereby acquires a degree of magnetism which is somewhat more permanent, owing, evidently, to the decomposition of that substance of which the magnites are the constituent principles being more complete, and the different magnites being more perfectly disengaged from each other, and accumulated in larger quantities

and in a more dense state, at or towards the poles of the bar, partly from the permeability of the iron being augmented, from the attraction between its particles being weakened, and partly from the attraction between the magnites themselves being also weakened by the heat or fire either generated or applied in these cases; and from the magnites, thus more perfectly separated from each other and more condensed at the poles of the bar, being more resisted in penetrating through the bar, from being more dense and the iron more contracted on its becoming cool, to combine together again on its being removed from the magnetic line, than they were on being separated from each other when the bar was hot or in a state of ignition.

13. Hard steel can not be rendered magnetical merely by placing it in the magnetic line of the earth, unless by allowing it to remain in that position for a very great length of time;---the magnetism of the earth being too weak for producing that effect in it in a short period of time. But if a bar of hard steel placed in that position is hammered, or filed briskly, or is heated, or has the electric spark passed through it, it very soon becomes magnetical; and the magnetism thus acquired when hot becomes so permanent in it on its cooling as not to be speedily destroyed but by heating the bar, whether by electricity or otherwise, when it is not in the magnetic line of the earth.---The permanency of the magnetism in this case is owing to the difficulty with which the magnites pervade hard steel when in a low temperature preventing their readily combining together again in a manner so intimately as to recompose that substance they formerly formed.

14. The preceding facts and reasonings prove in the clearest manner that fire contributes no further to the productions of magnetism, than by producing differences of temperature, whereby the iron or steel is first rendered by an increase of temperature so far permeable to the magnets as to admit of their being separated from each other to a certain extent; and then, by a diminution of temperature, is again rendered so far impermeable to them as to prevent their combining together again, so as to form again the same kind of substance they did before they were thus separated;---and that it contributes to the production of it only when the bars of iron or steel are in a certain position since heating them in the same manner and degree in

any

any other position does not render them magnetical;—that the magnetism seemingly generated in pieces of iron, and steel, &c. by means of electricity, or of the electrical spark, is the effect merely of those pieces having been heated to a certain degree, in certain positions, by means of the electrical fire or of these sparks, and not of any particular virtue in the electricity; since they evince that the same degrees of magnetism may be produced in these pieces of iron or steel by heating them in the same degrees, and in the same position, by any other means;—and that the magnetism seemingly produced by means of hammering, drilling, filing, or friction, is also the effect merely of the position, and the magnetism of the earth, since raising the temperature by these means in any other position is not the means of generating magnetism.

15. Hard steel, however, can be rendered highly and permanently magnetical even at a low temperature, and without heating and cooling or differences of temperature and in whatever position it may be placed with respect to the magnetic line of the earth, by placing it within the influence of a magnet or magnets, or by the immediate application of a magnet or magnets to it, natural or artificial; and the more powerful the magnet or magnets applied, the larger, *ceteris paribus*, the pieces or bars of steel they can render magnetical; and the higher the magnetic charge or magnetism produced by their agency in pieces or bars of the same size and form;—while the smaller the size, the greater, *ceteris paribus*, the magnetism induced in proportion to the size, or the more complete the decomposition of that substance contained in the bar or piece of steel which is thus resolvable into the magnites.—When a bar of hard steel is too long for the magnetic influence of a pole of the magnet applied to one of its extremities, to extend to its other extremity; or for the influence of the different poles of two different magnets applied to its extremities, one to each end of it, the authic pole of the one magnet being applied to the one end of it, and the orauthic pole of the other magnet to the other end of it, to reach the middle of the length of the bar, it becomes necessary to place these poles of the magnets near each other, and near the middle part of the bar and at equal distances from it, and to slide them along the surface of the bar, repeatedly, each from the point on which it was first placed to the extremity of the bar nearest to it, thus to separate, and conduct when separated,

the

the different magnites, so as to collect, accumulate, and condense them at or near the extremities of the bar, in such a manner as to form magnetic poles to it; and that this may be the more effectually accomplished the poles of the magnets applied should each cross the whole breadth of the bar, while the thickness of the bar should be proportioned to the power of the magnets employed so as not to exceed in extent the extent of the magnetic influence of the magnetic poles applied :---hence it is manifest that the most powesful artificial magnets must be formed of a combination of many different artificial magnets, each of which is the strongest producible by the magnets, natural or artificial, possessed by the operator, and thus applied for the purpose of producing magnetism, and forming magnets ; and that by means of one or two weak artificial magnets obtained by means of the agency of terrestrial magnetism other more powerful artificial magnets may by the method above described be obtained, and by means of these last others still more powerful, and so on in succession, till by a continued production of more and more powerful magnets, and by combinations of these, magnetism of the required strength, though very great, may be obtained.

16. It may seem strange and contrary to nature for a magnite of one kind in chemical combination with a portion of a magnite of a contrary kind, forming with it that substance which is resolvable into the different magnites, to have have more affinity to another portion of that contrary kind of magnite, seemingly at some distance from it and not so intimately combined with it, than it has to that portion of it with which it is in immediate chemical union, as by the above described methods of producing magnetism would appear to be the case; and, consequently, that it is impossible to account for decompositions by approach either in magnetism or in electricity. This, however, is not unexplicable: for it is not so much on affinity or attraction as on repulsion that decomposition by approach depends : as being rather the result of the repulsions between different portions of the same kind of magnite than of the attractions of those of different kinds; since, in these cases, the portion of magnite of a different kind from that of the pole of the magnet applied contained in that substance resident in the bar of iron or steel which is resolvable into the magnites, is attracted by two portions of the different kind of
                                                                                                    magnite

magnite to itself at the same time—to wit, by that portion of it contained in or adhering to the pole of the magnet applied, and by that portion of it resident in the iron or steel as a component part of the substance to be decomposed by the process—acting in direct opposition to each other and urging it in contrary directions, and thereby in a great degree counteracting each other, and preventing their producing any considerable effect on it; while the portion of the other kind of magnite contained in the substance resident in the iron or steel which is resolvable into the magnites, and is of the same nature with that contained in or adhering to the pole of the magnet applied, is repelled in consequence of that mutual repulsion which takes place between different portions of magnets of the same kind, and in consequence of there being little or no counteraction or opposition in this case as in the former, to their acting with full effect on each other—the magnite at the other pole of the magnet applied being too distant to produce much or any opposition in this case—and when the magnite of the pole applied has thus repelled the portion of the same kind of magnite with itself contained in the iron or steel, it will then be qualified, as being by this means in a great measure freed from its counteraction to attract, and would attract with effect that portion of magnite of a contrary kind contained in it; and on which it would no doubt act with some effect before if its quantity was much greater or more condensed than that of the portion of the magnite of the same kind which is contained in the iron or steel by which it is counteracted.

17. It is manifest, then, that if a magnet is applied to one end of a bar of steel, the further end of the bar will not be affected by that circumstance, if the length of the bar is too great for the power of the magnet, or magnetic influence, to extend to that end of it; and that, when this is the case, the one pole of the magnetism thus produced in the bar will be at that extremity of it that is nearest to the magnet applied, and the other not at the other extremity of it but in some other part of the bar, *ceteris paribus*, at a greater or shorter distance from the other pole, according to the power of the magnet applied; and that, if the length of the bar extends a considerable way beyond this last pole and the steel is not very hard and the magnetism induced in it weak, this last pole will produce magnetism in another portion of the bar beyond it, by repelling a

portion

portion of the same kind of magnite as its own to some distance from it, &c. which portion thus repelled forming another pole of the same kind, repels in its turn another portion of it forming another pole, and so on in succession, till these successive poles becoming gradually weaker and weaker in power as they recede from the magnetic pole applied, vanish entirely before they reach the further end of the bar.

18. There is no producing of the one magnite without producing the other at the same time; or of obtaining of either magnite in a state of complete disengagement from the other, or of obtaining a piece of steel, &c. in combination with one magnite only:---and if there were any such kind of magnets as pieces of steel, &c. charged with one magnite only, these magnets could possess no poles, and consequently no directive power if suspended in the manner of the magnetic needle:---a power which is necessarily much stronger than either the attractive or the repulsive powers of magnets acting or seemingly acting on each other at a distance; as, in that case, both the attractive and the repulsive powers contribute, and equally or nearly so, to the directive, if the distance between the acting magnets is great; while one of them only attracts, and one of them only repels.

19. The rendering of a piece of iron or steel magnetical neither adds to nor deducts from its weight. And if no substance is added to it, and no substance abstracted from it, on converting it into a magnet, and no other alteration takes place by the process than the resolving of one substance contained in it into other two different ones also contained in it, this must necessarily be the case, even though the substance thus decomposed should be a gravitating substance. It has been supposed, however, that rendering a body magnetical should add to, or at least conspire with and augment the effect of its gravity or tendency to the earth. But this on experiment is not found to be the case; and the reasons of it seem to be, 1st. the great distance of the magnetical body, or magnet, from the nearest pole of the earth, and the great diminution in the magnetic power of the earth on it from that circumstance; 2d. its being acted upon by both poles of the earth at once, and in some degree in opposite directions; each pole at the same time both attracting and repelling it; and each therefore in a great degree in both cases counteracting the other; 3d. the magnetical line of the earth not coinciding with the line of direction of gravity,

from

from its magnetic centre of attraction not being situated in its centre of magnitude; and 4th. its being *repelled* with the same, or nearly the same, force with which it is *attracted* by each magnetic pole of the earth, from its being possessed of both kinds of magnetism and of two poles, and from the difference of distance between its one pole and its other from either pole of the earth being by much too minute to produce any sensible difference in that respect.

20. It seems highly probable from many circumstances, though there is no direct or positive proof it, that both the magnites, and also that substance which is the result of their chemical union, are ungravitating substances. No gravitating bodies but iron or steel, nickel, cobalt, and chromum, seem to contain that substance which is resolvable into the different magnites; and no combinations of the magnites with gravitating substances but these are known; and their combinations with these are not chemical, the essential qualities of these bodies being no way affected or altered by their being rendered magnetical or unmagnetical:—no chemical combination of the magnites but with each other is known.

21. The magnites have no affinities, that are known at least, but with each other, and with such gravitating bodies as are capable of being rendered magnetic, and hence it is that they are not combinable with any other gravitating substances. The mutual attraction or affinity between the magnetic powers or fluids and magneticable gravitating substances as iron or steel, though not chemical, is very great; and, under certain circumstances, greater even than that between the different magnites themselves, as is proved by the applying of two very powerful magnetic bars of equal forms, sizes, and powers, longitudinally to each other, with the authic pole of the one in contact with the orauthic pole of the other, when all the phenomena and effects indicative of their possessing magnetical powers or properties, except that of adhering firmly to each other, disappear from all of their action that is not engaged in attracting the gravitating bodies being employed in acting upon and attracting each other; and by then separating again the bars from each other, when their different magnites, thus intimately combined and powerfully attracting each other, in place of having abandoned them to maintain this intimate union between themselves, are found adhering to their respective bars in equal force and in the same manner

ner as they did before the bars were thus applied to each other, the bar having instantly on their separation resumed their pristine powers and properties as magnets. But though the magnites cannot in consequence of their mutual attractions, by any known means, be separated from the gravitating substances to which they adhere, yet they admit of being con ducted by means of their mutual attraction along these gravitating substances to which they adhere, or from certain parts of them to others, and this is the principle on which artificial magnets are generated, as in placing the poles of different natures of two powerful magnets near each other on a bar of steel, and near the middle of the bar's length, and then sliding them repeatedly along its surface to its extremities in the same directions, till the substance contained in the bar resolvable into the different magnites is not only decomposed into the different magnites, but also till the magnites thus obtained are severally conducted to the extremities of the bar forming magnetical poles to it, and the bar is converted into a magnet, in consequence of the mutual attraction between the magnets of different kinds, and the repulsion between different portions of the same kind in these cases.

22. That magnets are possessed of widely extending atmospheres is proved by their effects:—that of each magnetic pole of the earth extending as far at least as a semi-diameter of the earth. And these atmospheres are a natural and in certain circumstances a necessary consequence of the essential elasticity or innate self-repellant power of the magnites. That these atmospheres, or the magnites, are substances or powers, is proved by their being capable of affecting and being affected, of acting and of being acted upon, and by the extent of their action; and that they are material, relatively at least to iron, steel, nickel, cobalt, and chromium, is proved by the slowness and difficulty with which they penetrate these gravitating substances; and that different portions of the same kind of magnite are so relatively to each other is proved by those solid orbs of magnetism whereby the poles of the same name, of iron wires freely suspended near each other by flexible threads, prevent these wires from coming into contact, and retain them at a distance from each other, though acting in opposition to their gravity, as long, *ceteris paribus*, as their magnetism lasts;—and that they are fluid substances is

proved

proved by their yielding, except in the case of the action of the magnetic orbs, mentioned above, on each other, to the least possible pressure.

23. It is known from experiments that magnetical attractions and repulsions, and consequently magnetical atmospheres, diminish as they recede from the surface or pole of a magnet in some high ratio, which differs in different magnites as influenced by different circumstances.

24. Though there is evidently a great analogy between magnetism and electricity in many respects; yet they nevertheless differ essentially from each other. For that substance which is resolvable into the magnites seems not to be contained in any kinds of gravitating matter except iron, steel, nickel, cobalt, and chromium; and the magnites have an affinity in as far as is known with these kinds only; while that substance which is resolvable into the electrites is contained in all gravitating bodies:—and with all gravitating bodies the electrites have affinity. Those gravitating substances that are more or less *impermeable* to the magnites are among those that are most *permeable* to the electrites, or that are the best conductors of electricity; while those that are most impermeable to the electrites are perfectly permeable to the magnites. The magnetic power of attraction seems to be stronger than the electrical; some magnets lifting more than 200 times their own weight.—The electrical poles of the tourmalin, or of a charged electric, are not attracted by the magnetical poles of the earth, as the magnetic poles of a magnet, or of a magnetically charged piece of steel, are. The different electrites are obtainable in a state of perfect disengagement from each other, which is not the case with the different magnites. The electrites combine *chemically* with most or all gravitating substances, the magnites with none. And fire is formed by a chemical combination of the electrites, but not of the magnites.

25. That fire is not the substance which is resolved into the different magites is proved: 1st. By the heating and cooling of bodies capable of being rendered magnetical not rendering them magnetical except when they are acted upon by magnets. 2d. By their being, even when of a very low temperature, rendered powerfully and permanently magnetical merely by the action of magnets on them without their being heated, and without differences of temperature. And, 3d. by fire not being resolvable into the

magnites, and by fire never being generated by any combinations of the magnets.

26. It seems probable that fire, the electrites, and the magnites, would severally be palpable to sense in most cases by mere mechanical action were it not for their perfect fluidity and extreme exility whereby they yield, when not in a condensed state, to the least possible pressure and resist not penetration.

27. On the same principle and from the same cause that the two electrites cannot unite together so intimately as to form fire in a free and sensible state while attracted by and in combination with gravitating matter, that of their being in intimate combination with it; and that that substance which they form by their union is latent or insensible to and incapable of acting upon other gravitating substances than that substance which is intimately combined with it when formed, while in intimate combination with that substance, that of its being in intimate combination with that substance; the two magnites while attracting and attracted by gravitating matter cannot generate by their union that substance of which they are the constituent principles in a free, disengaged, sensible and effective state whereby its nature and particular qualities might be discovered and known, or otherwise than in a latent or dormant state relatively to other substances, from their being thus intimately combined with the particular gravitating substance to which they attach and adhere. And it is not less to be regretted that there are no known means of detaching them from that gravitating matter with which they are in combination, and to which they adhere so strongly, in a separate, free, and thereby sensible and effective state, and of retaining them in that state, or at least in a state of less intimate combination, during pleasure, so as to admit of their particular natures and qualities being discovered and known, and of their being transferred to other gravitating substances, and even of their combining together in a free and disengaged state; since it is manifest that till some means and mode is discovered of detaching the different magnites separately from those substances to which they now so powerfully attach, and of retaining them in that state adhering loosely to substances with which they have less affinity till such time as they are from their mutual attraction allowed, by being brought into contact, to

combine

combine chemically together, forming by their union that particular substance of which they are the constituent principles in a free and disengaged state---in the same manner as takes place with the electrites and the substance they generate by their union---it must be impossible ever to discover the particular natures and qualities of the magnites further than as above ascertained, or to acquire any knowledge whatever of the nature and qualities of that substance they generate by their union.

The above are perhaps the only conclusions that are rationally and justly deducible from the magnetical phenomena and facts at present known, and comprehend all the theoretical or philosophical knowledge with regard to magnetism that can under the present circumstances with any degree of well-founded confidence be admitted and adopted.

ESSAY

ESSAY VII.

OF DURATION, SPACE, AND INFINITY.

---

1. IT is said there are some things which must have existed from eternity, because it is impossible for us to form a conception of their non-existence at any time. " For he that can suppose eternity" (absolute duration) " and " immensity" (absolute space) " removed out of the universe, may, if he " pleases, as easily remove the relation of equality between twice two and " four."*   This is, however, inverting all natural order and just reasoning, and making the existence of things depend on our conceptions of them, and not our conceptions of them on their existence.   It seems nevertheless to be the general opinion that duration and space are not only real entities, but such as would exist though all other things were annihilated, and such as possess an absolute, independent, and eternal existence :---existing from the necessity of their own nature and therefore neither creatible nor anni-hilable.   While some seem to regard this absolute duration, or time as they sometimes call it, not only as a real existence but as the very essence of all other existences; since, according to them, every thing that exists must necessarily exist in time: and it is on this principle that Dr. Franklin says time is the stuff that life is made of.   Others seem to regard it as a power, when they say time has produced as great wonders, the time favours, &c. and others again as a measure of capacity when they speak of it in the plural number as when they say the times are *full* of danger, &c.

* Dr. Samuel Clark's Demonstration of the Being and Attributes of God.—Prop. 3d.

2. The

2. The most common opinion, however, with respect to absolute dura-tion, seems to be, that it is something that is eternal, and is infinitely ex-tended, as existing always and every where; that it consists in a continued and successive flux of *instants* or *moments*, of which the present only exists; and therefore that it is successive, motive, and progressive; and that that of which it consists are evanescent and infinitely small portions of itself. This account of it, for it cannot be called a definition, it must be acknow-ledged, is far from satisfactory; as all that is to be learned from it is, that it is formed of itself, and that though infinitely extended and unannihilable an infinitely small portion only of it exists; and that it is motive and pro-gressive, but in what direction or through what there is no intimation; and though it is uncreatable and unannihilable, yet the instants or moments which form it are in an incessant state of mutation or of generation and destruction :---indeed, it is not only unsatisfactory, but also incomprehen-sible and absurd, as involving contradictions and impossibilities; and, therefore, is such as affords much reason for suspecting that this *absolute duration* is merely an imaginary being, having no real existence in nature; more especially as no proof can be adduced of, or reason assigned for, the existence of such a being :---a being that is not cognizable by sense or distinguishable by it from non-entity; a being possessing none of the known attributes or powers and properties of substances, or indeed any positive quality whatever; a being formed of negations, incapable of self-existence, and of preventing the existence of any thing else; and such therefore as necessarily must be excluded from nature, and the rank and list of actual existences.

3. The same is the case with respect to *absolute space.* It is indeed said to possess the properties of indivisibility, immobility, penetrability, capa-city, and infinite extension in all directions; but all these properties are with respect to this supposed being merely negative, and in place of prov-ing it to be a power, a substance or substratum, indicate only in this case the total absence or negation of all power, substance, or substratum, with their necessary modes and relations, for it is indivisible and immovable be-cause there is *nothing* to divide or to move, and it is penetrable and capa-cious because there is *nothing* to oppose, to limit, to bound, to obstruct, or to prevent the generation, the motion, and the distance of substance from

substance

substance or of extension in all directions.   What goes by the name of absolute space is neither an entity, as supposed, nor an attribute or relation of entities; but is in reality merely the absence and negation of all entity, attributes, and relations.   Absolute space has indeed been represented as being in its own nature immovably fixed, and as consisting of parts which it is impossible to separate from each other by any force however great; but it has been represented at the same time as being penetrable by all bodies without resistance, as refusing ingress to nothing whatever, and being the common receptacle and habitation of all beings or existences.   Also as being capable of no action, form, or quality, and yet as measuring the distances of things, and determining the velocities of their motions.   Thus inconstant and repugnant are the supposed attributes of absolute space.

4. But though absolute space is a non-entity, yet that is not the case with relative space, or space properly so called, which, though possessing no substantial existence, is yet an entity, as being either an attribute of substance, or a relation of substances, or of the different parts of the same substance with each other, for it is in reality nothing but merely the extensions of substances, and the distances between them: and these extensions and these distances are measured and determined by the application of some material body, directly or indirectly, which is adopted as the standard or measuring unit; and it is the particular extensions and distances thus ascertained which bodies in motion pass over that, the times being the same, measures and determines the relative velocities of their motions. And it is only the distances between material bodies not occupied by matter or substance of the same kind as that of which these bodies may be formed that can with propriety be regarded as vacant space, and as vacant relatively only to such bodies; and it is only to such relatively *vacant extension* that the term *space* as contradistinguishable from material substances or existences can with propriety be applied; space in this sense and in this sense only being distinct from body or at least from material substances.   It is not, however, even in this case, any thing positive, actually extended in itself, and endowed with real dimensions or other properties, and which, like Divine immensity, is through all and in all, but merely a relation of substances among themselves with regard to distance; and which, as being

necessarily

necessarily determined by their relative local situations, is neither uncreated, nor infinite, nor, as has been supposed, independent of the Deity the Author of all things.

5. In like manner though absolute duration is a non-entity, yet that is not the case with duration as relatively applied; which, though possessing no substantial existence, is yet an entity as being an attribute of substance. Duration, as an attribute or with respect to any particular thing and therefore with respect to all things as particulars, consists in, and may be defined to be *exemption from change of state with regard to any of its essential powers and properties*:---since that which changes not its essential powers and properties must necessarily endure or continue essentially the same. This is also a proper definition of identity. A thing essentially the same may, however, endure under various different accidental modifications; and duration with respect to any particular modification, and therefore with respect to accidents and modifications in general, must also consist in exemption from change, and may be defined to be, *the exemption of a thing from any change in its state of modification*. But as the termination of one state is only the commencement of another, no substance being annihilable by natural means, duration, as an attribute of things, is not limited to the continuance of any particular thing or things, or combination of elements, in the same state, but is continued from one state of existence to another, from generation to generation, or from thing to thing as they are severally destroyed and generated and follow each other in immediate succession; and as duration is an attribute of each individual of which this train or succession of individuals is formed, so must duration be an attribute also of the succession itself so formed, as consisting of all the particular durations of all the individuals forming the succession or series; and, if created things, of which it is an attribute, were eternal, duration would be so too, but not otherwise.

6. It is from the observation of these successive changes of state in external things, and of that succession of sensations and thought they thereby occasion in our minds, and from the observation of the changes which take place in some particular things relatively to those in others, that we acquire the knowledge of that attribute of things to which we give the name of duration. And it is from these observations also that we have been enabled

to

to discover and practise a method whereby it may be measured, appreciated, and determined, in particular cases; and it is to this measure of duration that we have given the denomination of time. Succession, or successive changes of state, or of place, in any thing, necessarily, of its own nature, signifies and implies prior and posterior states, or the occupation of certain places subsequent to others; or past, present, and future states, progression and motion; and thereby duration in those things whose respective states, or places, are undergoing successive changes, even though their continuance in each particular state should be too short for our perception. From this, and from the observation that certain things are liable to frequent and successive changes in their respective states or places while others are exempted from these, and that in cases of motion the durations or times are as the spaces passed over when the motion or velocity is equable, we acquire the knowledge of the comparative durations or continuances in the same state of things among themselves, and are thereby enabled to measure the durations of certain things by the changes in others. Thus, certain natural changes of state in certain bodies, from equable regular motions in them or nearly so, afford a standard proper for measuring the particular durations of things:---as the successive and regular changes of the seasons, of light and darkness or of day and night, of the phases of the moon, of the rising and setting of the stars, &c. and more especially the intervals between the successive appearances of the sun in the same point of the zodiac or what we call years, and between the successive appearances of the sun in the meridian or what we call natural days, which we again divide and subdivide into smaller intervals, which we call hours, minutes, &c. by means of such contrivances as sand-glasses, clepsydra, dials, clocks, &c. and in years, days, hours, &c. does time consist, or that standard whereby we measure and estimate the *real* duration of things.

7. With regard to sentient beings both duration and space seem to be merely sensible and relative, relative to the then state of their respective minds, and therefore *apparent* only, in as far as the sensations and thoughts of such beings do not of themselves afford any proper, steady, and just standard for determining the *real* durations and extensions of things with regard to each other as they actually are in nature:---thus in certain cases of pain and affliction an hour will appear to us as long as a day does in

common,

common, while in cases of pleasure and enjoyment a day will often not appear to us so long as an hour does at other times. These effects seem to depend in a great degree on their respective accompaniments of pleasure and pain. But, independent of these, our conceptions of duration with respect to the same portions of time vary as the numbers of the changes of state, or of the successive sensations and thoughts, which take place in our respective minds during these portions of time, as it is by means of these only, and the pleasures or pains attending them, that we are conscious of duration with respect to our own existence, and therefore in that case by these only necessarily measure it: and hence it is that in profound sleep, when no such changes take place, we are altogether insensible of duration with respect to ourselves and to every thing else. The mental conceptions of duration and space with respect to the same portions of time and of extension seem to depend also in a very great degree on the nature and size of the sentient being, and on those of the organs of sense of that being:—thus, an hour to a being particularly constituted may appear an age, as to certain diminitive insects whose existence is seldom much longer, while to another differently constituted an age may appear but an hour; to a being a thousand times larger than the sun, if such could be supposed, the earth which we inhabit would appear only as a foot-ball, while to certain microscopic animals a foot-ball may appear as large as this earth does to us: and hence it is evident that duration and space in these cases depend more upon the standard by which they are measured, the medium through which they are perceived, and the nature of that which perceives them, than on any thing else.

8. But though this is the case with respect to the mental conceptions of them, or to the sensations they produce or are the consequences of, and the appearances they thereby exhibit to minds differently constituted, yet it is not so with respect to duration and space themselves as attributes of things, for they do not vary thus but always remain steadily the same; and though mental conceptions of duration and space are thus liable to give various and different reports with respect to the same thing, and therefore do not of themselves afford a standard proper for determining the durations and extensions of things with regard to each other, yet there are in nature other standards to be found which are not liable to this defect

and which determines these in most cases with a sufficient degree of accuracy. It has already been shewn how duration as an attribute is accurately measured by means of *time;* and space, whether as an attribute of substance or as a relation between different substances or bodies, admits also of being measured with a considerable degree of correctness; nothing further being required for this purpose than employing the particular extension of any particular thing as a standard for measuring the extensions of other things by, or the space or extension between different things, and applying it to those things and those distances or extensions between different things, accordingly. -The steadiness and accuracy of the results or measurements obtained by these methods, and the unsteadiness and consequently inaccuracy of those by mental conception, prove in the clearest manner that duration and space exist not in mental conception only, but that they actually have a real existence in the nature of things as attributes and relations; and it is alone from their having such that the mind can acquire any conception or knowledge of them whatever.

9. Duration and space not only cannot exist otherwise in reality than as attributes or relations of things, but also cannot even be conceived by the mind as existing otherwise, or as perfectly abstracted from things. They may indeed in mental conception be abstracted from any particular thing, and from all things as particulars, but they cannot from things in general; it must still be something, that is some existence or entity real or imaginary, or some relations of things or existences or their relations in general, that the mind conceives to endure, and to be extended. The mind must always have real existence in view and attached to these conceptions; and if the terms absolute duration, and absolute space, are ever used in any other meaning, they must be terms merely *negative,* as signifying only a total want of external restrictions, limits, bounds, or obstructions to the extension or duration of any thing, as not being expressive of a single *power*, or even of one *positive property.*

10. It is not by means of abstraction, but, as has been already observed, from the succession which takes place in our own sensations and thoughts, and from our perception and observation of the successive changes of state which take place in some things relatively to others, that we acquire any conception or knowledge of duration, and of that measure of duration we call

call time; that is of duration as an attribute of things, and an attribute which some things possess in a more eminent degree than others, as being much less liable to corruption or change of state; for of duration as abstracted from things, and as existing absolutely, we cannot possibly have any conception or knowledge at all, as there actually is no such existence in nature. It is merely from the natures of things, from the progressive motion of some things from place to place while others remain at rest, and from our state of existence as well as that of most or of all other things of which we have any knowledge, being transient, fleeting, and progressive, as well as our sensations and thoughts, which, when we are vigilant, follow each other in a continued train or succession : and from the present sensation or thought, and the present state of things or present thing of each series, only, existing, that it has been concluded that duration is an absolute existence which is in itself liable to change of state, or which consists in a successive flow of fleeting moments of which the present only exists; in the same manner and on the same principle that people sailing on board a ship suppose the neighbouring coast to be in motion, and that the vulgar still believe that the sun moves round the earth and that the earth remains stationary. The duration, the succession, progression and motion, are all in the things themselves, and not in any being ABSTRACTED from them, and existing ABSOLUTELY and independent of them. In supposing such existences as absolute duration and absolute space we only deceive ourselves, and in endeavouring to substantiate them " only give to airy nothing a local habitation and a name."

11. It must also be acknowledged that in the supposed well established doctrine of the infinite divisibility of space, and of duration, and thereby of the infinite divisibility of substance and of matter, and indeed in the whole doctrine of infinities as given by mathematicians and metaphysicians, there is something not only mysterious but also incomprehensible and absurd. They have defined a point to be that which has no parts or magnitude, and yet have advanced that a line is formed of points, a superficies of lines, and a solid of superficies, and thus have left nothing in nature, not even space; and might as well have said at once that a solid is made up of points, or of what is destitute of all magnitude, as amounting in effect to the same thing. All this has however been regarded as demonstrated, and therefore

T 2

acquiesced

acquiesced in, though merely assumed in definition, a circumstance which has given rise to many fundamental errors in the principles and practice of the mathematical sciences, and to many absurd metaphysical reasonings and theories.   Thus it has from the supposed infinite divisibility of matter been inferred that all the bodies in the universe might be mechanically formed out of any quantity of matter however small; and indeed according to the above definitions and principles, it might with equal propriety and truth have been inferred that they might all be formed out of nothing, nothing and something on these suppositions being the same.   From the doctrine of infinite divisibility it has also been inferred that nothing can be so small but it may be divided into others infinitely smaller, and that there may be and actually are infinitesimals of infinitesimals in infinitum.   And these more than seeming paradoxes have been supported by mathematical proofs seemingly demonstrative, and with so much ingenuity and acuteness of argument as to be regarded as being established on the most unexceptionable and most conclusive evidence, though it is manifest that if this was the case there could be no such things in nature as instants of time, points of space, or atoms of matter, and that motion could never gradually diminish into rest, as in that case it might approach nearer and nearer to it in infinitum without ever attaining it.

12. But, if there actually were any such existences in nature as infinities, since infinity does not admit of the relations of great and small, all infinites would necessarily be equal; and since every number and every magnitude, however great or small, must necessarily be finite, and that which is finite in quantity cannot possibly consist of parts infinite, it necessarily follows that there cannot possibly be in nature any such things either as infinites, or as finites consisting of parts infinite.   There are in fact no such existences among created things as absolute quantity or infinity, absolute duration or eternity, absolute space or immensity, absolute motion, absolute place or local situation, &c. nor if there were would they possibly admit of computation or measurement from there being nothing of the same kind to compare them with or measure them by.   In infinity there is no whole, nor consequently any parts; and where there is no beginning or end there can be no middle.   Our senses are evidently adapted to take in and our faculties to perceive finite or limited existences only, and all our conceptions having
been

been of course ultimately derived from finite objects by means of finite sensations and finite faculties, it must necessarily be utterly impossible for us to form any positive conception of infinity of any kind. Faculties which are limited and finite cannot measure what is infinite and eternal; and to pretend to define eternity and immensity, and to comprehend infinity, is to pretend to put limits and ends to what admits of none, and to comprehend what is incomprehensible.

The subject of infinity will be resumed, and more fully discussed, in each of the three parts of the subsequent Essay.

ESSAY

ESSAY VIII.

OF THE PRINCIPLES OF THE MATHEMATICAL SCIENCES.

COMPUTATION and mensuration are the only objects of mathematical science. In investigating, discovering, and determining the means most proper for effecting these does it exclusively consist. And hence quantity of every kind, or whatever is capable of being numbered or being measured, or which, as being divisible into parts or portions, admits of degrees, as of more and less, or of increase and decrease, or that bears any ratio in these respects to any thing else, and which may be referred to any other thing as a standard of measure, is the object of mathematical science. In these sciences every quantity is numbered or is measured by an entity or magnitude of the same kind with itself, called the measuring unit; and quantity means only the number or the magnitude of the thing treated of as ascertained by means of this unit or standard of measure, to which in every case there is a reference either expressed or implied; and, hence, " by number we understand," as has been justly observed by the sagacious Newton, " not so much a multitude of units as the abstracted ratio of any " quantity to another quantity of the same kind, which we take for unity."

On the excellence and usefulness of mathematical knowledge, Doctor Barrow in his inaugural oration on being appointed Professor of Mathematics in the University of Cambridge, gives the following very eloquent description and encomium, viz. " The mathematics effectually exercise, not " vainly delude nor vexatiously torment studious minds with obscure sub- " tleties, but plainly demonstrate every thing within their reach, draw cer- " tain conclusions, instruct by profitable rules, and unfold pleasant questions. " These

" These disciplines likewise inure and corroborate the mind to a constant
" diligence in study; they wholly deliver us from a credulous simplicity,
" most strongly fortify us against the vanity of scepticism, effectually re-
" strain us from a rash presumption, most easily incline us to a due assent,
" and perfectly subject us to the government of right reason. While the
" mind is abstracted and elevated from sensible matter, distinctly views pure
" forms, conceives the beauty of ideas, and investigates the harmony of pro-
" portions; the manners themselves are sensibly corrected and improved,
" the affections composed and rectified, the fancy calmed and settled, and
" the understanding raised and excited to more divine contemplations."

The mathematical sciences are, 1st. Arithmetic—computation having
probably preceded mensuration. 2d. Geometry. 3d. Algebra. 4th. Fluctions and the infinitesimal calculus. The principles of the first, or of common or vulgar arithmetic, are too well understood to require any further investigation or rational discussion. Those of the others shall be treated of
in the above order.

PART

PART I.

OF GEOMETRY.

1. THE observation is common, and of great antiquity, that pure mathematics has the advantage of other branches of learning, in occasioning no contests among wrangling disputants, owing to the peculiar accuracy with which the terms have been defined, to the fundamental principles of the science being self-evident, and to the mode of reasoning employed in it being such as not to admit of doubt with respect to the justness of the conclusions, and doctrines deduced; yet, certain it is, that there is no entering on the study even of the Elements of Geometry, as they are found in the treatises on this subject, without being immediately involved in metaphysical subtilties and labarynths, in mystery and paradox; and, upon an accurate and deep investigation into the nature and foundation of the mathematical sciences, they will be found, there is much reason to believe, to rest upon other principles than those which have been hitherto supposed.

2. Every treatise on the elements of geometry begins with the definitions; and on the first reading of the first of these, viz. " A point is that which " hath no parts, or which hath no magnitude"* the understanding is struck with astonishment, the mind revolts at the thought of adopting a principle so repugnant to prevailing opinion, and the judgment refuses its assent to a proposition so contradictory to experience and the plainest dictates of sense. The student, from this first and introductory definition being beyond his apprehension, and from the information he had previously received with regard to the undoubted certainty of the principles of this science, and which he finds confirmed by those of his acquaintance most learned in it whom he may have consulted on the subject, is apt to mistrust his senses,

---

* Simson's Euclid.

to

to suspect the soundness of his judgment, and to regard himself as altogether unqualified for what, from these circumstances, appears to him such profound investigation. If experimental proof of this definition of a point, and those of a line, and of a superficies, being the 2d and 5th of Euclid, which are equally incomprehensible as the first—viz.—" A line is length " without breadth. A superficies is that which hath only length and " breadth,"*---is required, he is informed that the mathematics is a science purely speculative, which therefore does not admit or require any proofs, but such only as are drawn from intellectual sources, the most satisfactory and convincing of any, and that of these there are abundance to be found in the writings of the mathematicians, far more than sufficient to remove all the doubts and difficulties which novices in the science are liable to entertain and be embarrassed with in regard to the above definitions; which mathematical proofs and demonstrations it is the more necessary to consult, that it is a maxim never to be dispensed with in mathematical science, that nothing is to be taken for granted without sufficient proof of its certainty having first been obtained.

3. For these proofs and demonstrations the student is referred, principally, to the celebrated Introduction to Natural Philosophy by the very learned and ingenious Dr. John Keil, by much the ablest of all the advocates for the propriety and justness of these definitions, and the doctrines thence resulting, as that of the infinite divisibility of magnitude, &c. The arguments and proofs adduced by Dr. Keil, in that work, in favour of these doctrines, are so ingenious and important as to merit and require a candid and particular discussion.

4. Dr. Keil, in premising—that " † by Divisibility we would not here be " understood to mean an actual separation of parts from one another, " which supposes motion, which indeed the nature of space does not admit, " nor do the demonstrations borrowed from Geometry prove such a separa- " tion; but the divisibility which we here endeavour to evince, is only the " resolution of any magnitude into its parts, or their distinction and assign- " ment. As, for example, when Euclid, in the ninth Proposition of his " Third Book, teaches how to cut a rectilineal angle into two equal parts, " he does not in that method undertake to shew, how one of the equal

---

* Simson's Euclid.　　　† Keil's Introduction to Philosophy, page 20, &c.

" parts being separated from the others recedes and is placed from it at a
" given distance, but only delivers a method whereby a line may be drawn,
" dividing the angle in such a manner into two other angles, that the angle
" which lies on one side of this line shall be equal to the angle that lies
" on the other side the same line. So likewise when, in the following Pro-
" position, he teaches how to bisect any right line, he only shews how to
" assign a middle point, dividing the given right line into two equal parts,
" which point is the common termination of both the parts; namely,
" where one of the equal parts ends, and the other begins. This resolution
" of magnitude into its parts is so intimate and essential to it, as that which
" has no parts, as, for instance, a Point, is not said to be a magnitude,
" but the Beginning or End of magnitude: nor can any magnitude be pro-
" duced by any number of points, though infinite; for every magnitude is
" not compounded of Points, but Parts; that is, other magnitudes of the
" same kind, whereof every one is constituted of other parts, and each of
" these is still made up of others, and so on *in infinitum;* nor can we ever
" arrive at a magnitude so small, but it may be yet further divided into
" Parts; nor is there given, in any species of magnitude, an absolute *mini-*
" *mum;* but whatever is divided, is still farther divisible into Parts. This
" constant farther resolution of matter into parts, is by the philosophers
" called its *Divisibility in infinitum;* and that very truly, since there cannot
" be assigned any quantity of matter so minute, and any finite number so
" great, but that the number of parts composing that magnitude, that is,
" into which it may be resolved, shall be greater than that number, how
" large soever it be: *for we call that infinite which exceeds any finite"*—ju-
diciously avoids that absurdity into which so many other geometricians
have fallen of representing a line as being formed of geometrical points, or
of that which has no magnitude; a superficies of geometrical lines, or of
that which has no breadth; and a solid of superficies, or of that which has
no thickness; and has properly and justly represented vacant extension, or
space, as not being divisible into parts, from its possessing none, and given
a true account of what is meant by Divisibility in Geometry; but inad-
vertently, in this paragraph, draws some conclusions which the premises,
as here stated, not only do not warrant, but actually oppose and prove to
be erroneous; as when it is asserted that " a Point is the Beginning or End

" of

" of magnitude :"—at the same time that it is acknowledged that " a mag-
" nitude cannot be produced of any number of Points, though infinite;
" for every magnitude is not compounded of Points, but Parts; that is,
" other magnitudes of the same kind;" which necessarily implies an
absurdity; since it is contradictory, and impossible in the nature of things,
for a magnitude to originate and terminate in Points, or in that of which,
according to this acknowledgment, it neither is nor can be generated:—
it is, however, upon this unstable foundation, that the whole doctrine of
terminating ratios rests.

5. And there is also nothing in the premises, or indeed in nature and
reason, that authorises " *the calling that Infinite, which exceeds any Finite;*"
or, as here explained, any assignable quantity; since it is manifest, that
every quantity or number, or number of parts, and therefore every magnitude as consisting of parts, however great or small, must necessarily be
finite, though it may far exceed any finite quantity of which human beings
have any knowledge or conception, and consequently any quantity they
are capable of assigning. He then proceeds as follows:—" but because
" this infinite Divisibility of Matter can be demonstrated by arguments
" taken from Geometry, and since there are now-a-days some philosophers
" who attempt to banish Geometry out of Physics, by reason they are
" ignorant of that divine science; and as these gentlemen would be reck-
" oned amongst the most learned, they leave no means untried, whereby,
" though in vain, they may overturn the force of these Demonstrations:
" it will be therefore necessary, before we produce our geometrical argu-
" ments, to establish their strength, and to answer some objections.

" As amongst the philosophers of this class, the famous *John Baptist du*
" *Hamel,* the author of the *Burgundian* Philosophy, is of the greatest emi-
" nence, we shall produce his opinion on this subject. He says, then,
" that geometrical hypotheses are neither true nor possible, since neither
" points, nor lines, nor surfaces, as the Geometers conceive them, do
" truly exist in the nature of things; and therefore that the demonstra-
" tions that are produced from these cannot be applied to things actually
" existing, when none of these exist any where but in our ideas. He
" desires, therefore, the Geometers to keep their Demonstrations to them-
" selves, and not to make use of them in Philosophy, because, according
" to him, they spread over this science not light, but darkness.

" I admire

" I admire at the unskilfulness of this otherwise most learned person, in
" this affair; he might certainly with some justice take away all physical
" suppositions whatsoever, since geometrical hypotheses are equally certain,
" and equally possible and real, as those which he calls physical. Certainly
" if body exists, there must of necessity exist real points, real lines, and
" real surfaces, even such as are conceived by geometers; as we can easily
" make appear. For if body be given, that, since it is not infinite, has
" its terminations; but the terminations of body are surfaces, and these
" surfaces have no depth: for if they had they would thereby be bodies,
" which bodies would have still other terminations, which would be surfaces,
" and therefore there would be a superficies of a superficies. Either then
" this superficies is destitute of all depth, or not: if the first, we have what
" we require; if the latter, we come again to another superficies, and so
" we should proceed *in infinitum*, which is absurd. Wherefore we must
" conclude, that those terminations are deprived of all depth, and are
" therefore true surfaces, and as they are conceived by the geometers
" without any depth, or such as have only length and breadth to constitute
" their essence.

" Again, since this surface is not infinite, it is likewise bounded by its
" terminations; but those terminations are called lines, which have really
" no breadth: for otherwise they would be surfaces, and would have also
" their terminations, which we ought to conceive as destitute of all breadth;
" for, as we said before, there cannot be given a progression *in infinitum*;
" whence there are really given lines, which are only extended in length,
" without any breadth. After the same manner, lines also have their ter-
" minations, which are called points, to which belong neither length, nor
" breadth, nor depth. Wherefore, if body may be supposed to exist, it
" necessarily follows, that geometrical surfaces, lines, and points, may be
" said not only as possible to be, but also to be actually existing."

6. This reasoning, though truly ingenious and generally deemed un-
answerable, is however in reality more perplexing than solid; as resting
-entirely upon the ambiguity in the meanings of the terms termination,
surface, and superficies; and upon its not being expressly declared according to what particular meanings they are here to be understood; or upon
their not having been defined in this case further than in asserting that they
form no part of the body of which they are the termination and super-

ficies,

ficies, and that they are length and breadth without thickness or depth; definitions better adapted for creating wonder and confusion of thought, for misleading the reason and confounding the judgment, than for removing difficulties and elucidating the subject; for it being far from easy to conceive the actual existence of an entity distinct from the body on which it depends and of which it does not form a part, and which consists in and possesses no other attributes than those of length and breadth without thickness, or how that which consists in length and breadth only should be capable of producing sensible effects as the terminations or superficies of bodies are known to do, as when they affect the feeling on reacting on being touched by the hand and the sight on reflecting the rays of light incident on them on the eye, &c. and the arguments adduced above in favour of these doctrines being at the same time seemingly so pertinent cogent and convincing as not to admit of being easily and readily refuted, if it is at all possible, the mind becomes confounded and remains in suspence with respect to what to believe; whether to trust to the dictates of its senses, or to put implicit reliance on the validity of conclusions so ingeniously deduced and supported.

7. Had the Geometricians themselves clearly and distinctly conceived what it was they wished to be understood as the termination, surface or superficies of a body, what they wished to define, and had accordingly defined it clearly and distinctly, this state of suspense, doubt, and perplexity, could never have taken place. Had they been sensible that what they here attempt to define, and here represent as the termination, surface, or superficies of a body, or as that which in the common acceptation of these terms is understood to mean those bounding or terminating parts of a body which produce the sensible effects above described, can in reality with no propriety or justice be regarded as such, since, according to their own statement or definition of it, a termination or superficies forms no part of a body, is not a body of itself, and is possessed of no power, and is consequently altogether incapable of producing the sensible effects mentioned above, or any effects whatever; and, therefore, that what they represent as the termination or superficies, in place of being actually the termination or superficies of a body, is in reality nothing but the *area or extent* of the termination or superficies of a body, which really consists in length and

breadth

breadth only; and which, in these arguments, being *nominally* substituted for the *superficies itself*, produces that perplexity of thought so favourable to the reception of erroneous opinions, and confers on these arguments that plausibility which has impressed a general conviction of those doctrines they are brought to support being well founded and just. It is solely on the ambiguity and equivocation resulting from this misconception, misrepresentation, and misapplication of the terms termination, surface and SUPERFICIES of a body, for the AREA of the superficies of a body, or of certain properties of a superficies, as its extension in different directions, for the superficies itself, that all the perplexing difficulties in this case are to be attributed, and it is solely on these that the subtilty of argumentation rests, on which the above mysterious doctrines depend. The area of any particular body, or what in effect is the same thing in as far as mensuration or geometry is concerned, an equivalent area, can be transferred from one body to another without any ways affecting that particular body; thus the area of the superficies of a plain side of a body can be transferred to and be accurately delineated on paper, but the superficies itself of a side of a body cannot be so transferred without affecting the form and solid contents, &c. of the body, from the body in its terminating parts or superficies being formed of other materials besides a compound of length and breadth: all that can properly be meant by defining a superficies to be length and breadth only is that the area of a superficies is of two dimensions only, or that it extends only in length and in breadth; so that in fact this is not, if properly understood, a definition of a superficies itself, but of its area, measurement, or extent in two directions as ascertained and determined by means of some standard or measuring unit. If the justness of the above reasoning is admitted, no refutation of the inferences deduced from this geometrical definition of superficies with respect to its terminations of lines and points can be required, since these must necessarily, as being the terminations of measurement or area, be merely imaginary or suppositious.

8. Dr. Keil then adds, " but it will be answered, that these points, lines, " and surfaces are not material. What then? Who ever asserted that a " mathematical point was matter? Who ever fancied a material superficies? " If it was material, it would have its superficies or termination: but the " superficies of a superficies, who ever imagined? However, though neither
                                                          " surfaces,

" surfaces, nor lines, nor points, are real matter, yet they exist or may
" exist in it, as its modes, terminations, or accidents; just after the same
" manner as figure is not body itself, but only its affection, whereby it is
" contained under given terminations, and this has real properties wholly
" distinct from those of body."

9. After what has been advanced above, it is presumable there can be
no difficulty in admitting that what Mathematicians represent as and
denominate the superficies of a body is not real matter or material—but
only an affection or property of matter or body—or in discovering the
property or affection of the body thus represented and denominated, since
it manifestly can be no other than its area or the extension of its surface or
superficies in length and breadth.

10. Before entering on an examination of the geometrical demonstrations adduced in proof of these doctrines, it may be proper to discuss the
argument with which this lecture ends,* viz.—" But because the philoso-
" phers, against whom we dispute, are not acquainted enough with geome-
" trical demonstrations, and therefore do not easily perceive their evidence,
" before we end this lecture we shall produce one physical argument taken
" from motion, for the infinite divisibility of quantity: namely, if quan-
" tity consisted of indivisibles, it would follow, that all motion would be
" equally swift, nor would a slow snail pass over a less space in the same
" time than the swift footed Achilles. For let us suppose Achilles to run
" very swiftly, and the snail to creep sluggishly along, if extension con-
" sisted of indivisibles, the snail could not in any given time pass over less
" space than Achilles: for if in a moment's time Achilles passes over an
" indivisible space, the snail cannot in the same moment of time pass over
" less space; by reason, from the hypothesis, there cannot be a less. For
" one indivisible cannot be less than another, therefore it will pass over an
" equal space. The same may be said of any other moment of time:
" therefore the spaces passed over by them both would be equal; and
" consequently the swift footed Achilles cannot pass over more space than
" the slow snail, which is absurd. Other absurdities of the like sort may
" be deduced from the same hypothesis of indivisibles; but what we have
" already said, is sufficient."

* Keil's Introduction, Pp. 31 and 32.

11. This

11. This argument though ingenious is neither conclusive nor just: for though it is admitted that Achilles and the snail may pass over an indefinitely small space in an indefinitely small time, and consequently each pass over the same indefinite space in the same indefinite time, yet, it by no means follows from this as a necessary consequence that both will pass over any longer given space, as here inferred, in the same time; since the snail may, and from the known slowness of its motion in passing over a longer space, it is justly inferible, necessarily must require a much longer interval of time between each exertion in moving, whereby it passes over one of these indefinitely small spaces, to recover from the former, and prepare itself for a new exertion to enable it to move over another of these, and so on in succession; and though these intervals of cessation from motion should each be of so short duration as not to be individually perceptible to us, yet, from their number being so great, as recurring almost instantaneously and incessantly, they would necessarily diminish the velocity of the motion on the whole over any longer space in a very considerable degree; and the velocity of the motion of Achilles could not on the whole, though their velocities in passing over an indefinitely small space should be the same, equal that of the snail, unless the amount of the intervals of cessation from motion in Achilles in passing over the given space was equal to the amount of those in the snail in passing over the same space, which, from the known differences in the relative velocities of their motions, the former being styled the swift footed Achilles, and the other the sluggish snail, it would be absurd to suppose.

12. It is, however, on what has been called the geometrical demonstrations, that the greatest reliance has been placed in the attempts to prove the infinite divisibility of all extension, whether corporeal or incorporeal, viz. " Having now," says Doctor Keil,* " settled these principles, we re-" turn to our purpose; which was to demonstrate that all extension, whe-" ther corporeal or incorporeal, was divisible *in infinitum*, or had an infinite " number of parts; which we shall endeavour to prove by many invincible " arguments. Of which, this shall be the first: let A B (see fig. 1st) repre-" sent a right line, I say it is divisible, into parts exceeding any finite

---

* Keil's Introduction, Pp. 26, 27, 28, 29, and 30.

" number

" number whatever. Through A let be drawn any right line A C, and paral-
" lel to it let be drawn through B the right line B D, and in A C let there be
" taken any point, as C : if therefore the right line A B is not divisible into
" an infinite number of parts, let it be divisible only into a finite number of
" parts ; and let that number, for example, be six. In the line B D on the
" side opposite to C let there be taken any number of points exceeding
" six ; for example, the points C, F, G, H, I, K, L, and let there be drawn
" by the first postulate of *Euclid*, C E, C F, C G, C H, C I, C K, C L.
" These thus drawn, divide the right line A B into as many parts as there
" are right lines ; for if they do not, then some of the right lines intersect
" A B in one and the same point : but all of them intersect one another in
" the common point C, whence some two right lines will cut one another
" twice, or will have the same common segment ; both which is contrary
" to an axiom in the *Elements.* A B is therefore divided into as many dif-
" ferent parts as there are right lines ; but there are as many right lines as
" there were points taken in the right line B D : wherefore since there were
" taken more points than six, the right line A B is divisible into more parts
" than six. After the same manner, how great soever the number assumed
" shall be, it may be shewn that the line A B is divisible into a number of
" parts greater than that number, namely, by taking in the right line B D
" a greater number of points, (which may be easily done, since no finite
" number is so great but a greater may be assumed, and that in any given
" ratio of a greater inequality) and by drawing right lines from the point
" C to the points taken in the right line B D ; for these right lines will di-
" vide the right line A B into as many parts as there are right lines, and
" therefore into more parts than the number first assumed (how great so-
" ever it was) contains units ; and consequently the right line A B is
" divisible into more parts than can be expressed by any finite number,
" and therefore is divisible *in infinitum.* Q. E. D."

   " The second argument. Let A B (fig. 2d) represent any right line, I
" say it is divisible into an infinite number of parts ; for if it is not divi-
" sible into an infinite number of parts let it be divisible into a finite num-
" ber of parts, and let that number be, for example, five. Let any right
" line A K be drawn, making any angle with A B, and in it, produced if
" necessary, let there be taken as many points as you please above five,

" which let be C, D, E, F, G, H, K; join K B, and through the points
" C, D, E, F, G, H, let right lines be drawn parallel to K B: these will
" necessarily divide the right line A B into as many parts as there are right
" lines; for, if they do not, more right lines must concur in one and the
" same point: but they cannot concur since they are parallel; wherefore
" each right line will intersect the right line A B in a different point, and all
" will divide the right line A B into as many parts as there were right lines
" drawn parallel. But there were more drawn than five, therefore the right
" line A B will be divided into more parts than five. And the same may
" be affirmed of any other number. Wherefore no number is so great
" but the number of parts the right line is divisible into is still greater, and
" consequently the right line A B is divisible *in infinitum.*

" Thirdly, if quantity is not divisible *in infinitum*, it must be divisible
" into parts, that are not further divisible; but there is no part that cannot
" still be farther divided, because there can be given no quantity so small
" but there may be still taken a smaller, and that in any given ratio of
" lesser inequality. For let A B be a right line (fig. 3d), and let A C be
" an exceedingly small part of it, I say there may be a line less than A C
" in any ratio of less inequality, as, for example, one to three. From the
" point A draw any right line A D, and in it let be taken the equal right
" lines A E, E F, F G; join G C, and through E draw E H parallel to
" G C, the right line A H will be a third part of A C: the demonstration
" thereof is manifest from the *ninth proposition of the sixth book of the Ele-*
" *ments.* And therefore the right line A C will not be the least that can
" be taken. The same may be demonstrated of any right line whatsoever;
" and consequently there is not in nature an absolute *minimum.*

" Again, if quantity was composed of indivisibles, many absurdities
" would thence follow : for let there be, for example, two concentric circles
" (fig. 4th), A B C D, E F G H, and let the circumference of the greater be
" divided into its indivisible parts, and let be drawn from the centre Q to
" each of these parts, the right lines Q O M, Q P N, which will divide
" both the circumferences into an equal number of parts, but the greater
" circumference A B C D was divided into its smallest parts; and there-
" fore the less circumference E F G will consist of as many indivisibles, or
" smaller parts possible, as the greater circumference A B C: and conse-
                                                            " quently

" quently sinee an indivisible is equal to an indivisible, the circumference
" E F G H will be equal to the circumference A B C D, a lesser to a
" greater, which is absurd."

" Lastly, from this composition of quantity of indivisibles, there can be
" no incommensurate magnitude; which is contrary to what Geometers
" frequently demonstrate. For if all magnitude consisted of indivisibles,
" an indivisible would be an adequate and common measure of all magni-
" tudes of the same kind; for it would be exactly contained the same
" number of times in all, and therefore all magnitudes would have a com-
" mon measure, and the side of a square would be commensurate to its
" diagonal; contrary to the *last proposition of the tenth book of Euclid's*
" *Elements*."

13. These demonstrations however, as they are called, and which are
pronounced to be invincible, are in reality only either different ways of
begging the question by assuming in the premises that which is required
to be proved, as in the first case by the assumption of there being no indivisibles; or attempts to divide space---and thereby to prove its infinite di-
visibility---by the instrumentality of what cannot possibly divide or produce any effect whatever, an entity, merely nominal and fictitious, called a
geometrical line, having neither breadth nor thickness, and which neither
does, nor in the nature of things possibly can exist, not even in imagination,
since of such it is impossible to form any mental image or representation. In these cases, however, not only the possibility of its existence but
its actual existence is supposed and assumed, and it is on the above assumptions alone that the validity of the conclusions deduced by these irrefragable geometrical demonstrations exclusively depend. Thus, in the
first and second of these geometrical propositions, if the lines A B, A B,
in their respective appropriate diagrams, are formed of indivisibles, it is
manifest they cannot be cut and divided in the manner supposed in
these propositions: that they are not formed of indivisibles is assumed in
these propositions, since they are stated in them as being divisible by certain lines in *infinitum*; but these propositions afford no proof whatever,
and far less any invincible demonstration, of that being really the case, or
that they are not formed of actual indivisibles, though it is that which is
most necessary and is required to be proved to evince that divisibility in

infinitum

infinitum which in the proposition is only assumed. It is said indeed, " if " therefore the right line A B is not divisible into an infinite number of " parts, let it be divisible only into a finite number of parts : and let that " number, for example, be six." That is in the first proposition, and in the second it is said " and let that number be, for example, five." But notwithstanding these expressions it is manifest they are not regarded, or intended to be represented, as being formed of actual indivisibles ; since in that case it is evident they could not be divided further than into the number of finite parts given, it being manifestly impossible to divide what is indivisible ; and the notion of divisible indivisibles one would suppose is too absurd to be adopted. The third proposition proceeds also on the assumption of there being no indivisibles. The fourth proposition however —that of the concentric circles with its pretended demonstration—proceeds nevertheless it must be acknowledged on the very absurd suppositions of there actually being divisible indivisibles, or of the real indivisibles, or smallest parts possible of which the circumference of the inner and smaller circle E F G H is stated to be formed, being divisible :—yet this proposition is given as an instance of the absurdities resulting from the adoption of the opinion of there really being in nature actual indivisibles. The object of these propositions and conclusions seems to be the proving that those parts which are stated in these propositions to be indivisibles are not so in reality ; but if not so in reality, why are they stated to be so ? such mis-representation of data, such mis-statement of the facts on which the proofs are founded, can serve no good purpose ; and, indeed, no purpose but that of rendering the propositions altogether nugatory, and the conclusions deduced from them invalid.

14. It is added " Lastly, from this composition of quantity of indivi-" sibles, there can be no incommensurate magnitudes ; which is contrary " to what the geometers frequently demonstrate, &c." It is a sufficient answer to this argument merely to observe that this proposition of Euclid to which he refers, viz. the last of the tenth book of his Elements, is also founded upon a mere gratuitous assumption, in the ninth proposition of the same book, no where proved, of there being actually lines and quantities which are of their own nature incommensurable ; and, this being the case, that no reliance can be placed on the conclusions deduced from a proposition

tion founded on such dubious if not false data as is this famous last proposition of the tenth book of the Elements; which, in the estimation of Plato, was of such importance that he deemed those who understood it not more deserving of the name of brute than of man.

Should the lines A B, A B, in the diagrams of the first and second of these propositions be regarded as not consisting of parts of any kind, either divisible or indivisible, but merely as indicating, in the first diagram, the distance between the parallel lines A C and B D; and, in the second, the distance between the extremities A and B on the lines A K and B K; and thereby the extent, at those parts and in these directions, of the space or vacuity between them: and should the purpose of these propositions be to prove the divisibility of simple extension unoccupied by matter as represented by the lines A B, A B; and that either by means of lines drawn from the point C to different points in the line B D as in diagram first, or by lines drawn parallel to K B as in the second diagram, and then by representing that as the number of points may be infinite in the line B D of diagram first the lines drawn to those infinite points from the point C and cutting the line A B in different places must be the same or infinite also; and likewise as the number of lines drawn parallel to K B in diagram second may be infinite and cutting A B in different places these places may be infinite also; it follows that the unoccupied extension or space as represented by the lines A B, A B, must each be infinitely divided as being cut by an infinite number of lines in an infinite number of different places. In complete refutation, however, of this supposed demonstration it is only necessary to observe that this cannot possibly be the case if the lines by which the extension or space is divided are physical lines possessing breadth; since a finite number of these dividing it into a finite number of portions must necessarily occupy the whole extent of space, after which it is manifest there can be no further division by their means; and the same is the case with respect to other spaces, as that of an angle formed by a straight line and any curve:—that extension should be divisible by geometrical lines, or by what exists not and cannot exist, is a position that surely must be allowed to be inadmisible as necessarily implying an impossibility and being therefore absurd: indeed it seems strange it should ever have been supposed.

15. It

15. It is admitted, in lecture 4th,[*] that an infinite magnitude cannot be contained in a finite magnitude: but it is asserted that an infinite number may be contained in a finite; and consequently that a finite magnitude, from magnitude being divisible in infinitum, may contain an infinite number of parts. To this it may justly be answered, that every number however great or small is necessarily finite. There may be an indefinite, but there cannot possibly be an infinite number; and every series, however many or however few the number of its terms, must necessarily have a finite value or amount; and the value being finite the number of terms must necessarily be so likewise; so that no series can possibly be infinite. The expression an infinite number, as being a contradiction in terms involving an impossibility, is absurd, and ought never to be used. A number is not infinite for being indefinite or unassignable by human powers:—numeration must not be limited by human abilities so as to render it either dependent upon them or correspondent to them.

16. It is said[†] " But besides, there are many examples brought both " from arithmetic as well as geometry, where, by the confession of our ad- " versaries themselves, the number of parts will be infinite, but the magni- " tude composed of those parts shall be finite. Let the first example be a " series of numbers decreasing in any proportion, which shall be equal " to a finite number, as, for example, $\frac{1}{2}$, $\frac{1}{4}$, $\frac{1}{8}$, $\frac{1}{16}$, $\frac{1}{32}$, $\frac{1}{64}$, &c. the sum of this " series continued in *infinitum*, will be equal to a unit; but since the series " is continued in *infinitum*, its terms will be infinite in number: wherefore " in this case the parts of a quantity, that are infinite in number, will make " a finite quantity. And in like manner the sum of this series, $\frac{1}{3}$, $\frac{1}{9}$, $\frac{1}{27}$, $\frac{1}{81}$, " &c. when continued in *infinitum* will be equal to half an unit, as may be " demonstrated from arithmetic. But nobody will deny, that this series " being continued in *infinitum*, has an infinite number of parts; wherefore " there may be an infinite number of parts of a quantity, which however " shall not exceed one half of an unit. And in geometry it is known that " there may be given a space infinitely long, which however shall be ex- " actly equal to a finite space; and this in an infinite number of examples

* Keil's Introduction to Natural Philosophy, p. 33.

† Keil's Introduction, pp. 35 and 36.

" has

" has been demonstrated by the famous geometers Torricellius, Wallis,
" Barrow, and others; from whom we shall produce a few instances." This
opinion, though generally adopted, is certainly erroneous:—for an infinite
series is an impossibility in nature; and if it were possible, it could not
equal a finite quantity, as having no determinate limits to its number of
terms.   Or though it should have a beginning, or a first term—as in the
above examples of indefinite series in geometrical progression—which, on
that account though there were no other objections, is improperly stiled infinite though its number of terms are indeterminate, and its last term unknown; or though it is what in this case is called infinite, from its having
but one end or a first term or beginning and its being supposed to have but
one end only, it cannot possibly if infinite, as having no last term as assumed
in the hypothesis, have a finite value, or be equal to any finite quantity;
the sum or amount of such a progression when finite being always equal
to the quotient of the product of the last term multiplied into the common
ratio diminished by the first term divided by the common ratio diminished
by unity, and therefore always necessarily determined by the value of
the first and last given terms of the series, and that of the common ratio:
and when infinite, or when there is no first or last term, were it possible, it
could have no finite or determinate value.   The same reasoning is applicable to the geometrical examples which are given from the logarithmical
curve, and the hyperbola, with the intention of proving that there are
parts of space infinite in number, from their increasing in number in geometrical progression, which when added together are equal to a finite
space, as depending entirely on the same erroneous principles as the above.

17. It is surely carrying the argument too far when it is asserted,* " But
" since we have already demonstrated that there cannot be given any par-
" ticle of matter, however small, which may not be still divided into other
" infinite particles; it is thence manifest, that God cannot so divide matter,
" as that there shall be given its ultimate indivisible." Lastly, it is
attempted to prove geometrically that there actually are infinitesimals of infinitesimals, or fluctions of fluctions, *in infinitum;* or to demonstrate that
there are quantities infinitely less *in infinitum* than quantities that are infi-

---

* Keil's Introduction, p. 39.

nitely

nitely small ; and three geometrical propositions or examples are given with
this intention.   But they are such as cannot, when fully investigated and
well understood, be deemed satisfactory, or well adapted for conveying
conviction to the mind with regard to the truth of those doctrines they are
brought to prove.   For the proof, in the third and last of them, rests entirely on the erroneous supposition of an angular space being divisible, and
divisible *in infinitum*, by means of what cannot possibly divide, those nominal and fictitious entities geometrical lines since it is evidently impossible for it to be so divided by such as are physical ; and, in the other
two, the proof rests on the unwarrantably assuming of finite quantities
as quantities infinitely small; and on the equal unwarrantable inference
thence deduced of infinitely small quantities being infinitely divisible, merely
because finite quantities, or those finite quantities thus assumed are divisible.   On this arbitrary and gratuitous assumption, and on the divisibility
of the finite quantities thus assumed, is any finite part obtained by the
dividing of any of them pronounced to be an infinitesimal of an infinitesimal, or a fluction of a fluction ; and this procedure is given as a demonstration of it.

18. A mathematical demonstration, which is represented as purely and
rigidly geometrical, in proof of these paradoxes, of this mystical doctrine
of the actual existence of entities palpable to sense which possess not
magnitude, is also attempted by the learned Doctor Simson in a note to
the first definition of his edition of the Elements of Euclid.   But this
demonstration in reality proves nothing but this, which no one ever
doubted, that the superficies of any particular solid cannot be the superficies of any other similar solid to which it may be temporarily and occasionally applied, and thereby decisively refutes the doctrine it is
brought to support, or the hypothesis assumed in the proposition with
the intention of proving that a superficies has no thickness, of the two
solids thus applied having at their junction but one common superficies
only to their respective sides thus applied, which is in the one as well
as in the other solid ; and consequently the conclusions deduced from it,
since it necessarily follows from the above, that each solid has in this
case as well as in others a superficies to each of its sides exclusively its
own : to those thus applied as well as to the others.

From

From the above observations it must be manifest, how prodigiously different the speculations of the mathematicians, concerning the natures of things, are from the things themselves. It must have, however, required no common degree of ingenuity, ability, eloquence, and address, in those who conceived, adopted, and supported, doctrines so remote from common apprehension, and so repugnant to prevailing opinion, as well as to the real natures of things, as those of the geometrical definitions of points, lines, and surfaces—as that of the infinite divisibility of magnitude—and indeed the whole doctrine of infinites—to have propagated them with such entire success as to have enforced on nearly the whole philosophical world---the most learned, the most intelligent, and most judicious among mankind---a full conviction of their validity, and of their being so securely established on irrefragable mathematical demonstration as to defy refutation :---many of these doctrines have prevailed for upwards of two thousand years ; a circumstance which could not possibly have taken place, if those who conceived and adopted them had not supported them with great ability.

19. For the refutation of that opinion so long and so universally entertained of the mathematics---though applicable to practical purposes--- being a science purely speculative, the result merely of pure intellection, of mental resources and mental exertion having no dependence whatever on experience or experiment or on the nature of things, it is necessary only to observe with proper attention the procedure by means of which the science is formed, carried on, and developed, as given in the Elements of Euclid, as that of itself will afford a decisive proof of this in reality not being the case. It has indeed in a certain degree already been proved in the second of these Essays that mathematical science, like all other human sciences, is founded on and derived from experiments ; and that it consists of known facts, the result either of casual experience or of experiments made for the express purpose of ascertaining them, and of rational deductions from these or the facts thus ascertained. And, as this is the case, all the proofs, or demonstrations as they are called, being evidently founded on and evidently depending upon experiments, either made at the time or formerly made and referred to, there necessarily must be much impropriety and manifest disadvantage in attempting, as is often the case, to prove

those propositions, the truth of which is manifest from mere inspection of the diagram, or which admit of being proved experimentally or intuitively by an immediate direct appeal to the discriminating and judging faculty of the mind through the medium of the senses, by means of a long, tedious, disagreeable process called a demonstration; especially, as these other methods are often more accurate and unexceptionable, often more to be relied upon, and are much more obvious, easy, and concise, than that of demonstration; with which in these cases there is no necessity for burdening the memory. Such attempts are not only most egregious trifling and loss of time, but also when the propositions are such as admit of no other proof than experimental absurd in the extreme :---and, indeed, in any case no other proof can be so valid and satisfactory as the intuitive or experimental; since any degree of validity any other may possess must necessarily depend upon and be ultimately derived from experiment.

20. Most of the definitions given in the Elements of Geometry are merely descriptive and nominal; and the meaning of these can be properly explained, so as to be distinctly understood, only by exhibiting to the senses the objects themselves of which they are the descriptions and names. Euclid's 10th definition of book 1st, (Simson's Euclid) is " when a straight " line standing on another straight line makes the adjacent angles equal to " one another, each of the angles is called a right angle; and the straight " line which stands on the other is called a perpendicular to it." But how can this equality, in this case, be determined and known? not by mere intellection surely, nor from any thing that has proceeded since nothing has proceeded from which it can be justly and rationally deduced :---it can then be determined only by actual experiment. That they are ever or in any case equal to one another is however not proved by experiment or any otherwise here or in any other part of the Elements; and yet this equality is assumed and is given as an axiom (11th of book 1st), though far from being obvious, without any proof, merely from this definition. The 15th definition of the first Book of Euclid's Elements is " a circle is a plain figure " contained by one line, which is called the circumference, and is such that " all straight lines drawn from a certain point within the figure to the cir- " cumference, are equal to one another." But by what means that certain point is to be known, or the equality of the lines drawn from it to the circumference

cumference has been ascertained or may be ascertained and proved, is not to be discovered from this definition; which, inverting the natural and *proper* order of things, makes this equality to depend on the figure necessarily resulting from it, and intended to be defined from that circumstance, in place of making the figure depend on the equality of all the lines proceeding from a certain point given within it.

21. These propositions, however, of " all the radii of a circle being " equal to each other," and of " all right angles being equal to one ano‑ " ther," which are no where proved and only assumed, form the basis, the very fundamental pillars and principles of the science; a science which boasts of taking nothing for granted, but, proceeding from proof to proof in a necessarily connected series, deduces inferences the truth of which does not admit of doubt or uncertainty. This is an important defect in the Elements, and would essentially affect the validity of the science, were it not that these arbitrary assumptions on which it is founded and proceeds admit of proof.

22. It is on this assumption of all the radii of a circle being equal that Euclid founds his first demonstrations. The 3d proposition of the Elements ought to have been the first, since the two that precede it depend upon it. This 3d proposition is " from the greater of two given straight lines to " cut off a part equal to the less." The method proposed and practised by Euclid both of effecting, and of demonstrating this, appears really preposterous: what occasion is there for drawing the line A D, (see Simson's Euclid) when A E could be taken at once, and without the intervention of A D, equal to C; and that by the very means, and with the very same certainty, that A D is? this seems a very absurd procedure; and the demonstrations, as they are called, of this and of the two preceding propositions are made to rest on the mere assumption, never demonstrated as was above observed, of all the radii of a circle being equal among themselves. The fact is the equation or equality in this and the two preceding propositions is proved, and that in the most satisfactory manner, experimentally, by means of the compass and diagram; and it cannot be proved any otherwise than experimentally. This manner of proof by the compass is applicable to most or all of the immediately succeeding propositions; but to call it demonstration must be truly ridi-

culous.

culous. The prop. 4th, 5th, 6th, 7th, and 8th of this book, are all founded on and proved by experiment, or on the coincidence or not of triangles similar or dis-similar applied to one another:—these propositions might be proved in a manner at least equally correct and convincing, and much more obvious and easy, by applying a compass to the diagrams; or by the actual application of small triangles of metal, ivory, or wood, formed according to the diagrams, directly to one another; whereby their coincidence or non-coincidence would immediately appear. The problems that immediately follow, being propositions 9th, 10th, 11th, and 12th, seem to be effected in a very proper manner, but they may be proved much easier by applying a compass to the diagrams, or small metallic triangles (as the triangles A D F, and A E F, of proposition 9th) to each other, and with equal accuracy with the manner here given; as its degree of accuracy, even supposing the application and deduction to be perfectly just, must depend entirely on the degree of exactness with which the preceding propositions or facts from which they are deduced have been experimentally proved and ascertained. The propositions 13th and 14th are self-evident; or are so manifest to sense from mere inspection of the diagram as to require no other proof:—the same might have been said of some of the preceding propositions, and may be said of several which follow. Proposition 15th is so obviously and easily deduced from facts already experimentally ascertained, and that directly without the intervention of any medium, that there seems little occasion in this case for a direct experimental proof by means of a compass or otherwise; and indeed it must be in a great measure manifest to sense from a bare inspection of the diagram. Propositions 16, 17, 18, 19, 20, and 21 could all be easily proved by direct experiment, were they not evident to sense from viewing the diagrams. Of the problem, prop. 22d, the same may be said that was said of the problem, prop. 3d. Propositions 23d, 24th, 25th, and 26th, are proved by applying angles, and triangles, respectively to each other, which might be done with more ease and perspicuity by immediate direct experiments, than by inferences deduced from prior experiments, or indirectly from supposed applications of one figure to another: but indeed these propositions are so evident from mere inspection of the figures as to require no other proof.

23. Propositions

23. Propositions 27, 28, 29, 30, and 31, may be all easily and accurately proved by immediate direct experiment, either by means of a compass and the diagrams, or by means of two similar rods of brass or ivory---each having a smaller rod of the same kind fastened to that point which divides its length into equal parts and there moveable on a pivot so that it may be made to form at pleasure any required angle with the rod to which it is fastened---being applied to each other in different manners, as by placing them parallel to each other while the smaller rods are made to meet together forming one straight line crossing the larger rods at different angles as required; and also by placing the one immediately above the other while each makes the same angle with the smaller rod, and in such a manner as that the angular points, and the corresponding sides of the angles, of both may exactly coincide. The 32d Proposition also admits of being easily proved by experiment, or mensuration by means of the compass and diagram. Euclid in demonstrating it takes an exterior angle equal to one of the interior and opposite angles by means of the compass and actual mensuration; and if he had taken the other also in the same manner, it would have been the easiest way of proving the proposition, and have saved the unnecessary trouble of studying and remembering what is called a demonstration. Prop. 33 is manifest to sense, and can be easily proved by applying a compass to the diagram. Prop. 34 is also manifest to sense, and can be proved by applying a compass to the diagram, with more ease, and with equal accuracy with the method employed by Euclid to prove it, viz. by proving the equality of the several sides and angles of the two triangles to each other respectively, from having actually formed them so by mensuration by means of the compass; and then inferring, merely from the equality of the sides and angles thus obtained, the equality of the two triangles themselves to each other. The same kind of observations is applicable to many of the other Propositions, though in some of them with this difference of their areas not being measured immediately and directly by means of lines and angles, but by the intervention of other areas which manifestly form a half, fourth, or other determinate part of the areas required to be measured, or by the addition or subtraction of equal areas to or from equal areas; and it is unnecessary to pursue this reasoning further, since it is sufficiently evident from what has been already advanced,

and

and from the frequent references in the Elements to those propositions whose proofs rest on immediate direct experiment, as the 3d, 4th, &c. of Book I., that the mathematical sciences, like all others, depend upon experience or experiment.

24. It would however be an egregious mistake to suppose that Geometry, though ultimately founded on experience and experiments, is a science merely experimental, and admits in every case of being taught experimentally, since the principal and higher parts of it consist almost entirely in investigation by rational deduction, rational deduction from facts previously ascertained whether by means of direct experiments or of conclusions logically and justly deduced from them. It is on just reasoning that this science principally depends, and it is principally by the use and application of just reasoning that a knowledge of it is to be acquired.

25. For, though no opinion can be worse founded than that of the mathematical sciences being the result of pure intellection only, and that Geometry is merely the application of metaphysics to magnitudes; and though many geometrical propositions cannot with propriety and advantage be proved otherwise than experimentally, and several of them admit of no other proof, yet these are only the first and fundamental parts and propositions of the science, and there are numerous others which not being proveable by immediate actual experiment require being proved in a manner less obvious and direct, by means of rational and just deductions from the fundamental propositions, or those which have been proved by immediate direct experiment, through the instrumentality of intermedia, or of diagrams, &c. adapted to the purpose; and it is in this procedure that that which is called geometrical demonstration properly consists; and in the successful prosecution of which much ingenuity, judgment, and address are often required. The measures, or the ratios, of certain magnitudes being ascertained, by means of actual experiment, or by means of the direct application either of the magnitudes themselves to each other, or of the measuring unit or standard to them respectively, the end and object of geometrical science is, by rational deductions from these without the aid of more experiments, to determine incontrovertibly the measures, and the ratios, of other magnitudes; and to point out the manner and means by which this may be effected:—the excellence of mathematical science

does

does not consist in its not being founded in experiment, but in its deducing from so few experiments so many just and important conclusions.

26. Though points, and lines, as represented by geometricians, cannot possibly have any actual existence in nature, or cannot exist otherwise than hypothetically and in name only; and though geometrical surfaces are only attributes of bodies, or the areas or extensions of their surfaces in length and breadth, no doubt can be entertained with respect to the actual existence of physical bodies, and that of their essential attributes extension, figure, &c. since of these we have every evidence human nature admits of; and consequently of the physical superficies, lines, and points or parts, of these bodies, each of which is itself a body or physical solid of a certain particular figure forming a constituent portion of that particular body or physical solid of which it is a superficies, line, or point or part; and each therefore is necessarily extended, even a physical point or atom, or possesses extension as one of its essential attributes; and, being extended, is necessarily a magnitude: magnitude consisting in EXTENSION, and not in PARTS—as supposed by the geometricians—for extension consists in distance; in the distance between bodies as well as between the parts or extremities of a particular body, though that distance should be unoccupied, and therefore constitutes what is called vacant extension or space as distinguished from corporeal or material extension; which, though not consisting in parts, as being unoccupied, is yet a magnitude as being extended; and which, though not divisible into parts, as not being formed of parts, is yet, as being a magnitude, distinguishable into portions by the proper application to it of physical lines or bodies for that purpose. And, though it is only magnitudes that consist of parts or portions, or that are divisible or are distinguishable into these, that admit of being measured; yet that affords not any sufficient reason for supposing, and far less for laying it down as an incontrovertible position, since it by no means necessarily follows from it, that an indivisible, or that which has no parts, has no magnitude; and thence for concluding that magnitude is divisible *in infinitum.*

27. The terms extension and distance are properly of the same import. Distance or extension is inferred from, and consists in, the admission, or possibility of admission, of entities between other entities, real or supposed; and these entities which admit of such interposition are, on that

account,

account, regarded as and said to be distant from each other, whether they are separate distinct beings or bodies, or the extremities or other parts of the same body or substance; and this distance, as ascertained by means of interposing bodies, is regarded as and is denominated the *extension* either of the body between its extremities, or other particular parts, when the objects of distance are thus connected, or of the *space* between different bodies which are not thus connected. Distance or mere extension, whether the distance between the extremities or other parts of a rod or other body or between separate distinct bodies, admits of being diminished to annihilation by making these parts or bodies approach each other till coming into contact it vanishes or becomes equal O, there then being no admission, without moving and thereby separating them again from each other, for that interposition of any other body between them from which distance or extension is inferible.

28. The annihilation of extension or distance by this means affords an experimental or intuitive and therefore decisive proof of the invalidity of that doctrine which invests extension with the attribute of infinite divisibility; since the admission of the possibility of its being annihilable by the division and diminution of its parts or portions necessarily precludes the possibility of its being divisible *in infinitum*; and since bodies moving towards each other could never come into contact if distance or extension could be divided, or diminished and contracted *in infinitum* without being exhausted by that means. It, however, by no means follows from this that a material entity or atom admits either of being diminished to annihilation or of being infinitely divided; and it is manifest that the contrary must necessarily be the case, since a material atom, from its essential solidity, must necessarily effectually resist the contact of its extremities and its consequent annihilation; and since all further division or diminution of solid magnitude must necessarily terminate when the extremities are so near to each other as not to admit of being nearer without coming into contact and so terminating in the annihilation of the atom. To suppose that substance or matter should be *annihilable* by mere mechanic division of it, as distance or vacant extension may be, would not be less absurd than the supposition of its being formed of geometrical points, lines, and superficies, or of *entities not possessing magnitude:*---or than that of its being *infinitely divisible.*

But,

But, if neither divisible in *infinitum*, nor to annihilation, it necessarily follows that the division of it must be finite, and must terminate in a finite time, and terminate in indivisibles, that is, in physical points or atoms ; which, though not consisting of parts, as being indivisibles, are yet magnitudes as possessing extension ; and which, though not divisible and therefore not measurable themselves as individuals, may yet form a standard by which other magnitudes may be measured or computed ; and, in nature, a physical point necessarily must be the universal standard or measuring unit, since it is of physical points that all the other magnitudes in nature are formed :---and, this being the case, it necessarily follows that there cannot possibly be in nature any absolute incommensurables ; though there may be many magnitudes that are so relatively to human abilities.

29. Though the terms magnitude and extension are both often used as synonimous with quantity, and though extension is magnitude, yet they are also frequently employed in a meaning peculiar to each as expressing different things ; the terms a magnitude and magnitudes being often used to signify a body and bodies, whereas the term extension is never used as signifying body---but is used only as signifying an essential attribute or quality of body---and not even as signifying a geometrical solid, unless when the epithet triple is prefixed to it, or when it is said to be of three dimensions. Though the extension of a body is properly in every direction, it is usual to regard a body as extended in three directions only, viz. length, breadth, and thickness, and to regard each of these as perpendicular to the other two ; and hence both a body and a geometrical solid are said to be of three dimensions as possessing extension in the three directions of length, breadth, and thickness---a geometrical superficies to be of two dimensions as possessing only length and breadth---and a geometrical line of one dimension, as possessing length only.

30. Mensuration is the comparing of magnitudes together, either by the direct application of the one, as the measuring standard or unit, to the other ; or by the direct application of an intermediate magnitude, as a measuring standard or unit better suited to the purpose, to one or to both, and thereby determining either their relative extensions and magnitudes, as to equality, greater, or less---though the exact degree of greater or less may not always be obtained by this means---or the extent of one, or of

both, either in one, two, or three dimensions, or in length, in surface, or in solid contents, relatively to the intermediate magnitude used as the measuring standard or unit. As magnitudes are of three different kinds, viz. linear, superficial, and solid, and as each can be compared and measured by means only of a magnitude of the same kind with itself, so there necessarily must be three different kinds of measuring standards also, a linear, a superficial, and a solid ; a line being measured by a line, a surface by a surface, and a solid by a solid.

31. Geometry is the science of mensuration, both theoretical and practical, as rationally deduced from the extensions and properties of figures, as ascertained by means of experiment and induction, and of rational inferences from these. And, hence, it comprehends methods of ascertaining and determining whatever is capable of being ascertained and determined by means of mensuration ; as not only those properties and relations of figures that depend on the position and form of the lines or planes that bound them, &c.---and thereby the centres of magnitude, &c. of bodies---but also the particular extents of surface, and the solid contents of bodies, together with their several ratios and properties in as far as these are discoverable by human abilities, &c.

32. Ratio is a mutual relation of two magnitudes of the same kind to one another in respect of quantity. This is the definition of ratio given by Euclid in his Elements, being definition 3d of book 5th, Simson's edition, which seems to me, as including those quantities which are incommensurable by human abilities as well as those that are commensurable by them, perfectly proper and unexceptionable. It follows from this definition of it, and from the nature of things, that geometrical relation or ratio in respect of quantity, must necessarily, as differing in degree, be with respect to degree, of three species, viz. those of equality, greater, and less, since every particular magnitude must necessarily in the nature of things be either in the relation of equality, or of greater or of less, in respect of quantity to every other magnitude. Ratio consists in two terms only however numerous the magnitudes to which the same ratio may be applicable. Ratio is discovered and determined either by comparing and measuring the one term or magnitude by the other, or by measuring both by means of some magnitude which from its aptness for that purpose is adopted as a

standard

standard or measuring unit, and by then comparing together their respective measures thus ascertained. Some have regarded ratios as magnitudes, and have treated of them as such; unmindful of their being only the geometrical relations of magnitudes in place of being magnitudes themselves; and though there are different kinds of magnitudes, as linear, superficial, and solid, there is no difference on that account in their respective ratios, mathematical ratios differing not in kind but in degree only.

33. Proportion is equality of ratios, not of magnitudes. And therefore necessarily consists in two ratios at least. It also necessarily refers to three or more magnitudes, and on that account necessarily consists of three or more terms, but never of less than three, and when of three only the second always supplies the place of two:---as 2:4::4:8. In Doctor Barrow's edition of Euclid's Elements the definition of proportion is given as the fourth definition of the 5th book, and with much more propriety, since those that follow manifestly refer to it and depend on it, though in the observation he has annexed to it he confounds its meaning with that of ratio. This definition according to his edition is, " proportion is a similitude of ratios," and the observation annexed to it is, " That which is here " termed proportion, is more rightly called proportionality or analogy; for " proportion commonly denotes no more than the ratio betwixt two mag- " nitudes." Doctor Simson in his edition makes it the 8th definition, and gives it in these words: " Analogy, or proportion, is the similitude of ra- " tios." In Doctor Keil's edition it is also made the 8th, and is thus expressed: " Analogy is a similitude of proportions." This seems to imply that proportion and analogy are terms of different significations; and that as proportion is the equality, or similitude as they are pleased to express it, of ratios, so is analogy the similitude of proportions. What are given by Dr. Barrow as the 6th and 8th, and Doctors Keil and Simson as the 5th and 7th definitions of this book, are in reality not definitions, but propositions requiring proof; and that which is here denominated the 5th definition should be thus expressed, viz.---Theorem. When the equi-multiples of the 1st and 3d of four magnitudes, compared with the equi-multiples of the 2d and 4th, according to any multiplication whatsoever, are such that when the multiple of the 1st is greater, equal, or less, than that of the 2d, the multiple of the 3d is greater, equal, or less, than that of the 4th, each

to each respectively, both together are either greater, equal, or less, than the equi-multiples of the 2d and 4th, if these be taken that answer each other, then are these four magnitudes, of which they are the multiples, proportional; or the 3d of the four magnitudes is to the 4th, in the same ratio that the 1st is to the 2d. And that which is here termed the 7th definition should be expressed thus, viz.—Theorem. When, of equi-multiples, the multiple of the 1st magnitude exceeds the multiple of the 2d, but the multiple of the 3d does not exceed that of the 4th, then these four magnitudes are not proportional. This method of giving propositions unproved for definitions, on a subject otherwise rendered extremely abstruse by the inaccurate manner in which it has been treated, both by Euclid and his expounders who differ widely in opinion among themselves concerning it, has contributed very much to that obscurity so much complained of in these pretended definitions, and to render the geometrical doctrines of ratio and proportion almost incomprehensible, or, at least, so perplexed and embarrassing as to prove extremely irksome and disgusting to the student in geometry.

34. This practice of giving propositions unproved for definitions is not peculiar to this fifth book: the Elements commence with it. Passing over for the present those of this kind that precede, as being propositions which admit not of proof, and taking into consideration what is given as the definition of a circle, being the 5th of book 1st, it will be found to include the following unproved theorem, viz. All the radii of a circle, that is all the lines drawn from a certain point within the figure to the circumference, are equal to one another. A theorem in the truth of which the very essence of the figure consists, this assumed property being essential to it, since without it it cannot possibly exist, and yet of this theorem no proof is given or even attempted. This procedure is in every point of view very improper; it being of the utmost importance in science that it should be founded on clear and well established principles, since, if that is not the case, the conclusions rationally and fairly deduced from them may justly incur the suspicion of being erroneous and false; and therefore this manner of proceeding, without evidence, on assumed facts, must necessarily detract much from that supposed certainty for which mathematical science has been so much celebrated. Since it is impossible to define a term

term expressive of an object of sense in such a manner as to be intelligible to those who never perceived that object, and are unacquainted with it and its construction, there is no other way of rendering the meaning of the word intelligible to them, than either by exhibiting to their inspection the object itself of which the term is the nominal sign; or by describing to them the means and manner by which they may form and obtain the object or figure, and thereby satisfy themselves with respect to its appearance and properties, in as far as these can be discovered from the manner of its construction, and from the inspection of it when formed. Thus the figure denominated by the term a circle, being an object of sense, the meaning of that term may be intelligibly defined either by the exhibition of that figure as the object which the term expresses: or by means of a proposition descriptive of its construction, if such with propriety can be called a definition of it. Thus. Problem. To describe a circle, viz. Apply one point of a pair of compasses opened to and retained at any required distance, or one extremity of a rod, cord, or chain, of any required length, to any particular point in a plain surface, to be retained there revolving on that point as a pivot, while the other point of the compass, or the other extremity of the rod, cord, or chain, is made to move completely round it, describing a line as it moves along on the plain surface: and then the figure thus described is a circle, the line thus described is that which is denominated the circumference of the circle, the fixed point round which it is described on which the point of the compass or extremity of the rod, &c. rested in describing it, is that which is called the centre of the circle, and all straight lines drawn from the centre to the circumference are called radii of the circle.

35. From the mode of construction given in this descriptive definition, which in reality is only the solution of the problem to describe a circle given as a definition, the proof of the theorem or axiom, " All the radii of " a circle are equal to one another," is justly inferible, or rather, it follows as a corollary or necessary consequence from it, as being experimentally and decisively proved by it, from the distance between the two points of the compass, or between the extremities of the rod, &c. remaining invariably the same, and reaching precisely from the centre to the circumference, while the circle is describing; and the distance being thus proved to be

be always the same between the centre and circumference, it necessarily follows that all lines drawn from the centre to the circumference are equal among themselves.

36. Perhaps Euclid's tenth definition to his first book of Elements might be improved by rendering it thus, viz. When one right line crosses another, and all the angles thus formed are equal among themselves, these angles are called right angles, and the one line is said to be perpendicular to the other. And to this with much propriety and advantage may be added in a note, or as an axiom, the following proposition, which easily admits of being ascertained and proved experimentally, viz. that four angles and four angles only can be formed at the point of contact or intersection by one right line crossing another: since from these propositions the proofs of many other propositions may be easily and obviously deduced as rational and just inferences; and indeed are corollaries or necessary consequences of them. Thus, since there are necessarily, in this case, two angles on each side of either line, or on the same side of the same line, and since these two angles are each right angles when they are equal to each other, it necessarily follows, that "The angles which one straight line makes with another "on the same side of it, are either two right angles, or are together equal "to two right angles," being the 13th prop. book 1st, Simson's Euclid. And conversely, that " If at a point in a straight line, two other straight "lines upon the opposite sides of it, make the adjacent angles together "equal to two right angles, these two straight lines shall be in one and the "same straight line," being prop. 14th, ditto. Also the proposition "That "if two straight lines cut one another, the angles they make at the point "where they cut, are together equal to four right angles," being cor. 1st to prop. 15th, ditto; and the proposition "That all the angles made by any "number of lines meeting in one point, are together equal to four right angles," being cor. 2d of do. And likewise the proposition "That all right "angles are equal to one another," assumed by Euclid as an axiom, but no where proved by him. Since if four angles and four angles only can be formed by one right line crossing another on the same plane, and since the four angles thus formed, are equal to one another when they are right angles, it necessarily follows that they must quadrate, or divide the whole of that area immediately surrounding the angular point or point of intersection into

four

four equal portions, each of them or each right angle in this case necessarily comprehending or occupying precisely one of these portions, or one fourth of that area; and the areas immediately surrounding all points being from the nature of things equal to one another, it follows as a necessary consequence that the aliquot parts or portions of them, as that of one fourth, being that portion comprehended under a right angle, must also in every instance be equal to one another; and this being the case that all right lined angles under which these equal portions are comprehended must also be equal to one another, and therefore that all right angles, whether proceeding from the same or different angular points, as comprehending equal portions, must in every case necessarily be equal to one another. Q. E. D. This proposition admits also of being proved by means of immediate direct experiment and induction.

37. The definition of parallel lines, the 35th of book 1st, given by Euclid, viz. " Parallel straight lines are such as are in the same plane, and " which being produced ever so far both ways do not meet," Simson's edit. is not so proper as that since given by others, viz. " Parallel lines are lines " which however far extended always preserve the same distance between " themselves." Since it is in always preserving the same distance that parallelism consists---this properly being essential to it---and since it is manifest that lines always preserving the same distance between themselves however far extended not only do never meet, but also that neither they, nor any part or parts of them, can ever approach nearer to, or recede further from each other.

38. With the intention of affording entire conviction with regard to the validity of the conclusions of the 27th, 28th, and 29th propositions of the first book of the Elements of Euclid, by removing the scruples and doubts of those who are dissatisfied with the indirect method of proof employed by Euclid in these propositions, direct demonstrations of them are given in a Supplement to this Part of this Essay; and also easy and obvious demonstrations, differing in manner and in principle from those given by Euclid, of propositions 32d, 41st, &c. with their corollaries.

39. What in the Elements of Euclid are given as the definitions of a point, a line, and a superficies, being the 1st, 2d, and 5th of book first, are in reality, as has already been shewn, only unfounded hypotheses not

admitting

admitting of proof. These pretended definitions, these hypotheses are so inconsistent with the real natures of things, so repugnant to reason, and so incomprehensible; are so aptly suited to the purposes of mysticism, to serving as a basis to a fanciful and visionary philosophy, and are so ill adapted for the forming of a solid and stable foundation for real science, as to make it presumable that they could not possibly have been the fundamental geometrical doctrines originally given by the discoverers of the science, but must be corruptions of these original doctrines, in consequence of the misapprehensions, mistakes, or prepossessions in consequence of favourite hypotheses of those who have attempted to expound and improve them :---most probably the result of the subtilties and supposed refinements of the Greek philosophers on the discoveries and knowledge of more enlightened nations.

40. The figures denominated by the terms a point, a line, and a superficies, being real entities and objects of sense, the terms expressing them cannot be intelligibly defined to those who are ignorant of their meaning any otherwise than by exhibiting the figures themselves as the objects these terms express ; and this only proper method, from its being the natural method or that which first occurs to the mind from its being the most obvious and easy, there can be no doubt must have been the original method of defining these terms, or of rendering their meaning intelligible. And as these figures are employed in geometry only as marks, symbols, or representations, of place, position, direction, termination, form, &c. of length without breadth or thickness, of length and breadth without thickness, and of length, breadth, and thickness, as differently applied and disposed for the purpose of effecting and facilitating the mensuration of those bodies, or of those surfaces, of which they are employed to represent the boundaries, forms, or figures, &c. and as it would necessarily render mensuration and calculation more complex and embarrassing, and detract from the accuracy and precision of the conclusions, if these symbols should, in the calculations and mensurations, be supposed to possess any other kinds of extension or magnitude besides those they are employed to represent, no doubt can possibly be entertained but that it must originally have been postulated, with the intention of preventing those effects, that these figures or symbols, though actually possessing other extensions and magnitudes
besides

besides those they are employed to represent, are nevertheless in mensuration and calculation to be regarded as possessing these only, their real extensions and magnitudes in other respects being in these cases to be entirely neglected: and this reasonable request has no doubt been expressed more particularly in postulates; in such perhaps as those that follow, or in others to the same effect, viz. Post. 1st, Let it be granted that a geometrical point, or a point as employed in delineating diagrams in geometry, is to be regarded not as entirely destitute of magnitude—as such could not in reality possibly exist, and, though endowed with a suppositious and hypothetical existence, could not answer the purpose intended by it, of being a sensible mark of place, as not being cognizable to sense—but, for the sake of accuracy in the conclusions, as a magnitude too minute either to embarrass the operations and computations, or sensibly to affect or invalidate their results. Post. 2d. Let it be granted that a geometrical line, or a line as employed in the purposes of geometry, may be regarded not as length entirely destitute of breadth and thickness—as in that case it would not be palpable to sense, and therefore would be altogether improper for answering the purposes intended by it of sensibly indicating and denoting length, direction, the boundaries of areas or what are commonly called geometrical superficies, and for distinguishing these into portions or divisions—but, for the sake of accuracy in the calculations, as of a breadth and thickness too minute sensibly to affect or invalidate the correctness of the results. Post. 3d.—Let it be granted that a geometrical superficies may be regarded as an exact representation of a corresponding physical or material superficies as to figure and area only, and therefore as consisting of length and breadth without thickness, or of length and breadth only; since extent or measurement of area, whatever its figure may be, is in every case ascertained and determined by its length and breadth only. From postulates such as these, or from others nearly to the same effect, do these hypotheses or pretended definitions of a point, a line, and a superficies, most probably derive their origin.

41. Postulates ought to be either reasonable requests, the utility and advantage necessarily resulting from the granting of which is so manifest that they cannot consistently with the rules of right reason be denied—as those given above—or problems founded on and deduced from experience, and

which admit of being experimentally proved at any time, but which are nevertheless required to be granted without proof from a conviction that the practibility and truth of them must have fallen so often under every one's experience and observation that no further proof can be necessary :---of this kind are those given by Euclid; to which the following should have been added, since he proceeds upon the faith of its having been granted, though never required to be granted, in the eleventh book of his Elements, viz. Let it be granted that geometrical solids may, for the purpose of facilitating the proofs and of giving accuracy to the calculations, be regarded as capable of mutual penetration, though real physical material solids do not admit of it.

42. Axioms are theorems, and theorems that form the fundamental propositions of the science. They are all conclusions rationally deduced either from casual experience and observation, or from experiments purposely made, and these generally of the most obvious, familiar, and easy kinds; and such is their nature that they admit at any time of being proved by means of immediate, direct, easy and accurate experiments. But that which forms, or ought to form, the characteristic of geometrical axioms, though it has never been observed before, is their being altogether incapable of any other PROOF but EXPERIMENTAL; since, as forming the first and fundamental propositions and principles of the science, they admit not of demonstrative proof, there being no others from which they can be rationally deduced, or from which the conclusions or truths they annunciate can be demonstrated. Those truths of which axioms are expressive, though not perhaps those truths that are first known, are truths that must be known or granted before those other propositions or truths constituting the science can be rationally deduced from them. And so far are these fundamental principles or first truths called axioms from being innate truths---immutable, necessary, and eternal, self existent, coeval with the Deity, and totally independent not only of all created things but even of the Deity also, or such as are evident of themselves, and which from the constitution of our nature or by a law of human thought we are, antecedent to experience and without proof, obliged to believe---as they are usually represented, that it is this incapability of their being known or proved any otherwise than experimentally that distinguishes axioms from other geometrical theorems :---

a truth

a truth necessarily fatal to that hypothesis which deduces science, and mathematical science in particular, from sources purely intellectual.

43. Entirely analogous to, and equally unfounded with this way of representing the axioms of geometry as self evident, necessary and eternal truths, is that principle which has been adopted both by metaphysicians and geometricians, and which is so often quoted—viz. that though a circle had never existed the demonstrated truths concerning it, as being of their own nature independent necessary and eternal would nevertheless exist—as being contrary to nature and right reason; as investing non-entity with attributes and relations; and conferring on attributes and relations an independent existence, as in giving existence to attributes both before those entities of which they are the attributes existed, and after those entities of which they were the attributes no longer exist or are annihilated:—thus the proposition all the radii of a circle are equal among themselves could not be a truth if no circle or radii had ever existed, since this truth, or a proposition expressing it, could have had no existence independent of the existence of a circle and radii and of these radii being equal among themselves, as it is the annunciation of this property as experimentally ascertained from actually existing circles and radii that constitutes this supposed independent eternal truth, or is that in which it allenarly consists and which manifestly never could have existed if that of which it is the attribute or property had never existed. The same reasoning is applicable to all the axioms of geometry; of which indeed the above proposition of all the radii of a circle being equal among themselves ought to be one. Geometrical axioms should not be restricted to those given by Euclid. Every geometrical proposition that possesses the distinguishing characteristic of admitting of experimental proof only is intrinsically and essentially an axiom; or one of these first and fundamental propositions and principles of the science from which its other propositions are rationally deduced. And on this account they should not only be given as such, but should also as such be proved experimentally.

44. Though the preceding investigation into the nature and fundamental principles of geometrical science deprives it of that pure intellectual origin, and perfect independence on things and the attributes of things external to the mind, or on the powers, properties, and mutual relations of things as they

actually

actually exist in nature, which has erroneously been attributed to it, though things and the properties and mutual relations of things or their attributes of extension or magnitude are the only objects of it, and the only things treated of in the science. And though the result of this investigation detracts considerably from the supposed infallibility of geometrical demonstration in every case, and from that supposed perfection in the science so inconsistent with every thing of human invention and human acquirement; and though it brings all mathematical evidence on a level with that in which all other human knowledge---except that respecting the human mind itself as resulting from the consciousness of its own operations---rests; as entirely depending on and being deduced from, in common with other sciences, experience or experiments; and as having also in common with them the discovery only of the properties and mutual relations of external things for its object; yet as these results of the investigation are only freeing the science from ill-founded prepossessions, from abstruse, intricate, and enigmatical doctrines, originating in and productive of error, it is evident it must even on that account be of much utility and importance; as well as in substituting for these erroneous principles thus rejected others not liable to these objections, and thereby establishing the science on the solid and permanent basis of reason and of nature. At the same time that by means of the natural, plain, and simple representations and reasonings and the conclusions deduced from them in the course of this investigation all the obscurity so much complained of is dispelled, no ambiguity with respect to the first and fundamental principles of the science remains, the veil of mystery in which they were involved is withdrawn, the paradoxes disappear, and the student in geometry, having now no reason to doubt or disbelieve his senses, to blame the dullness of his apprehension for not understanding what is unintelligible, and on that account to regard himself as unqualified for the study, may now with entire confidence in his powers, and in the justness, solidity, and stability, of the fundamental principles on which the science rests, pursue his object without being perplexed with these embarrassing doubts and difficulties which such abstruse, erroneous, and deceitful doctrines as those now rejected naturally inspire, and with the reasonable expectation of learning it with the more facility, and the more effect, utility, and advantage, from his understanding what he learns.

SUP-

SUPPLEMENT TO PART FIRST

OF THE ESSAY ON THE PRINCIPLES OF THE MATHEMATICAL SCIENCES.

DEFINITION.—Parallel lines are lines which however far extended both ways always preserve the same distance between themselves.

PROPOSITION, THEOREM, (being the 27th of book 1st of Euclid.) " If a " straight line falls on other two straight lines, and the alternate angles are " equal, these two straight lines shall be parallel," may be demonstrated *directly*, in place of *indirectly* as done by Euclid, in the following manner, viz.

Let the straight line EF which falls upon the two straight lines AB, CD, make the alternate angles CFE, BEF, equal to one another; AB is parallel to CD. (Figure 5th).

From E let fall the perpendicular EG on the line CD; take EH equal to GF, and join HF. Then, since the side EH of the triangle EHF is equal to the side GF of the triangle EGF, and the side EF is common to both triangles; and since the angle EFE of the triangle EGF is also equal to the angle BEF of the triangle EHF, prop. 4th, b. 1st, of Euclid, the remaining sides of these triangles EG, and HF, must also be equal to one another; and therefore the remaining angles must also, each to each, be equal to one another, that is, the angle EFH to the angle FEG, and the angle EHF to the angle EGF; but the angle EGF being a right one from EG being perpendicular to CD, the angle EHF must also be a right one, and the line FH must be perpendicular to the line AB: but, if the lines EG, HF, placed at a distance from each other, and making the same or equal angles with the lines AB and CD, are equal to one another the lines AB and CD must be parallel; that is they must always preserve the same distance between themselves, since it is the lengths of these lines which determines the distance between them at different places. Q. E. D.

Corollary,

Corollary,-(being prop. 33d, b. 1st, of Euclid,) the straight lines which join the extremities of two equal and parallel straight lines, towards the same parts, are also themselves equal and parallel.

The proposition 28th, b. 1st, of Euclid, viz. " If a straight line falling " upon two other straight lines makes the exterior angle equal to the inte- " rior and opposite angle on the same side of the line; or makes the inte- " rior angles on the same side together equal to two right angles; the two " straight lines shall be parallel to one another." And prop. 29th, b. 1st, of Euclid, which is only the converse of prop. 27th and 28th, may be demonstrated *directly* as follows, viz. (See last figure.)

Since it is proved by the last proposition that if the alternate angles are equal the lines must be parallel, it necessarily follows, as supposing the contrary would imply a contradiction and absurdity, that if the lines are parallel the alternate angles must be equal: but, if the alternate angle C F E is equal to the alternate angle F E B, it must also be equal to the angle A E M, since F E B and A E M are vertical angles; and since the angles A E M and A E F are equal to two right angles, the angles A E F and C F E, being the two interior angles on the same side, must also be equal to two right angles, since the angle C F E is equal to the angle A E M, and the angle A E F is common to both. Wherefore if a straight line falling upon two parallel straight lines makes the exterior angle equal to the interior and opposite angle on the same side of the line; or makes the interior angles on the same side together equal to two right angles; the two straight lines shall be parallel to one another: and if a straight line falls upon two parallel straight lines, it makes the alternate angles equal to one another; and the exterior angle equal to the interior and opposite angle upon the same side; and likewise the two interior angles upon the same side equal to two right angles. Q. E. D.

After these the following proposition---a proposition replete with important consequences as including in it propositions 34th, 35th, 36th, 37th, 38th, 39th, 40th, and 41st of the first book of Euclid's Elements of Geometry---ought to be introduced, viz.

PROPOSITION. THEOREM.—All the angles of every parallelogram are equal to four right angles. (Fig. 6.)

Let

Let A C B D be any parallelogram whatever; extend the line A B indefinitely, from the point D let fall the line D E perpendicularly upon it, and from the point C let fall the line C B also perpendicularly upon it. Then the lines C D and A E being parallel, the lines C B and D E must necessarily be parallel also, by prop. 29th, as making the same angles with the line A E and the two interior angles they make upon the same side of it are together equal to two right angles; but this being the case, at the same time that these lines C B and D E must be equal to each other, as being perpendicular to and extending between and terminating in the same two parallel lines and each making the same angle with them, the figure B C D E must be a parallelogram; and the four angles of it must be four right angles, for the angles C B E and B E D being, by the construction, each a right angle, its other two angles B C D and C D E must, by Prop. 29th, be so also, the two interior angles B E D and E D C being equal to two right angles, and the other two interior angles D C B and C B E being also equal to two right angles. And the parallelogram B C D E being formed into two triangles B E D, and B C D, by the diagonal D B, whereof the side C D of the one is equal to the side B E of the other, and the side C B of the one also equal to the side D E of the other, and the side D B common; and the angles of the one being also equal to the angles of the other, each to each respectively, from their being either alternate or right angles, it follows, from prop. 26th, book I. that these triangles must be equal to each other in every respect. But this being the case, and the triangle C B A being in every respect equal to the triangle C B D, for the same reasons that C B D was found to be equal to D B E, viz. equality both of sides and angles each to each respectively, it necessarily follows that the parallelogram A B C D is equal to the parallelogram B C D E; and that the four angles of the parallelogram A B C D, and consequently of every parallelogram whatever, are equal to four right angles. Q. E. D.

It likewise necessarily follows, as corollaries from this Proposition, 1. That the diagonal of a parallelogram divides it into two equal parts. 2. That all the three angles of every triangle are equal to two right angles; the diagonals dividing the angles as well as the areas of parallelograms into equal portions. 3. That if a parallelogram and a triangle are upon the same base, or upon equal bases, and between the same parallels the triangle
angle

angle is precisely one half of the parallelogram. 4. That parallelograms upon the same base, or on equal bases, and between the same parallels, are equal to each other. 5. The converse of the last Proposition. 6. That triangles upon the same base, or on equal bases, and between the same parallels, are equal to one another. 7. The converse of the last proposition.

Proposition 32, of Book I. of Euclid, viz. " If a side of any triangle " be produced, the exterior angle is equal to the two interior and opposite " angles," may, without having recourse to the compass and ruler to form an angle equal to one of the interior angles, be demonstrated in the following simple manner from preceding propositions, viz. (fig. 7.)

The side A B of the triangle A B C being produced towards D, the exterior angle C B D is equal to the two interior and opposite angles B A C, and A C B. For the three angles of a triangle being, by last proposition, equal to two right angles; and the angles C B D and C B A together being, by Prop. 13, Book I. of Euclid, also equal to two right angles; and the angle C B A being common both to the triangle, and to the angles made by one right line falling on another on the one side of that line; and since, if equals are taken from equals the remainders are equal, it necessarily follows that the external angle C B D must be equal to the two opposite and internal angles B A C and A C B. Q. E. D.

From this and the immediately preceding proposition the following corollaries are deducible, viz. 1. All the interior angles of any rectilineal figure, together with four right angles, are equal to twice as many right angles as the figure has sides. 2. All the exterior angles of any rectilineal figure are together equal to four right angles.

PART

PART II.

OF ALGEBRA.

1. ALGEBRA is a mode of Investigation and Computation founded on the invention, intent, and use, of the signs + and —; and on the known properties of Ratios; to suit which a particular manner of annotation has been invented and adopted: and in the theory thence rationally deduced, and in the expert application of the rules and operations thence resulting to practice, does the Science, and the Art, of Algebra consist.

2. Though Algebra has been a favourite study with the moderns, and great improvements have been made in the practical parts of it, particularly in the discovery and adoption of a more appropriate notation than that found in the works of Diophantes, and in those of the authors who first cultivated it on its being introduced into Europe by the Arabians—in the discovery of many most ingenious, effectual, and useful expedients and devices for facilitating and expediting the operations—and more especially for approximating to the values of quantities which have no known ratio to unity—and in applying Algebra to Geometry, and both Algebra and Geometry to Physics; for which the world is indebted to Harriot, Vieta, Anderson, Des Cartes, Fermat, Wallis, Newton, the Gregorys, Leibnitz, Mercator, Huygens, Halley, the Bernoulis, Maclauren, Euler, and others of high celebrity of former times, as well as to several very eminent mathematicians now alive; yet there is reason to apprehend—from the differences of opinion which prevail, from a deficiency of precision in many cases, and from the causes of many of the essential operations and their effects never having been satisfactorily explained—that the scientific part of it has not made equal progress, or advanced *pari passu* with the practical; and perhaps it may be found on a rational investigation into its present state, that some erroneous opinions are still entertained, without even

a suspicion of their being so, with regard both to the nature and fundamental principles of Algebra as a science, and with regard to the reasons
of several of the rules and operations of it as an art.

3. The intent and use of the signs + and —, as used in common Arithmetic in denoting addition and subtraction, are well understood. But in
the science of Algebra it is allowed, by all considerate and judicious Mathematicians, that the proper meanings of these signs, and the reasons of
their various applications, though they were no doubt known to the original
inventors of the science, have hitherto with respect to the moderns been
involved in impenetrable obscurity and mystery, and are still desiderata in
the science of Algebra, no rational and satisfactory explanation of their
intent and use in that science, though it forms the very base on which the
superstructure rests, and though numerous attempts have been made for
that purpose, having hitherto been given. The latest of these attempts—
besides a long dissertation in French, inserted in the Philosophical Trans-
actions of the Royal Society of London for the year 1806, being little more
than two years previous to the printing of this Essay, by Abbé Buée—
have been made by the learned Baron Maseres, in a pretty large quarto
volume, on the use of the negative sign in Algebra; and by the celebrated
Mons. Carnot, ex-minister of war in France, in a work entitled *Géometrie
de Position*, said to contain 540 quarto pages, both published within these
few years. These two last-mentioned works I have not seen; but it seems
to be the general opinion, in as far as my information reaches, of those
who have perused them, that these works, though learned and ingenious,
do not, more than that of the Abbé Buée, afford new and satisfactory information sufficient for removing the difficulties and dispelling the mysterious obscurity in which this intricate subject has hitherto been involved.

4. Perhaps the following observations, which for the sake of the greater
perspicuity are illustrated by the most simple, obvious, and familiar examples, may tend to the elucidation of this very abstruse subject by withdrawing from it, in whole or in part, that veil of mystery in which it has
hitherto been enveloped.

5. Though it is represented in every treatise on Algebra, that the algebraical sign +, known by the designation of the positive sign, always indicates addition, and denotes an increment, and therefore is denominated

plus;

plus; and that the algebraical sign —, known by the designation of the negative sign, always indicates subtraction, and denotes a decrement, and therefore is denominated *minus;* yet a due consideration of all circumstances will, I have no doubt, prove that this is not a true statement with respect to the meaning, intent, and use of these signs. For, if I am not deceived, these signs in the science of Algebra have properly and in fact no reference or relation whatever to *number,* or to *magnitude,* merely as such—*these* being exclusively represented and denoted by the letters of the Alphabet, and the numeral co-efficients—and are appropriated solely for the purpose of denoting the *nature or qualities of the physical quantities* with respect to each other, to which they are respectively prefixed; and indicate merely, in algebraical addition and subtraction, that that quantity to which one of these signs is prefixed is either of a directly contrary nature or quality, or acts in a direction precisely opposite, to that of any quantity to which the other sign is prefixed; their action and effects on each other being reciprocal: and hence it is that equal quantities having different signs destroy each other's effect, and that their amount thereby becomes equal to nothing. The sign + is no more the mark of addition than the sign — is; nor is the sign — more the mark of subtraction than the sign + is: they are merely indications of properties of opposite natures, or of powers acting in opposite directions; the one no more denoting an increment or decrement than the other; and a negative quantity in place of being less than nothing, as has been represented and inculcated, is necessarily and in fact equivalent in power to a positive of equal value, since otherwise it could not possibly destroy its effects.

6. From its being usual in practice to appropriate the sign + to any given quantity from which another given quantity is a deduction, or is to be deduced by algebraical addition with unlike signs; and to prefix the sign — to that quantity which either is a deduction or is to be deduced from the other by the same means; has arisen, I imagine, the general opinion that the real intent and use of the negative sign is to indicate subtraction; that + denotes an increment, and — a decrement; and hence that they may be aptly compared to the credit and debit of an account.

7. In algebraical addition of quantities, a negative quantity does not subtract from another negative quantity, more than a positive quantity does from

another positive quantity; but on the contrary adds to it: thus, $-2a$ added to $-3a$ gives $-5a$ for the amount; in the same manner as $+2a$ added to $+3a$ gives $+5a$ for the sum: so that neither the one nor the other are decrements, and $-2a$ is as much an increment to $-3a$, as $+2a$ is to $+3a$. Also, a positive quantity deducts or subtracts, *ceteris paribus*, from a negative quantity as much, and on the same principle of the contrariety of their respective natures, or of the directions in which they act, as a negative quantity does from a positive quantity: thus, in adding $+2a$ to $-3a$, the sum is $-a$, so that $+2a$ is deducted from $-3a$ by this addition, in the same manner and degree that $+3a$ is reduced to $+a$ by adding $-2a$ to it. In this case, then, the one is as much a decrement as the other; and from the contrariety of their respective natures or modes of action, it is impossible for any increment to result from this kind of addition, the smaller quantity always deducting from the larger, and the remainder or sum, for in this case they signify the same thing, becomes either positive or negative according as the quantity of which it is a remainder is either positive or negative. Besides the sign $+$ does not in other respects indicate addition more than the sign $-$ does: since in adding *unlike* quantities together they are both used: thus, $\begin{smallmatrix} +3a \\ -4x \end{smallmatrix}$ gives $+3a-4x$ for the sum, and it is understood that these two quantities in the sum are added together, though $-$ in place of $+$ interposes between $3a$ and $4x$; and though it is not expressed $+3a+-4x$, which it should be if $+$ denoted addition, to signify that $-4x$ either is or is to be added to $+3a$.

8. Since it is the nature of subtraction to be the inverse of addition, and thereby to produce effects the very reverse of those produced by addition; and since it is also the nature of these signs to invert, when changed, the qualities, &c. of the particular quantities to which they are prefixed, it must be evident that adding one quantity of which the sign has been changed to another quantity the sign of which has not been changed, must, in effect, be equivalent to subtracting the quantity whose sign is thus changed from the other: and that this is actually the case is proved by the effect thus produced being precisely the reverse of that of algebraical addition, as giving a directly contrary result; thus $+3$ added to $+5$, -3 to $+5$, $+3$ to -5, -3 to -5, give respectively $+8, +2, -2, -8$, for their sum; whereas, on changing the signs of the quantities added, they give $+2, +8,$

—8,—2, for the remainders; so that the quantities to which they are thus added are effected by it in a way the very reverse of what they are when these several quantities are added to them without having their signs changed.

9. As algebraical addition with unlike signs is equivalent to arithmetical subtraction; so algebraical subtraction with unlike signs is equivalent to arithmetical addition: thus, $\frac{+5}{\frac{-3}{+2}}$ and $\frac{-5}{\frac{+3}{-2}}$ added algebraically is arithmetically subtracted; and $\frac{+5}{\frac{-3}{+8}}$ and $\frac{-5}{\frac{+3}{-8}}$ subtracted algebraically is arithmetically added. Also $+5-5$ added algebraically $=0$, and 5 subtracted from 5, arithmetically, also gives 0; but -5 subtracted, algebraically, from $+5$ gives $+10$, and $+5$ from -5 gives -10; at the same time that on being added algebraically together they give 0. The algebraical addition of equal quantities with unlike signs annihilates them, while subtracting the one from the other algebraically gives a result or remainder equal to the sum or amount of both of them; and the algebraical addition of equal quantities with like signs gives a sum equal to double the amount of either of them, while algebraical subtraction annihilates them.

10. That the sign — is not used in algebra to denote subtraction, as it sometimes is in common arithmetic, must be manifest when it is considered that, though any positive quantity requires to have its sign changed from + to — before it can be subtracted algebraically from any other quantity; on the other hand any negative quantity requires its sign to be changed from — to + before it admits of being subtracted algebraically from any other quantity, positive or negative, so far is the sign — from being the sign of subtraction in algebra.

11. Though to alter the sign prefixed to any quantity is to invert its quality, position, or direction; and though the two different signs of + and — still produce effects directly the reverse of each other; yet, in algebraical multiplication and division, it is, according to my conception, the — sign only, or a — multiplier or divisor only, that can with propriety alter or more properly reverse the quality or direction of the quantity multiplied or divided, and thereby that of the product or quotient: and this I imagine is the real and only reason, and not any of those hitherto assigned, why like signs give +, and unlike —, in these cases.

12. On

12. On this principle there necessarily must be two different ways of multiplying and dividing the same quantity---the one positively or directly, and the other negatively or inversely---and hence to multiply any quantity positively or directly, or with a positive factor, must be to add it to itself positively, or as it actually is, or without its sign and thereby its qualities being changed or reversed, as often as there are units•in the multiplier; and to multiply any quantity negatively or inversely, or with a negative factor, must be to it add to itself negatively, or with its sign, and thereby its qualities changed and reversed, as often as there are units in the multiplier. Thus $+10$ is equivalent to $+5 \times +2$ and -10 to $-5 \times +2$, both these quantities $+5$ and -5, being multiplied positively, or by a positive factor, $+2$, and therefore without having their respective signs and qualities thereby changed and reversed; and -10 is also equivalent to $+5$ added twice to itself with its sign changed, or to $+5 \times -2$, or negatively by 2, and therefore with its sign changed and qualities reversed; and $+10$ is also equivalent to -5 added twice to itself with its sign changed, or to -5×-2, or by 2 negatively and therefore with its sign changed. Though it is generally allowed that multiplication by a positive number implies a repeated addition, yet it seems to be as generally maintained that multiplication by a negative implies a repeated subtraction. But a repeated subtraction cannot possibly be multiplication: and to change the sign of any quantity does not subtract that quantity from itself, or affect it in any manner further than in inverting its quality, position, or direction; in all other respects it remains the same as before, and no quantity admits of repeated algebraical subtractions, since no quantity can be subtracted algebraically from itself without giving 0 for the remainder, beyond which there is no proceeding: thus $+a$ algebraically subtracted from $+a$, or itself, and $-a$ from $-a$, both give 0 for the remainder.

13. Since the algebraical involution, and evolution, of quantities are only particular cases of algebraical multiplication, and division, it is evident that the same rules with respect to the signs must obtain in these as in those; and hence that there must be two different ways of involving or evolving the same quantity having the same sign prefixed, the one positively or directly, the other negatively or inversely; that is either with its nature, or quality, position, and direction retained, or with these reversed:

versed : thus, any simple quantity is involved positively, or as it is, by multiplying the exponent by that of the power required, and retaining and prefixing in all cases the same sign with that of the root or quantity involved ; and any simple quantity is involved negatively or with its qualities, position, or direction reversed, by multiplying the exponent by that of the power required, and prefixing in all cases the contrary sign to that prefixed to the root. But there can in any case be no reason or cause for involving any quantity otherwise than as it actually is, or with its sign changed, and thereby with qualities the very reverse of those the root possesses, unless there is a special indication of its being absolutely required in the particular case, by the negative sign being prefixed to its own proper sign ; for to involve a quantity otherwise than as it is, or with qualities the very reverse of those it actually.possesses, when such contrary sign is not prefixed, requiring it and rendering it necessary in that particular case, would be to invert its nature, quality, position, or direction, without any reason or cause whatever ; and in fact would not only be doing more than is required or necessary in simply involving it, but by doing so would render the result erroneous by rendering it the very reverse of what it ought to be.

14. If the preceding principles are just, it follows that $-a$, multiplied by $-a$, or multiplied inversely, gives $+aa$ for the product, &c. yet $-a$ involved positively, or simply added to itself as it actually is as often as there are units in the multiplier, gives $-aa, -aaa, -aaaa$, for the 2d, 3d, 4th, powers, &c. there being no indication, cause, or reason, in this case of simply involving it, for multiplying it otherwise than as it actually is, as there is in the other case where $-a$ is expressly required by the negative sign being prefixed to the multiplier, or by its being multiplied by a negative factor, to be multiplied or added to itself negatively, or with its sign changed, as often as there are units in the multiplier :—and for the same reason though $\sqrt{-a} \times \sqrt{-a}$ gives $\sqrt{aa}$, or $+a$ for the product, and though $\sqrt{-3} \times \sqrt{-3}$ gives $\sqrt{+9}$, or $+3$; yet $\sqrt{-a}$ on being simply involved must give $-a -aa$, $-aaa, -aaaa$, &c. for its powers; and $\sqrt{-3}$ must give $-3, -9, -27, -81$, &c. But when the negative sign is prefixed to the radical sign of the quantity to be involved, it then becomes necessary for obtaining the proper result, to involve it negatively or with its sign changed, and thereby

with

with its qualities, position, or direction inverted ; the prefixing of the negative sign to the proper sign of the quantity being a special indication of its being absolutely required in that particular case : thus the first power of $-\sqrt{+a}$ ought to be $-a$, the 2d $-aa$, the 3d $-aaa$, the 4th $-aaaa$, &c. and $-\sqrt{-a}$ ought to be involved $+a, +a^2, +a^3, +a^{4th}$, &c. though $-\sqrt{+a}\times$ $-\sqrt{+a}$; and $-\sqrt{-a}\times-\sqrt{-a}$; should both give $\sqrt{+aa}$, or $+a$, for their respective products, as being equivalent to $+a\times+a$, and to $-a\times-a$.

15. The involution of compound quantities is more difficult—especially when the binomial has one term positive and another negative, and when the negative term is of greater value than the positive—so as the powers shall always retain the proper signs.; except in the case of involving them by merely placing the exponents of the different powers over the root, as in involving the binomial $\overline{a-b}$, &c. thus $\overline{a-b}$, $\overline{a-b})^2$, $\overline{a-b})^3$, $\overline{a-b})^{4th}$, &c. which is involving it, after this manner, positively, or as it is with the signs in the powers the same as in the root ; but if it is required and necessary to involve it in this manner negatively or inversely, the signs in the powers must be inverted or be the reverse of those in the root : thus the powers of the root $a-b$ would become $\overline{-a+b}^2$, $\overline{-a+b}^3$, $\overline{-a+b}^{4th}$, &c. When the compound quantity to be involved positively is positive, the proper signs are always retained by the common method of involution. But if it is required and necessary from any particular cause to involve a positive compound quantity negatively, then the signs in the powers must be changed to the reverse of what they would be were it involved positively.

16. When it is necessary to involve a binomial in such a manner as to express all the different terms included in each power, in place of expressing the several powers generally as by the above method, it becomes necessary for obtaining the proper results or real powers of the root, to observe the following rules with regard to the signs, viz. If the terms of the binomial to be involved are both of the same nature or quality, that is either both positive or both negative as $\overline{+a+b}$, or $\overline{-a-b}$; and it is required to involve them positively or as they are, the first kind, as $\overline{+a+b}$, when involved in the usual manner, gives the proper results ; but this is not the case with the other or $\overline{-a-b}$, which to give the true powers of the root requires to be involved positively, or by repeated multiplications of the root by the same quantities as those of the root having the contrary sign prefixed

to

to them; or, in this case, by multiplying repeatedly the root $-a-b$ by $\overline{+a+b}$: so that to obtain the proper results, in this case of positively involving both of these roots with their proper signs prefixed must be repeatedly multiplied by the same quantities as those of the roots with positive signs prefixed. The case however is quite the reverse when it is required to involve such binomial quantities negatively or inversely; it being necessary, in that event, for obtaining the proper results, to change the signs of the roots, those terms which are positive to negative and those which are negative to positive, and then to multiply each root with its signs thus changed repeatedly by the same quantities as those of the roots with the positive signs prefixed: and, hence, such binomials as $-a-b$ when involved in the usual manner in place of giving the true powers of the root give its inverse powers.

17. When a binomial does not express a sum, but a difference, as $-a+b=-P$, or $-a+b=+P$, or as $-5+3=-2$, or $-3+5=+2$, of which the sign is either positive or negative, according as the greatest quantity of that binomial of which it is a remainder is either positive or negative; and if it is required to involve it positively, it is necessary for obtaining the true powers of the root or binomial, if that root or binomial is negative, that is expresses a negative difference, as $-a+b=-P$, or $-5+3=-2$, to multiply repeatedly the root by the same quantities as those of the root with the signs reversed :—as thus,

$$-5+3=-2$$
$$\times +5-3=+2$$
$$\overline{}$$
$$-25+15$$
$$+15-9$$
$$\overline{}$$
$$-25+30-9=-4$$
$$\times +5-3$$
$$\overline{}$$
$$-125+150-45$$
$$+75-90+27$$
$$\overline{}$$
$$-125+225-135+27=-8$$
$$\times +5-3$$
$$\overline{}$$
$$-625+1125-675+135$$
$$+375-675+405-81$$
$$\overline{}$$
$$-625+1500-1350+540-81=-16$$

C C Whence

Whence it appears that the true powers in this case, or of $-5+3=-2$ are thus obtained, viz. $-4, -8, -16$, &c.---When the binomial or root is positive, as $-a+b=+P$, or $-3+5=+2$, the proper positive results are always obtained by involving it in the usual way.

18. It is evident from the foregoing example that -2, or any other negative quantity, though in the form of a binomial, may be involved so that all the powers of it shall retain the same sign, and thereby the same qualities, position, or direction, with itself; and that this object is obtained on the same principle as in the case of the involution of simple quantities, and by the same expedient, that of multiplying the quantity to be involved positively, or by a positive factor of equal value with itself, and thereby adding it to itself as it is, or without its signs or qualities being changed or altered, as often as is necessary for obtaining the powers required. But if it is required to involve $-\overline{+a-}b$, or $-\overline{+2-5}$, that is $--3$, or -3 negatively or inversely, that is $+3$, then the signs of the binomial must be changed for that purpose, and in place of $\overline{+a-}b$, or of $\overline{+2-5}$; $\overline{-a+}b$, or $-2+5=+3$, must be involved after the common manner as being a positive quantity for obtaining the proper result.

19. The manner in which the signs ought to be employed in the evolution of quantities is easily deducible from the foregoing principles. Thus $\sqrt{-aa}=-a$, $\sqrt[3]{-a^3}, =-a$; $\sqrt[4]{-a^4}=-a$, &c. so that all these quantities are evolved positively into $-a$: also, $a-\sqrt{+aa}$, &c. is evolved into $a-a$, and $a-\sqrt{-aa}$, &c. into $a+a$, from being evolved negatively, &c. When quantities are involved or evolved by the celebrated binomial theorem it is necessary for obtaining the proper results, or the true powers of the roots and the true roots of the powers by that means, to accommodate the signs of the terms according to the above principles, or according to the real meaning, intent, and use of these signs.

20. In involution and evolution of algebraical quantities affected by different signs, it is the quantities only that are to be involved or evolved; their signs neither requiring nor admitting of it, since a sign cannot possibly be multiplied or divided. And, hence, the only rule for the signs in involution of simple quantities is to prefix the same sign to the powers obtained by involving the quantity that was prefixed to the root of which they are the powers; and in evolution to prefix the same sign to the root that

was

was prefixed to those powers of which it is the root. It is absurd, contradictory in itself, and perfectly impossible in the nature of things, for the powers to be of a kind, or of a nature and quality, the very reverse of the root, or of that of which they form the powers ; or for a root to be of a kind or quality contrary to that of the powers from which it is extracted, and of which it forms the root. And consequently $+x^3$, or $+5^3$, can with propriety and justice mean only that the quantity x or 5 is to involved to the power expressed by its exponent; that is that 5 is in this case to be multiplied three times into itself, thereby giving 125 for its cube or third power, at the same times that it retains the same sign with the root, or with that quantity of which it is the third power; and so of other cases. And $-x^3$, or -5^3, can also with propriety and justice be understood to mean only that these quantities are to be involved, as denoted by their exponents, into powers of the same kind or quality with themselves and which therefore retain the same sign. And likewise $\sqrt[3]{x^3}$ or $\sqrt[3]{125}$ can with propriety and justice be understood to mean x or 5 only :---while $\sqrt{-x^2}$, $\sqrt{-25}$, or $\sqrt[4]{-x^4}$ $\sqrt[4]{-625}$ as well as $\sqrt[3]{-x^3}$ $\sqrt[3]{-125}$ cannot with any propriety or justice be regarded as signifying anything besides $-x$, -5 : all the powers of the same quantity, and of the same kind or quality, necessarily having the same root and the same sign.

21. On the same principle the algebraical expression $-\overline{+x^3}$ or $-\overline{+5^3}$ can with propriety and justice be understood to mean only, that $+x$, in consequence of the negative sign prefixed to it, is inverted into $-x$, or is to be involved negatively ; and that when so involved its powers are the powers of $-x$; or what comes to the same thing that $+\overline{-x^3}$ means only that $-x$ is to be involved positively, or as it actually is as indicated by its proper sign which in this case is negative ; and that $-\overline{-x^3}$ means only that $-x^3$ is to be involved negatively or with its sign changed from $-$ to $+$ and thereby its qualities, &c. inverted. Also the algebraical expression $-\sqrt[3]{-x^3}$ can justly and properly be understood to mean only that the nature or quality, &c. of the quantity $-x^3$ is inverted by the operation of the negative sign which precedes the radical sign, and is therefore to be evolved negatively or with its sign and qualities, &c. inverted ; while $-\sqrt[3]{+x^3}$ means that $+x^3$ is to be evolved negatively also, or with

its

its sign changed and qualities altered, in virtue of the negative sign which precedes the quantity $\sqrt[3]{+x'}$; and $+\sqrt{-x'}$ can properly and justly be understood to mean only that it is to be evolved positively or as it actually is, and therefore without its sign being changed and its qualities thereby inverted.

22. It is perfectly impossible in the nature of things for the same power to have two roots and these of kinds and qualities the very reverse of each other, and therefore one of them necessarily of a kind and quality the very reverse of that of the power itself, since the power cannot possibly be possessed of the qualities of both of these roots of contrary natures, or of qualities which are repugnant and destructive of each other, and therefore such as are necessarily incapable of existing together as qualities of the same being or entity. Powers may have their signs, and thereby qualities, in certain cases and for certain good reasons, inverted, and then may be regarded as powers of the same root of which they were before such alteration in their signs and qualities took place, or as the inverse powers of these roots; but there are in fact, properly, no such powers in nature, and they really become by such alteration powers not of their former root, but of that quantity which formed that root with its signs and qualities inverted.

23. In algebraical multiplication, though $-x \times -x$ gives $+x'$ for the product or second power, yet the second power thus obtained is not in reality, though apparently, the second power of $-x$; but the second power of $+x$, the sign of the multiplicand being necessarily reversed or rendered the very contrary of what it was, and that even antecedent to the multiplication, since that is an effect necessarily resulting from the same quantity having two negative signs prefixed to it; $-x \times -x$ and $\overline{--x'}$ being identical, in as far as they have properly and justly one and the same meaning, each signifying the inverse product or inverse second power of $-x$; that is, the second power of $+x$, or what is the same thing of $-x$ with its sign inverted or changed so as to become $+x$: and so of other powers thus obtained. And the root of the power thus obtained, as of $\overline{--x'}$, is $\overline{--x}$; that is, $+x$; $+x$ and $-\overline{-x}$ being identical in every thing except the mode of expression, or the mode of employing the signs for expressing

pressing the same thing. And for the very same reason that a negative root becomes a positive root, and on being positively involved produces positive powers, does a positive root become a negative root, and on being positively involved produces negative powers, that of having a negative sign prefixed to its own proper sign: and hence it is that $-\overline{+x}$, and $+\overline{-x}$, have precisely the same signification, each being equivalent to $-x$; and that the powers both of $-\overline{+x}$, and of $+\overline{-x}$, are negative; while those of $+\overline{+x}$, as well as those of $-\overline{-x}$, are positive.

24. The involution and evolution of binomials may be effected in a simpler and easier way than any hitherto proposed, when the values of the several terms are known, by involving or evolving their respective sums, or any symbol or letter representing them, when all the terms have the same sign prefixed, whether positive or negative; and by involving or evolving their respective differences, or any symbol or letter representing them, when the different terms have different signs prefixed to them. Thus, if $+p$ is substituted for $+a+b$, or the sum of the terms, or if $+a+b=+p$, then the powers of $+a+b$ are $+p$, $+p^2$, $+p^3$, &c. if $+a^2+2ab+b^2$ is taken $=+p^2$, then $\sqrt{+a^2+2ab+b^2}=+p$; if $-a^2-x^2=-p^2$, then $-p=\sqrt{-a^2-x^2}$; and if $-a+b=+q$, then the powers of $-a+b$ are $+q$, $+q^2+q^3$, &c. and if $-a+b=-q$, then the powers of $-a+b$ are $-q$, $-q^2$, $-q^3$, &c. and if $-2+5=+3$ is the root, then the powers of it are the powers of $+3$; or if $-5+2=-3$ is the root, its powers are then those of -3; and so of other cases: in the above cases q represents the differences between the quantities or terms of the binomials, and is either positive or negative according as the largest of the two quantities of which it is a remainder is either positive or negative. By such means may any compound quantities be reduced to simple ones: and this method may perhaps be found useful even in certain cases where the values of the terms are not known.

25. The sign $-$ is often prefixed to the exponent of a quantity; as a^{+2-3} or as it is commonly expressed a^{2-3}, and as a^{-2}, &c. In this case the mark or sign $-$ denotes division, or that, in the first example given above, a^2 is to be divided by a^3; and in the second example of a^{-2} that unity is to be divided by a^2; or otherwise that a^2 is the denominator of a fraction in the first example of which a^2 is the numerator; and that a^2 in the second example is the denominator of a fraction of which unity forms the numerator: and hence the

the mark or sign — cannot in these cases with propriety be regarded as the negative sign; though expressed by the same mark or notation the negative sign is; and though these exponents to which it is prefixed are *improperly* called the negative powers of the quantities; for any positive power of any quantity, as of a, multiplied by adding to it, the common way of multiplying powers, what is called a negative power of the same quantity, or of a, of an equal exponent, gives unit for the sum, or product, as $a^{-3} \times a^{+3}$, or a^{-3+3}, $=1$, or unit, which could not be the case if $^{-3}$, the first exponent of a, was negative, since in that event the positive and negative exponents of a, as being of equal value, on being added together, would mutually destroy each other, giving 0, or zero, for the sum or product, in place of unity: what is called the negative exponent of a quantity, as of a in the case a^{-3}, in reality expresses no power of that quantity, or of a, whatever; and nothing, merely, but the quotient of unity divided by a^3, or $\frac{1}{a^3}$; and hence it is that a^{-3+3}, as being equivalent to $\frac{1}{a^3} \times a^3$, $=\frac{a^3}{a^3}$, gives unity for the sum, product, or quotient, according as it is regarded as being the result either of addition, multiplication, or division. It is usual to employ a° as the symbol of unity: and hence it has sometimes been stated that $a^{\circ-1}=a^{-1}$; but very improperly, since a° represents unit only, and a may represent any simple quantity whatever; and since in that case $1^{-1}=a^{-1}$, or $\frac{1}{1}=\frac{1}{a}$ in place of $=\frac{1}{a^\circ}$, which is absurd.

26. The terms *plus* and *minus* are justly applicable to the signs $+$ and $-$ in no case, except as they are employed in common Arithmetic in denoting addition and subtraction: in Algebra they cannot be admitted: these signs are employed in that science for very different purposes. In Algebra the signs $+$ and $-$ have no meaning or use but as having a reference to each other; and therefore neither $+$ applied to any quantity, as $+a$, nor $-$ applied to any quantity, as $-a$, have any meaning or use but when the quantities or magnitudes to which they are respectively applied are of contrary natures, or in opposite positions, or act in contrary directions, and when they are employed to express that contrariety or opposition: neither $+a$, nor $-a$, differing from a, when that is not the case; the signs, then, in fact, having no signification, meaning, or use. And towards the proper understanding

standing of the intent, meaning, and use, of these signs, it is particularly to be observed, 1st, THAT THE NEGATIVE SIGN NOT ONLY COUNTERACTS AND IS CONTRARY TO AND SUBVERSIVE OF THE POSITIVE SIGN IN ALL CASES, BUT ALSO THAT IT COUNTERACTS AND IS SUBVERSIVE OF ITSELF WHEN TWICE REPEATED, OR WHEN TWO NEGATIVE SIGNS APPLY TO THE SAME QUANTITY: AND IT IS FROM ITS, THUS, IN THESE CASES COUNTER-ACTING ITSELF, THAT TWO NEGATIVE SIGNS MAKE A POSITIVE SIGN, THREE A NEGATIVE, FOUR A POSITIVE, FIVE A NEGATIVE, ETC. AND, 2dly, THAT THE POSITIVE SIGN COUNTERACTS ITSELF IN NO CASE, AND COUNTERACTS THE NEGATIVE IN CASES OF ADDITION AND SUBTRAC-TION ONLY, AND NOT IN THOSE OF MULTIPLICATION AND DIVISION, OR IN THOSE OF INVOLUTION AND EVOLUTION.

27. If the preceding principles and reasonings are well founded and just, they not only afford a most satisfactory, clear, and convincing explanation of the intent, meaning, and use of these signs in Algebra, but also prove incontestibly that neither the even powers of negative roots, nor the roots of even negative powers, are, as universally believed, imaginary and impossible: there actually being such negative powers, and these powers powers of negative roots; and it being impossible for positive even powers, as $+x^2$, $+x^4$, $+x^6$, &c. to have, as is supposed, either $+x$, or $-x$, for their root; or for the powers either to differ in nature and qualities from their root, or to possess the qualities of two different roots differing in natures, and the natures of which are contradictory, repugnant to, and subversive of each other. And, hence, that the doctrine of the imaginary and impossible powers of quantities, first conceived by Cardan and since so fully treated of by succeeding writers on Algebra, has no foundation in nature or in reason, and no other tendency than to perplex, deceive, and mislead. But though these powers and roots have hitherto, by the moderns at least, been regarded as imaginary and impossible without being so in reality, yet there are other powers and roots both of quantities and of equations which have been admitted by them into the science of Algebra as realities that are in fact merely imaginary and impossible. These are the supposed powers and roots of unity, and of cypher or zero.

28. Unity is indeed in one sense the root of every other quantity, inte-gral or fractional, simple or compound, since it is either in the addition of

units,

units, or in the division of unity into parts or fractions, and in combinations of these, that all other quantities consist; and it is also the root of all the different progressions of numbers, arithmetical, harmonical, and geometrical; but though the root of all the different geometrical progressions, as of 1, 2, 4, 8, &c. of 1, 3, 9, 27, &c. of 1, 4, 16, 64, &c. of 1, 5, 25, 125, &c. yet the powers of these progressions are not the powers of unity; for if that was the case unity would not have one second power, or one third power, only, &c. as other numbers have, but innumerable second powers, third powers, &c. thus, in the above progressions, 2, 3, 4, and 5, would all be second powers, and 4, 9, 16, and 25, third powers, of unity: and each of these powers would have as many different values as there are quantities included in them; but any given power of any given quantity cannot have different values relative to that quantity, since it is its retaining always the same relative value or ratio to that quantity as a root, that constitutes it a power of that quantity or root.

29. Every number, except unity, may be regarded as a root, and as having powers; though in reality it is not the number abstractly taken that constitutes the root of these powers, but the ratio of that number to unity: as the ratios of $2:1$, $3:1$, $4:1$, $5:1$, &c. and of their reciprocals $\frac{1}{2}:1$, $\frac{1}{3}:1$, $\frac{1}{4}:1$, $\frac{1}{5}:1$, &c. Powers and roots being the result of the involution and evolution of such ratios; each immediately succeeding term or power in a geometrical progression having the same ratio to the preceding, and, vice versâ, that the first term or power of it has to unity. Hence it is manifest that what are in Algebra supposed to be the powers and the roots of unity, as 1^2, 1^3, 1^4, &c. $x^3 - 1 = 0$, &c. $\sqrt[2]{1}$, $\sqrt[3]{1}$, $\sqrt[4]{1}$, &c. or 1, $\dfrac{-1+\sqrt{-3}}{2}$, and $\dfrac{-1-\sqrt{-3}}{2}$, as three different cube roots of unity, are only, when they have any meaning, unity under the disguise of another notation, since the only ratio of unity to unity is that of equality, or $1 = 1$, a ratio which admits not of involution or evolution; and of which all the supposed powers and roots must necessarily, in every thing but in the notation, be identical with unity, or that number of which they are supposed to be the powers and the roots: the supposed roots of unity will be more particularly considered in treating of equations. The employing of such terms as 1^2, 1^3, 1^4, &c. $x^3 - 1 = 0$, &c.

&c. $\sqrt[2]{1}$, $\sqrt[3]{1}$, $\sqrt[4]{1}$, &c. in Algebra, and in assigning in certain cases suppositious and erroneous values to them, cannot but be productive of bad effects, as necessarily leading to erroneous and absurd conclusions: yet such powers and roots are generally admitted in Algebra; and the admission of them is regarded as forming a fundamental and important principle in that science.

30. Unity is not only incapable of being involved, or multiplied into itself: but it also cannot, any more than 0, multiply or divide any other quantity. Thus 4×1, and 4×0, being each equal 4, the multiplicand or quantity to be multiplied, it is manifest that that quantity has not been multiplied by means of this process, or imaginary species of multiplication; since if that had been the case the product must necessarily have differed from the multiplicand. And, in cases of division, as $\frac{4}{1}$, and $\frac{4}{0}$, or 1)4(4, and 0)4(0, the dividend, or quantity to be divided, not being altered by the operation (there either being no quotient, or a quotient which does not differ from it), it is manifest that no division of it, by means of this imaginary species of it, can possibly have taken place. If 0 is divisible by 0, or what is the same thing if quantities each equal 0 are divisible by each other, the quotient must necessarily be 0, and not any real quantity; since 0 can be found in 0, 0 times only. Supposing the contrary involves the absurdity of 0 being actually divisible into real entities or quantities, and those of different and various kinds. For, if it is admitted that 0 may be taken from 0 once, it may be taken from 0 again, 0)0(1, 0)00(11, 0)000(111, &c. or nothing divided by nothing may have the different quotients 1, 2, 3, &c. And, on this principle, though $\frac{0}{0} = 1$, or gives 1 for the quotient; and though this is also the case of $\frac{1-1=0}{1-1=0}$, of $\frac{2-2=0}{2-2=0}$, &c. yet it is not so in many other cases; thus $\frac{2-2=0}{1-1=0} = 2$, or gives 2 for the quotient, $\frac{3-3}{1-1} = 3$, $\frac{4-4}{1-1} = 4$, $\frac{5-5}{1-1} = 5$, &c. and $\frac{6-6}{2-2} = 3$, $\frac{12-12}{3-3} = 4$, &c. and thus the quotients of $\frac{0}{0}$ are numerous and various, differing from each other according to each different statement of the case $\frac{0}{0}$. This doctrine besides involves the absurdity of 0, or non-entity, not only being divisible, and divisible by entities or real quantities, but also of its being divisible by itself or non-entity; and, moreover, that quantities or real entities are divisible by non-entity or nothing.

31. From the admission of the above erroneous principles into the science of Algebra has proceeded that doctrine, now almost generally adopted, which ascribes to vanishing fractions whose numerators and denominators become at the same time equal 0, or vanish, a real value; or which makes nothing divided by nothing equal to something, and thereby nothing and something the same: as the fraction $\frac{x-x^3}{1-x}=4$, when $x=1$, on the principles of 0 being divisible by 0 and of unity possessing powers, though in reality $=\frac{1-1}{1-1}=\frac{0}{0}=0$.

32. All human knowledge, mathematical as well as other kinds, must necessarily depend on experience---on physical data and physical principles---that is, on nature, or the natures of things as they and their relations among themselves appear to human beings; and on the degree of physical accuracy in the principles must the physical accuracy of the conclusions, mathematically deduced, necessarily depend. The science of Algebra, like all others, is founded on and is rationally deduced from experiment and induction; and like them proceeds progressively from what is simple to what is more complex, from particulars to generals. Its object and end is also the same as that of other sciences, the attainment of knowledge by the discovery of useful truths: and this object it effects partly by Composition or Synthesis, and partly by Resolution or Analysis, in first composing from the facts or data certain formula called equations---the name equation being given to a ratio of equality expressed symbolically and algebraically---which admit of being analysed or resolved by the rules of the science into their respective component parts called the roots of the equation; and secondly in resolving by these rules the equations thus formed into their roots, whereby that which is sought or required is discovered and ascertained, and the questions proposed answered. The peculiar excellence of the science of Algebra has been supposed to consist in its assuming that as known which is unknown; and thence by a retrograde process from quantities unknown and sought to quantities known deducing the proper conclusions. This, however, is by no means the case; it possesses no such quality; but, on the contrary, like every other kind of rational investigation, proceeds from what is known or given to what is unknown and sought; that is, for such is the nature of this science, from

known

known or given equations to other equations which are unknown and sought, and from thence deduces the proper conclusions: and though it is usual in the investigation to denote the unknown and sought quantities by means of particular symbols, as the letters x, y, z, &c. yet these symbols are never assumed as representing known quantities, but the contrary.

33. In the deducing, then, of just conclusions from what is known or given with respect to what is unknown and sought, by means of the composition and resolution of equations, does the science and the art of Algebra consist. Rules for various methods whereby this may in most cases be effected—in as far at least as depending on the known properties of ratios, the various alterations which may be made in equations without affecting the ratio of equality, and the formation of equations from known quantities and known relations—are to be found in all elementary treatises on Algebra detailed in a manner sufficiently correct, clear, and convincing; and an account of the natures, generation, and resolution, of the various kinds of equations is likewise given in these treatises; which is also sufficiently satisfactory with respect to simple equations at least, except in stating that there are such simple equations $x+a=0$, $x+b=0$, $x+c=0$, &c. and yet representing x, a, b, c, &c. in these cases as real quantities; or, as otherwise expressed, such simple equations as $+x=-a$, $+x=-b$, $+x=-c$, &c. since it is absolutely impossible, from the natures and contrariety of the signs $+$ and $-$, for $+x$ to equal $-a$, $+x$ to equal $-b$, $+x$ to equal $-c$, &c. for if $+x=+a$, x and a being of equivalent values, $+x$ cannot also $=-a$; as, in that case, $+a$ and $-a$ must necessarily express and signify the same thing; that is, the signs $+$ and $-$ must necessarily have the same signification, and thereby become insignificant and unnecessary in this science, which cannot be admitted: and, if x, a, b, c, &c. are real quantities, and not mere nothings or substitutes for cyphers, and are of equivalent values, though $+x-a=0$, $+x-b=0$, &c. yet $+x+a$, $+x+b$, &c. cannot also $=0$; since that supposition would involve the absurdity of $+x-a$ and $+x+a$ having the same signification and being of equal values; and since it is manifest that no positive quantity or quantities added together, and no negative quantity or quantities added together, though of equivalent values, can possibly $=0$: it being the addition of positive and negative quantities of equal value only that can have that effect, and that merely as

resulting

resulting from that contrariety which is denoted and expressed by the signs prefixed. To give just rules and reasons for the generation and resolution of compound equations, especially of the higher orders, is matter of great difficulty; and some of those which have been given seem not to be altogether unobjectionable. Among the first of these rules is the following: " Every equation has as many roots as it has dimensions:" and hence a quadratic has two, a cubic three, and a biquadratic four roots, &c. a rule which does not hold good in every case. Thus the equations $4x^2-4=60$, and $x^3-4=60$, have each but one root, namely 4, though the one is of two dimensions and the other of three: the same is the case with such equations as $x^3+3x^2+3x^2+x^3=64$ formed by the involution of $x+x$ to the third power when $x=2$; with such affected quadratics as $x^2+2x=24$, of which the root is 4, formed by the multiplication of $x+2$ by x; and, indeed, in all cases in which an equation has been raised to any particular dimension by means of involution: and it is not in these cases only that this rule fails, as will afterwards appear.

34. That compound equations are generated by a successive multiplication of simple equations, as by multiplying the simple equations $x-a=0$, $x-b=0$, $x-c=0$, $x-d=0$, &c. into each other, was a discovery of Harriot's; and a valuable discovery, though there are many compound equations, besides the several kinds mentioned above, which are not so formed : and it was a mistake to state $x+d=0$, $x+e=0$, &c. as equations, and at the same time represent x, d, and e, &c. as real quantities. In this, however, as well as in his manner of accounting for the generation of compound equations, he has been generally followed.

35. In generating equations by this method it is manifest the different unknown quantities, or unknown quantities of different values, are represented by the same symbol or letter, commonly x; and that what are called the powers of this letter in equations thus generated are in reality not POWERS OF ANY ROOT, but PRODUCTS of the multiplications of these different values of x, or of the unknown quantities which it represents, into each other; and, hence, that these different values of x cannot with propriety be regarded as roots of powers at least; and perhaps might more properly be denominated the factors for generating, and for resolving or decyphering the equation, than the roots of it; as giving the same name

to

to powers and to products, and the same name to roots and to factors of multiplication, renders the meanings and uses of these terms indeterminate, equivocal, and ambiguous, and by that means those doctrines they are employed to unfold obscure and dubious.

36. This distinction between the powers and products of equations is of the utmost importance with respect to the acquiring a just conception of the true nature of equations, and thereby towards the discovery of the proper means of resolving them. For hence it is manifest, that every equation has not as many roots as dimensions; that it is those equations only that are products of as many different quantities multiplied into each other that have so; and that, as these equations that are products are generated and raised to those dimensions they respectively possess by multiplication and not by involution, the reduction of their respective dimensions must be effected by division and not by evolution; that is, by reversing the process by which they were generated, as lowering them one dimension by dividing them by one of the generating and component simple equations or binomials, lowering them two by dividing them successively by two of these, &c. and also that the questions can be resolved by multiplying and not by involving the roots or keys found into the powers indicated by the exponents of the several equations thus formed.

37. What are regarded as negative roots, or negative values of x, are in reality not keys, though factors of equations; and though, when substituted for x in them, and multiplied, not involved, agreeable to the indices and co-efficients of the terms in these, they generate other and different equations, though the absolute terms, or the right-hand sides, of these are the same with those of the original equations; for these negative keys do not belong to those equations of which they are supposed to be the keys; or they are not keys of these, but of others having terms of different quantities and of different signs from those in these, into which they convert these, when substituted for x in them, though the sum or the difference of the first and second terms in quadratics, forming either the absolute terms, or the other side of the equations, in these cases, are in the corresponding equations the same; for the equations thus generated give the sum when the difference is required and is given, and the difference when the sum is required and is given, by the original equations; and these the sums and the differ-

ences

ences of quantities different from those of the original equations. Thus, in quadratics, affected quadratic equations are commonly distinguished into three different cases, viz. 1st, into the form of $x^2+px-r=0$, or $x^2+px=r$, in which r or the absolute term is equal to the sum of the other two terms of the equation; 2d, into the form of $x^2-px-r=0$, or $x^2-px=r$, in which the absolute term is not equal to the sum but to the difference between the other two terms of the equation, when that difference is positive; and, 3d, into the form of $x^2-px+r=0$, or $x^2-px=-r$, in which the absolute term is equal to the difference between the other two terms of the equation, when that difference is negative: and if the affected quadratic equation of the first form $x^2+4x=60$, of which $+6$ is a true root, and -10 is supposed to be another, has -10 substituted for x in it the equation $+100-40=60$ is generated; differing from the original equation $36+24=60$, not only in the quantities forming its terms, but also in the sign of the second term, and in thereby giving an equation of the second form instead of the first, or the difference in place of the sum of the two first terms for the absolute term, or the other side of the equation; as well as in its root: so that it is in reality an equation essentially different from that of which $+6=x$ is the root. If the equation $x^2-4x=12$, of the second form, of which $+6$ is the root, and -2 a supposed root, has this supposed root substituted for x in it by the common method, the equation $4+8=12$ is generated, differing in every respect in the same way as in the former case from the original equation, except in giving the first form in place of the second, or in giving the sum when the difference is required and is given in the original, and therefore likewise differing essentially from the original equation. And hence it is manifest that these supposed negative values of x do not in either case form a root of the original equation. In the equation $x^2-8x=-12$, of the third form, there are two values of x both positive and both real roots of the equation; since when substituted for x each gives the difference of the two first terms for the other side of the equation, agreeable to the statement and as required, and the same quantity for the difference: thus, substituting 6 for x gives the equation $36-48=-12$; as substituting 2 for x, gives $4-16=-12$ also.

38. This reasoning will appear more clear and convincing on exhibiting the different manners of the respective generations of these equations; and then

then substituting the roots, real and supposed, for x in them: thus, in the first case, the equation $x^2+4x=60$ is generated by multiplying the simple equation $x-6$, or $6-6$, $=0$, by the positive binomial $x+10$, or $10+10$; thus,

$$
\begin{aligned}
x-\ 6 &= 0 \\
\times x +10 & \\
\hline
x^2-\ 6x & \\
+10x-60 & \\
\hline
x^2+\ 4x-60 &= 0
\end{aligned}
$$

gives the equation $x^2+4x=60$, or an equation of the first form or case, which in substituting $+6$ for x in it becomes $36+24=60$; an equation differing in no respect from the original equation except in the substitution of figures for symbols: whereas in substituting -10, the other supposed root, for x in it, it becomes $100-40=60$; an equation differing essentially and in every thing from the original equation except in giving the same absolute term; and of which, notwithstanding, -10 could not be a key, or resolve the question according to which the original equation was formed, as the equation thus formed could not possibly, as thus differing from the original, answer or accord with the conditions of the question on which it was formed; and as it is in fact an equation of the second case in place of the first, giving the difference instead of the sum of the first terms for the absolute term.

39. The equation $x^2-4x=60$, of the second case, is generated by multiplying the simple equation $x-10=0$ by the positive binomial $x+6$, or $6+6$: thus,

$$
\begin{aligned}
x-10 &= 0 \\
\times x +\ 6 & \\
\hline
x^2-10x & \\
+\ 6x-60 & \\
\hline
x^2-\ 4x-60 &= 0
\end{aligned}
$$

giving $x^2-4x=60$, or an equation of the second form or case, which on substituting 10 for x in it becomes $100-40=60$; an equation differing in no respect from the original equation except in the substitution of figures

for

for symbols; whereas, on substituting -6, the other supposed root, for x in it, it becomes $36+24=60$; an equation differing essentially from the original one, as being of the first form or case in place of the second, giving the sum instead of the difference of the two first terms for the absolute term, &c. and hence it is manifest that -6 cannot possibly be a key to the original equation, or resolve the question or proposition according to which it is formed, as not answering the conditions on which it is formed.

40. And the equation $x^2-16x=-60$, of the third case, is generated by multiplying the simple equations $x-10=0$ and $x-6=0$ into each other; thus,

$$x-10=0$$
$$\times x-\ 6=0$$
$$\overline{\quad\quad\quad}$$
$$x^2-10x$$
$$-\ 6x+60$$
$$\overline{\quad\quad\quad}$$
$$x^2-16x+60=0$$

giving $x^2-16x=-60$, or an equation of the third form or case, which on substituting $+10$ for x in it becomes $100-160=-60$; and on substituting $+6$ for x in it becomes $36-96=-60$; equations differing in nothing from the original equation except in the substitution of figures for symbols, and therefore such as would severally resolve the equation, and answer the questions agreeable to which it may have been formed. When this last equation is generated by involution, &c. in place of as above, or by multiplying $x-16$ by x, when $x=10$, making $x^2-16x=-60$, or $100-160=-60$, it will on being resolved by the method of completing the square, &c. give the same two positive roots as above, namely, $+10$, and $+6$, but it is manifest that the first of these only is the real root of the equation in this case, and therefore the only key for resolving the proposition or question according to the conditions of which it has been composed; and that the other supposed root, though positive, is in reality not a root of the equation in this case.

41. Roots of equations which are regarded as impossible and imaginary, and which are denominated the impossible or imaginary roots of equations, are amply treated of in every system of Algebra; and in some of them the proper applications and uses, and even the *possibility*, of these *impossible* quantities

quantities are treated of. They are represented to be the roots of such equations as involve the square root of a negative quantity; and it is supposed that they always enter equations by pairs. " Of this kind is the " root of the quadratic $\sqrt{\overline{aa-bb}}=\sqrt{\overline{-xx}}$, when aa is a less quantity than " bb, supposed to be; because then both $\overline{aa-bb}$ and $-xx$ are negative quan- " tities, and the square root of a negative quantity is impossible. For " every possible root, whether it be affirmative or negative, if it be multi- " plied by itself, produces an affirmative square; therefore that would " be an impossible one which is to produce a negative square." And also, for the same reasons, the roots of such affected quadratics as $\sqrt{x^2-20x}=\sqrt{-8^2}$. That these conclusions are deduced from a misconception of the meaning, intent, and use of the signs $+$ and $-$, and from not making the proper distinction between multiplication and involution in Algebra, and consequently that these reasons are unfounded and these conclusions erroneous, has already been attempted to be proved; and these equations themselves (when translated or transformed into the numeral ones $\sqrt{36-100}=\sqrt{-64}=-8$; in the first case when $a=6$, $b=10$; and $\sqrt{16-80}=\sqrt{-64}$, $=-8$, in the second case in which $x=4$) evince that it was not without sufficient cause: as they clearly testify their having roots, and possible roots though negative; and which require only to be involved or evolved positively, or as they actually are, to give the proper and just results.

42. The principal source, however, of impossible or imaginary roots is supposed to be such equations as $aa+bb=0$; of which the roots are supposed to be $a+\sqrt{-bb}$, and $a-\sqrt{-bb}$, and both supposed impossible. But, if such an equation can be supposed, it can mean only that nothing is equal to nothing; since the sum of $aa+bb$ is stated by it as equal to nothing: and nothing it must be admitted has no possible root. Moreover, if a and b are regarded as real quantities, in place of mere substitutions for 0; and, consequently, the quantities $a+\sqrt{-b^2}$ and $a-\sqrt{-b^2}$ also real; there is no possible way of either involving or of multiplying these supposed roots that will give $aa+bb$ for the power or the product: for these supposed roots, when the true meanings of their signs are properly understood, are only other expressions for $a-b$, and $a+b$, which when multiplied into each other will give a^2-b^2 for the product, but never a^2+b^2. When a real value is substituted for 0, in the above supposed equation,

aa and *bb* come by that means to have real values also, and the equation to be a proper one; as when stated thus, $aa + bb = x^2$; if $x = 5$ then *a* will $= 3$ and $b = 4$, and the equation when transformed into a numeral one will become $9 + 16 = 25$.

43. In reasonings and deductions such as these attempted to be refuted in the preceding sections must the supposition of what has been regarded as the cube of unity, or 1^3, have originated, and the supposition of the cube of unity having not only one root, but three different roots, and of these roots being the three following, viz. 1, $\frac{-1 + \sqrt{-3}}{2}$, and $\frac{-1 - \sqrt{-3}}{2}$; which may perhaps be regarded as the apex of this climax of erroneous and delusive doctrines. The absurdity of the supposition of a root and a power of that root being the same or the same quantity; also of 1^3 differing from 1, even when a symbol as y^3 is substituted for 1^3, has already been attempted to be pointed out; and this must appear still more manifest when it is stated, as in the proof attempted of this doctrine of unity having powers and of the third power of it having three different roots, that $y^3 - 1 = 0$, or otherwise that $1^3 - 1 = 0$, or that the power and the root are the same this equation being equivalent to $1^3 = 1$; and that two of these supposed roots of this supposed third power of unity differ essentially from unity or from that root of which this cube is supposed to be a power. This supposed proof consists in first stating $y^3 - 1 = 0$; then in stating $y - 1 = 0$; the inevitable consequence of which is that $y^3 - y = 0$, or $y^3 = y$; or, substituting their real values for them, that $1^3 = 1$: from which it is concluded that unity is one of the cube roots of unity; and, this being the case, that the equation $y - 1 = 0$, or $1 - 1 = 0$, is one of the simple equations of which the supposed cubical equation $y^3 - 1 = 0$ is generated (though it is above stated to be equivalent to this same simple equation $y - 1 = 0$), and that therefore it is necessary to reduce the equation $y^3 - 1 = 0$ one dimension by dividing it by the simple equation $y - 1 = 0$, for obtaining the other two roots, which will then be the two roots of a quadratic: that is in fact, that $1 - 1 = 0$ should be divided by $1 - 1 = 0$; or, in other words, that 0 should be divided by 0 to give the other two roots. Though it is manifest that 0 divided by 0, if such a division was possible, could only give 0 for the quotient; yet, in this case, the quotient is stated to be $y^2 + y + 1$; which, according to the

preceding

preceding data, should be $=3$, since $y=1$; and of this quotient the really *impossible* quadratic equation $y^2+y+1=0$ is formed, for though the symbols y^2 and y might in contradiction to the premises equal 0, it is utterly impossible for the last term $+1$ or unity to be the same with or to $=0$ or cypher, of which impossible equation it is attempted to obtain the roots by transforming it into the likewise *impossible* equation $y^2+y=-1$, which according to the preceding data is equivalent to $1+1=2=-1$; and, from these truly *impossible* premises, the other two supposed cube roots of unity $\frac{-1+\sqrt{-3}}{2}$ and $\frac{-1-\sqrt{-3}}{2}$ are *thus* supposed to be obtained, viz. $y^2+y+\frac{1}{4}=$ $1-+\frac{1}{4}=\frac{-3}{4} \therefore y+\frac{1}{2}\pm\frac{\sqrt{-3}}{2} \cdot y =\frac{-1\pm\sqrt{-3}}{2}$.

44. What exists not can neither be positive nor negative: and, in the application of Algebra to Geometry, the roots of these imaginary equations which are supposed to define intersections, &c. which exist not, and which in the nature of things cannot possibly exist, are impossible not because the roots or the symbols or terms denoting them are marked and represented as negative; but these terms are marked and represented as negative because these intersections, &c. are impossible, and exist not, from the data or physical principles on which these equations are formed being impossible; there being in these cases no such intersections, &c. as those stated in the data on which these imaginary equations are formed: and though the roots of equations which are merely imaginary and impossible may justly be regarded as impossible also, and are marked negative because they have no actual existence and are impossible, it by no means follows as a necessary consequence that the negative roots of real quantities and real equations are likewise imaginary and impossible.

45. From the preceding principles, and the facts just now stated, the following conclusions are rationally deduced, viz. 1st, That, contrary to the received opinion, every quadratic equation has not two roots; and that it is not because the square root of a positive square quantity may be either $+$ or $-$, the reason commonly assigned for quadratics having two roots and the one $+$ and the other $-$, as supposed, that certain affected quadratics, those of the third form, have each two roots. 2d, That real equations have neither negative, nor impossible roots. 3d, That every root that resolves the equation will not solve the proposition or question agreeable

to the conditions of which the equation has been composed; and, 4th, That every equation has not as many roots as dimensions, but only as many roots or keys as there are simple equations in their respective compositions, the number of roots in each equation being determined by the number of simple equations which enters into its composition; there being but one true root to each when one simple equation only enters into their respective compositions, as in the 1st and 2d cases of affected quadratic equations given above, and two true roots when two simple equations enter into their composition as in the 3d case or form of these equations. And indeed this rule holds universally, or with regard to equations of all orders: what are called the negative roots of equations not being so much as component parts of the simple equations in which the compound ones originate, but merely terms of those positive binomials by which these original equations have been multiplied.

46. It is likewise to be observed from the above statement, that, contrary to the common rule given with regard to the co-efficients of equations, the co-efficient of the second term is not always the arithmetical sum or amount of all the roots of the equation, real and supposed; but, on the contrary, is often the arithmetical difference between them: thus, in the two first cases of quadratics given above of $x^2 \pm 4x - 60 = 0$, the co-efficient of the second term is the arithmetical difference of the roots real and supposed of these equations, or of the first terms of those quantities by the multiplication of which they are formed; whereas, in the 3d case given above of $x^2 - 16x + 60 = 0$, the co-efficient of the second term is the sum of these roots or quantities. In all compound equations, however formed, whether by multiplying simple equations into each other, or by multiplying one or more simple equations by one or more positive binomials, in each of which the terms are of equal value, into each other, the co-efficient of the second term is always either the arithmetical sum, or the arithmetical difference, of the genitors or generating quantities; that is, of the first terms of these equations or binomials employed in generating them: it being their sum in the first case, and their difference in the last case.

47. All compound equations formed after the manner now described are possessed of the following properties, viz. In all those of the first case, or

that

that are formed by multiplying simple equations into each other, every complete quadratic has two different keys, or values of x capable of resolving the equation and answering the question; every cubic three; every biquadratic four, &c. In every quadratic so formed there are properly four terms, each of equal value; but on summing it, it is usual to add the two middle terms together, thereby forming one of double the value of either of the extreme terms, which are always of equal value to each other in all these equations; that is, the highest dimension of x in each equation is always equal to the absolute term of that equation; and it is from this addition of the two middle terms into one, and their then forming the second term of it, that the co-efficient of this term becomes equal to the sum of the different values of x, or of the generating quantities. In every complete cubic so formed there are properly eight terms, and each of equal value, but it is usual in summing them to add the 2d, 3d, and 4th together into one term, then forming the 2d, and consequently of precisely three times the value of the first or the last term, and also to add the 5th, 6th, and 7th together into one term, then forming the third of the equation and of precisely equal value with the second term of it: and it is owing to this addition in forming the second term that the co-efficient of that term is the sum of all the three different values of x in the equation. In every complete biquadratic so formed, there are properly sixteen terms and all of equal values, but by the usual mode of summing them they are reduced to five; of which the 2d and 4th are of equal value, and each of four times the value of the first or the last term; while the 3d term is of six times the value of the first or the last: and it is owing to this mode of summation that the co-efficient of the 2d term is the sum of all the four different values of x in the equation. And so with respect to equations of higher dimensions, the number of proper terms in each immediately succeeding equation being precisely double those of the preceding.

48. In each cubic there are not only three different values of x, but three different values of x^2 also, as formed by multiplying the three different values of x two and two together: and in a biquadratic there are not only four different values of x, and of x^2, but likewise four different values of x^3. But these facts will appear plainer from the following examples, viz.

Example

Example 1st.

$$x-2=0$$
$$\times\, x-3=0$$

$$\overline{\hphantom{xxxxxxxx}}$$

$$x^2-2x$$
$$\hphantom{xx}-3x+6$$

$$\overline{\hphantom{xxxxxxxx}}$$

$$x^2-5x+6=0 \text{ square,}$$
$$\times\, x-4=0$$

$$\overline{\hphantom{xxxxxxxx}}$$

$$x^3-5x^2+\hphantom{2}6x$$
$$\hphantom{xx}-4x^2+20x-24$$

$$\overline{\hphantom{xxxxxxxx}}$$

$$x^3-9x^2+26x-24=0 \text{ cube.}$$

Example 2d.

$$2-2=0$$
$$\times\, 3-3=0$$

$$\overline{\hphantom{xxxxxxxx}}$$

$$6-6$$
$$\hphantom{xx}-6+6$$

$$\overline{\hphantom{xxxxxxxx}}$$

$$6-12+6=0 \text{ square,}$$
$$\times\, 4-4=0$$

$$\overline{\hphantom{xxxxxxxx}}$$

$$24-48+24$$
$$\hphantom{xx}-24+48-24$$

$$\overline{\hphantom{xxxxxxxx}}$$

$$24-72+72-24=0 \text{ cube.}$$

Example 3d.

$$x-x=0$$
$$\times\, x-x=0$$

$$\overline{\hphantom{xxxxxxxx}}$$

$$x^2-x^2$$
$$\hphantom{xx}-x^2+x^2$$

$$\overline{\hphantom{xxxxxxxx}}$$

$$x^2-2x^2+x^2 \text{ square,}$$
$$\times\, x-x=0$$

$$\overline{\hphantom{xxxxxxxx}}$$

$$x^3-2x^3+\hphantom{2}x^3$$
$$\hphantom{xx}-\hphantom{2}x^3+2x^3-x^3$$

$$\overline{\hphantom{xxxxxxxx}}$$

$$x^3-3x^3+3x^3-x^3=0 \text{ cube.}$$

Example 4th.

$$x-2=0$$
$$\times\, x-3=0$$

$$\overline{\hphantom{xxxxxxxx}}$$

$$x^2-2x-3x+6=0 \text{ square,}$$
$$\times\, x\hphantom{xx}-4=0$$

$$\overline{\hphantom{xxxxxxxx}}$$

$$x^3-2x^2+\hphantom{2}6x-24$$
$$\hphantom{xx}-3x^2+\hphantom{2}8x$$
$$\hphantom{xx}-4x^2+12x$$

$$\overline{\hphantom{xxxxxxxx}}$$

$$x^3-9x^2+26x-24=0 \text{ cube.}$$

From the examples 1st and 4th it is manifest that in the quadratic $x^2-5x+6=0$ there are four terms of equal values which are reduced to three by adding the two middle ones together, then forming the second term of double the value of either of the others; and that x has two different values in it, the sum of which forms the co-efficient of the second term thus constituted; and that in the cubic of $x^3-9x^2+26x-24=0$, of that example, there are eight terms of equal values which are reduced to four by addition, whereof the 2d and 3d are of equal values, and each of thrice the value of either of the extreme terms, which are also equal to each other;

other; and likewise that not only x has three different values into it, the sum of which forms the co-efficient of the 2d of the four terms into which it is converted by addition, but also that there are three different values of x^2 in it, which on being added together, form the co-efficient of the third of these terms; and consequently that the co-efficient of the 2d term is equal to the sum of the values of the x's in the third, and the co-efficient of the third is equal to the sum of the x^2's in the 2d; for every proper term of which these compound 2d and 3d terms are formed are each equal to the absolute term, which absolute term is always equal to the highest dimension of x in the equation or to the first term of it, or each is equal to all the three different values of x in the equation multiplied into each other, which in this cubic are 2, 3, and 4, and of which the product is 24; thus, the co-efficient of $6x$, the first proper term of which the third compound term $26x$ of the 4th Example is formed, is generated by multiplying two of these values of x, 2 and 3, into each other, and their product 6 by x, in this case $=4$ the other value of it, giving 24 for the product, which is equal to the absolute term; the co-efficient of $8x$, the 2d proper term, is generated by multiplying the product of the two values of x, 2 and 4, by $x=3$, in this case the other value of x, giving 24 also for the product; and the co-efficient of $12x$, the 3d and last proper term, is generated by multiplying the product of the two values of x, 3 and 4, by $x=2$, in this case the other value of x, likewise giving 24 for the product: while the x^2 of $2x^2$, the first proper term of which the second compound term is formed, is generated by multiplying the two values of x, 3 and 4 into each other, giving 12 for the product $=x^2$ in this case, which multiplied by the co-efficient of the term 2, the other value of x, gives 24 for the value of the term; the x^2 of $3x^2$, the second proper term, is generated by multiplying the two values of x, 2 and 4, into each other, giving 8 for the product, $=x^2$ in this case, which multiplied by the co-efficient of the term 3, the other value of x, gives also 24 for the value of this term; and the x^2 of $4x^2$, the 3d and last proper term, is generated by multiplying the two values of x, 2 and 3 into each other, giving 6 for the product, $=x^2$ in this case, which multiplied by the co-efficient of the term 4, likewise gives 24 as the value of this term. This cubic may be expressed in any of the four following manners, viz.

1st.

$$\text{1st.}\quad x^3-9x^2+26x-24=0.$$
$$\text{2d.}\quad 24-72+72-24=0.$$
$$\text{3d.}\quad x^3-3x^2+3x^2-24=0.$$
$$\text{4th.}\quad abc-3abc+3abc-24=0.$$

It is manifest that what are called co-efficients in the 3d example are only the number of the proper terms contained in each of the compound ones.

49. Similar products,—except with respect to the signs, and that they do not form equations—are obtained by multiplying either positive or negative binomial factors into each other, of which the terms in each are equal to each other, and respectively of equal values with those of the radical simple equations by the multiplication of which into each other the preceding quadratics, cubics, &c. were generated: thus,

Example 5th.

$$+x+2=+4$$
$$\times\ +x+3=+6$$
$$\overline{\qquad\qquad\qquad}$$
$$x^2+2x$$
$$\quad\ +3x+6$$
$$\overline{\qquad\qquad\qquad}$$
$$x^2+5x+6$$
$$\times\ +x+4=+8$$
$$\overline{\qquad\qquad\qquad}$$
$$x^3+5x^2+6x$$
$$\quad\ +4x^2+20x+24$$
$$\overline{\qquad\qquad\qquad}$$
$$+x^3+9x^2+26x+24.$$

50. In all compound equations of the second case generated as described above, or of which the co-efficients of the second terms express not the arithmetical sums but the arithmetical differences of the generating quantities, every complete quadratic has but one key or value of x capable of resolving the equation and answering the question to which it refers; a cubic may have either one or two keys in this case, according as one or two radical equations have entered into its composition, but it cannot possibly have three; a biquadratic may have one, two, or three keys,

keys, but cannot have four; and so of equations of this kind of higher orders: they have all as many keys as there are simple equations in their respective compositions; but none of them can have as many keys as dimensions, since none of them are generated entirely, as in the former case, by the multiplication of simple equations into each other. On the algebraical summation of quadratics of this kind, or of which the two middle terms have contrary signs, the co-efficient of the second or middle term, thus formed, gives not the sum of the generating quantities, but their difference; and this algebraical summation of symbolical equations seems to give very different results from the algebraical summation of similar numeral ones of equal values:—thus,

Example 1st.

$$x-6=0$$
$$\times x+10=20$$
$$\overline{}$$
$$x^2-6x$$
$$+10x-60$$
$$\overline{}$$
$$x^2+4x-60=0$$

Example 2d.

$$6-6$$
$$\times 10+10$$
$$\overline{}$$
$$60-60$$
$$+60-60$$
$$\overline{}$$
$$60\quad{}_*-60=0$$

Example 3d.

$$x-10=0$$
$$\times x+6=12$$
$$\overline{}$$
$$x^2-10x$$
$$+6x-60$$
$$\overline{}$$
$$x^2-4x-60=0$$

Example 4th.

$$10-10$$
$$\times 6+6$$
$$\overline{}$$
$$60-60$$
$$+60-60$$
$$\overline{}$$
$$60\quad{}_*-60=0$$

This unexpected and seeming strange and unaccountable difference in the results is nevertheless a difference in their modes of expression only; the same or equal values being cancelled by both methods, or in each case values equal to the amount of both of the original middle terms, for the x's in the equations thus formed express neither the sum, nor the difference, nor yet the mean values of the generating quantities, or of the x's in the original equations; but one of these values only, and that the value which forms the key of the equation, and hence it is that these equations can be resolved and the questions they refer to answered by the substitution of that value for the x's in the equations thus formed; a result which could not be effected but by means of this expedient of expressing the equations symbolically, and then adding the middle terms thus expressed algebraically to each other. Thus, in *Ex.* 1st and 3d, the sum of the two first terms of each is only of equal value with the first term of the numeral equations of the 2d and 4th examples, as is proved by their equalling the same quantity that that term does; and hence it is manifest that equal values are cancelled by both these operations, or in reducing by the algebraical addition the symbolical quadratics $x^2 - 6x + 10x = 60$; and $x^2 - 10x + 6x = 60$; and the numeral one $60 - 60 + 60 = 60$; to the forms $x^2 + 4x = 60$, $x^2 - 4x = 60$, and $60 = 60$: and, since the co-efficient of the 2d term of the symbolical equations thus formed is the arithmetical difference between the generating quantities, substituting that value of x, which forms the key of the equations, for the x's in them, must necessarily give the true result, as being necessarily equivalent to multiplying the two generating quantities into each other: thus, $x = 6$, the key of the first of these equations, being one of these quantities, and x, $+4$ the co-efficient of the second term, $= 10$, the other generating quantity of that equation; while $x = 10$, the key of the other equation, is one of the generating quantities of that equation, and x, -4 the co-efficient of its second term, the other; the multiplying of $x + 4$ by x, when $x = 6$, must necessarily be equivalent to multiplying 10 by 6; and the multiplying of $x - 4$ by x, when $x = 10$ must necessarily be equivalent to multiplying 6 by 10. And hence it is that both necessarily give the same quantity for the absolute term, and that quantity the same with that given by similar numeral equations. The same mode of reasoning is with equal propriety and justice applicable to equations of these kinds of the higher orders.

51. From these properties of equations, or from the natures of these kinds of equations, thus discovered, may such equations be generated from any commensurate quantities given as their several absolute terms; it being manifest from the above facts, 1st, that every compound equation has as many generating quantities as dimensions; 2d, that, when the co-efficient of the second term in them is the sum and not the difference of these quantities, the 2d term exceeds the first term in value, and consequently its

equivalent

equivalent the absolute term, as many times as is expressed by the figure denoting the dimensions of the first term; 3d, that the relative values of the other terms may also be easily ascertained; and 4th, that these quantities, according in number with the dimensions of the equation, which on being multiplied into each other give the absolute term, or the given quantity, for their product, and of which either the sum or the difference is equal to the co-efficient of the second term of the equation required, must necessarily be the generating quantities of that equation.

52. Thus, if it is required to form, on these principles, a quadratic equation from the given term -6; it is evident in the first place, from the negative sign of the term given, that this must be a quadratic of the third case, and consequently that its second term must be negative; secondly, that being a quadratic, two numbers must be found which multiplied into each other give 6 for their product; thirdly, that these two numbers are 2 and 3; and fourthly, that the first term of the equation must be x^2, the 2d $-5x$, the co-efficient of it being the sum of the two keys, viz. 2 and 3; and consequently the complete equation $x^2-5x=-6$, which answers. If -60 is the term given there may be a variety of equations formed from it on these principles, each of which have different generating quantities, and each of these quantities a key to it, since there are several different numbers two of which multiplied into each other give 60 for their product; as 2 and 30, 3 and 20, 4 and 15, 5 and 12, 6 and 10; and therefore any or all of the following equations may be adopted in this case as circumstances may require; viz. $x^2-32x=-60$, $x^2-23x=-60$, $x^2-19x=-60$, $x^2-17x=-60$, $x^2-16x=-60$, of which the keys respectively are the numbers 2 and 30, 3 and 20, &c. as given above: all of which answer. If $+60$ is the term given, then the quadratic formed will be either of the first or of the second case, and of the one or the other as the second term of it is either positive or negative, the co-efficient of it being the difference and not the sum of the generating quantities; and the quadratics thus formed from it may also be various, as the following, viz. $x^2+28x=60$, $x^2+17x=60$, $x^2+11x=60$, $x^2+7x=60$, and $x^2+4x=60$; of which the keys are respectively the numbers 2, 3, 4, 5, and 6: or $x^2-28x=60$, $x^2-17x=60$, $x^2-11x=60$, $x^2-7x=60$, and $x^2-4x=60$; of which different equations the keys are respectively the numbers 30, 20, 15,

12, and

12, and 10; all of which answer. After the same manner may other qua-dratics be formed from any other given commensurate quantities.

53. If it is required to form on these principles a cubic equation from the given term 120; as any of the following groups of three figures each, when multiplied into each other give 120 for their product, viz. 2, 3, 20; 2, 4, 15; 2, 5, 12; 2, 6, 10; 3, 4, 10; 3, 5, 8; and 4, 5, 6; there may be as many different cubics having 120 for their absolute term, and having as many different groups of generating quantities of three numbers each; and this being the case I shall, for conciseness, give one of these only as an instance, viz. that of which the three numbers giving the product 120 are 4, 5, 6; of which the first term, equal to that product is x^3; the se-cond term $15x^2$, of which the co-efficient is the sum of these generating numbers; the third term is $74x$, of which the co-efficient is the sum of the products of the generating terms as multiplied two and two into each other; and the complete equation is therefore $x^3 - 15x^2 + 74x = 120$; and the keys of it are the numbers 4, 5, and 6; which answer. The same method is applicable to the formation of other cubics from this and from other given commensurate quantities; and also for forming other equa-tions of all the different higher orders by only accommodating it to the circumstances of these from given commensurate quantities; as by finding as many different quantities for each order, as are the dimensions of that order, which multiplied into each other will give the given quantity for their product, &c.

54. It is obvious that on these principles equations of all orders of which the quantities are commensurable, and which have been generated accord-ing to the manner formerly described by the multiplication of simple or radical equations either into each other or into binomial factors of which the terms of each are equal to each other, may easily and readily be re-solved; that is by first finding as many quantities as are indicated by the dimensions of each, that by being multiplied into each other will give the absolute term of the equation required to be resolved; and second that these quantities shall be such, as that either their sum or their difference, according to the circumstances of the case, shall be equal to the co-efficient of the second term of that equation. Thus, if $x^2 - 13x = -40$ is a quad-ratic equation of the third case required to be solved; it is necessary for

that

that purpose to find such different quantities as multiplied into each other will give 40 the absolute term of the equation for their product; and, as the equation is a quadratic, that the number of these quantities be limited to two; and further that the sum of these two quantities shall be 13, or the same quantity with the co-efficient of the second term of the given equation: and as the quantities 5 and 8 answer all these conditions in this case, it is manifest that the given equation is resolvable by them, or that they are keys of it. If it is required to solve a quadratic of the first case, as $x^2 + 7x = 60$, on the same principles and by the same means it will be found upon trial that the quantities 5 and 12 are the generating quantities of the equation, and that the quantity 5 is its key. If it is the quadratic $x^2 - 7x = 60$ of the second case that is required to be solved; it will be found upon trial that the same quantities 5 and 12 are its generating quantities, and that its key is 12. If it is required to solve a cubic equation as $x^3 - 16x + 79x = 120$, then it is necessary for that purpose to find THREE quantities the product of which shall be equal to the absolute term of the equation, and their sum to the co-efficient of the second term of it, &c. which three quantities in this case will upon trial be found to be 3, 5, and 8, each of which are keys to the equation. Or if it is required to solve a cubic of which the co-efficient of the second term is the arithmetical difference in place of the arithmetical sum of the generating quantities of the equation, as the equation $x^3 - 2x^2 - 33x + 90 = 0$, it is necessary to find three quantities of which the product is 90, and the difference 2; and these are the numbers 3, 5, and -6; of which 3 and 5 are keys, and -6 a factor.—Perhaps it may be proper to distinguish those genitors or generating quantities of equations which are capable of solving the equation and answering the question it refers to, from those that are not, by denominating the former keys of the equation, and the latter factors of it: a practice I have adopted in this Essay, though I believe not warranted by precedent.

55. On the same principles, and in similar manners, accommodated to the particular circumstances of the different cases, may equations of these kinds of the higher orders be easily and readily resolved. Even equations which seem incomplete, from the second or other term being wanting, may in some cases if their generating quantities are commensurable be re-

solved,

solved, merely by finding as many quantities as are indicated by their respective dimensions which multiplied into each other will give the absolute terms of these equations for their respective products :—thus the equations $x^3 - 9x + 10 = 0$, and $x^3 - 156x + 560 = 0$, both of the irreducible case of Cardan may be resolved by this method ; 2 multiplied by 5 gives 10 for the product, the absolute term of the former of these; and upon trial 2 will be found to be its key : and the numbers 4, 10, and 14, multiplied into each other give 560 for their product, the absolute term of the latter of these ; and upon trial 4 and 10 will be found to be keys to it.

56. There are however other kinds of equations of which the generating quantities are commensurate, which admit not of being resolved on these principles ; as those generated by the multiplication of positive binomial factors in part at least symbolically expressed into each other, and then inserting their products or values expressed in numbers as their absolute terms :—thus, the positive binomial $x + 2 = 4$ multiplied by the positive binomial $x + 8 = 16$ gives $x^2 + 10x + 16$ for the product, which reduced to numbers is 64, and hence the equations $x^2 + 10x + 16 - 64 = 0$, or $x^2 + 10x - 48 = 0$. By the method of completing the square the last of these equations may be as far resolved as to obtain a quantity which substituted for x in the equation will give 48 for the absolute term of it ; but that quantity will be none of its generating quantities, neither 2 nor 8, and therefore not such a quantity as is capable of resolving the proposition or answering the question for the resolving of which the equation was composed ; or in other words not such a quantity as gives any of the two true and original values of x, or consequently the values of any of the unknown quantities which entered into the composition of the equation, and which it is the object of the composition and resolution of the equation, of the whole algebraical process to discover. These values of x not being discoverable in cases such as the above by that, this, or any other known method, it becomes an object of some importance to discover a method whereby that purpose may be effected or that end obtained. Perhaps the following may answer in many or in all cases of the kind, viz. Since the second term of each equation formed as above is always positive, and always of precisely double the value of the first term of it ; and since there are but two terms in this case besides the absolute term, the absolute term comes to be divided

vided into three equal parts---in this case of 16 each---of which one comes to be the value of the first term of the equation, and the sum of the other two---or in this case 32---the value of the second term of it; all that can be necessary for discovering its two different generating quantities can be only the finding of two different quantities which multiplied into each other will give the value of the first term---in this case 16---and consequently of the absolute term also, if the equation had been complete and formed after Harriot's method; which two different quantities will in this case be found upon trial to be 2 and 8, the two generating quantities, and as there are no other integers but these capable of giving that result---for 16×1 cannot justly be regarded as being multiplied---these must, though the fact had not been otherwise known, necessarily be admitted to be the two generating quantities of the equation. This method, however, only gives the factors or generating quantities, and not any key for resolving the equation; and indeed equations of this kind have no keys, or at least none that will answer the question proposed to be resolved by them.

57. There are many other kinds of equations besides the above, and those formed by the involutions of roots to powers, which differ essentially in their properties, &c. from those generated agreeable to the manner first suggested by Harriot; and hence the impropriety of giving certain rules which apply to one or two species of equations only as general rules. When the quantities of which equations are generated are not commensurate recourse must be had for resolving them to the other known methods for the resolution of equations; and when the true generating quantities and keys are not obtainable by these means all that can be done is to endeavour to approximate to them as nearly as possible. Among the many improvements introduced into the science of Algebra by the moderns, or the mathematicians of the two last centuries, the various methods of approximation they have discovered are not among the least important; though the method of approximating to the values of x that will resolve such equations—first introduced into Europe by the Arabians, at the same time with the Indian arithmetic and arithmetical characters, and the science of algebra---known by the names of the method of trial and error, or the rule of double position, is still perhaps, though these values do not always answer the question, the easiest and most universal of any. The method

by

by series seems to have originated in the *Vera Circuli et Hyperbola Quadratura*, published at Padua in the year 1667, of the celebrated Professor James Gregory---one of the most illustrious ornaments of that mathematical century so auspiciously and successfully ushered in by the great discoveries of Copernicus, Galileo, Kepler, and Napier---in which is to be found the invention of an indefinitely converging series for the areas of the circle and hyperbola: a work which he reprinted the year following at Venice, and then added to it a new work entituled *Geometriæ Pars Universalis, inserviens Quantitatum Curvarum Transmutatione et Mensuræ*; in which, for the first time, a method for the transmutation of curves is given: and the same year, 1668, he published another work at London entituled *Exercitationes Geometricæ*, in which these subjects are further pursued.

58. It is however much to be regretted that such an inaccurate and indeed unfounded mode of expression should have been adopted in these cases as that of denominating certain series infinite; which, though indefinite or indeterminate, are in reality not infinite; nor is it possible in the nature of things for any series to be so : a mode of expression which, besides being founded on erroneous principles and thereby liable to lead to erroneous conclusions, has a direct tendency to render these doctrines into which it enters obscure and perplexing, and to involve them not apparently only but actually in mysticism and absurdity. No infinite series, if such there were, could possibly have a finite value; for that which is infinite cannot be finite: and to suppose it so, or to be both finite and infinite, is to suppose it invested with opposite, repugnant, and incompatible attributes. It must therefore be absurd to propose summing an infinite series; to speak of the sum of such a series; and to treat of infinites, or infinite series of different kinds and properties, of infinites having parts, proportions, and limitations, or of finite infinites, or of infinites contained within infinites; and to propose adding to, or subtracting from, multiplying or dividing infinity or infinite quantities, and thus pretend to give limits to that which admits of none, must also necessarily be absurd. If what is called an infinite series is equal to a finite quantity, it must itself necessarily be a finite quantity; and it is utterly impossible for any series to be finite in value, and yet infinite in the number of its terms.

59. In

59. In the method of infinite series by division---as by expanding the fraction ⅓ by division in decimals in the common manner into what is called the infinite series 0,33333, &c.---there always necessarily must be a remainder however small, and therefore that series though continued in infinitum, if such was possible, could not possibly equal ⅓; and hence it is altogether improper to represent it as being equal to it; the sum of the series always necessarily requiring the remainder to be added to it to form a sum equal in value to the finite quantity ⅓. The same reasoning is applicable to all cases of this kind, or to all series formed by a continued division. The doctrine of division in infinitum, however plausible it may appear in mere abstract speculation, which overleaps the bounds of nature, from there being no doubt that in the above case the figure 3 might be continued to be added to the figure 3 seemingly without end, or at least till limited by the limited powers and existence of the agent or agents by whom the addition is made, yet when applied to physics or actual existences it is perfectly inadmissible; for this division of something must, from the nature of created things or finite existences, necessarily terminate, and terminate either in something or in nothing; but, if it terminate in nothing, and there consequently is no remainder---the only supposition on which the sum of the series can equal the finite quantity it is intended to represent---this hypothesis necessarily involves the absurdity of something being reducible to nothing merely by division; and, consequently, by inverting the process, that something may be formed out of nothing by a mere aggregation of nothings, or of the parts of nothing, or of the parts of that which cannot possibly have any parts: and, if this hypothesis is rejected, and it is admitted that something cannot possibly be reduced to nothing by mere division however minute, it must necessarily be concluded that the division of something must necessarily terminate in something, and that that something in which it terminates must necessarily be an indivisible; and therefore must necessarily include in it what would have formed both the next descending term and the remainder if it had been further divisible.

60. That this is actually the case is proved by the results of these methods themselves employed for the summations of series; as by the precise value of an infinitely as it is called decreasing geometrical progression,

of which the first or highest term is known, being accurately ascertainable by these methods, and which could not possibly be the case if the remainder, as well as the sums of the terms in geometrical progression, was not included in the total amount: for to suppose 0 or cypher to be either the last and lowest term of a decreasing or the first term of an increasing progression or series, and to substitute it in them as such, is in fact only introducing an imaginary entity nominal and fictitious having no actual existence into the progression as a term of it, whereby either the real last term comes improperly to be denominated and regarded as the last term but one of it, or the real first term to be regarded as the second term of it and to be denominated such. I give the new formula $S = y + \frac{y-a}{r-1}$ for the sum of a geometrical progression of which the first and last terms are known; in which y denotes the highest term, a the lowest term, and r the common ratio: which formula I prefer to those hitherto in use of $S = \frac{yr-a}{r-1}$, and $S = \frac{ar^n - a}{r-1}$,---the last of which answers only when $a = r$, and therefore to render it general ought to be $S = \frac{r^n \times r - a}{r-1}$ ---because I think it conveys a more clear conception of the nature of the process and the reasons of the operations than either of these---which operations it also simplifies and renders more obvious and easy---especially when it is considered that this formula altered to $y + \frac{y}{r} + \frac{y}{r^2} + \frac{y}{r^3} + \frac{y}{r^4} + \frac{y}{r^5} +$, &c. is a general formula for decreasing geometrical progressions in which the number of terms is indefinite as being applicable to all the different varieties of them. In progressions of this kind when y denotes the highest or greatest term, the expression $y + \frac{y}{r}$ denotes the sum of the greatest and next greatest terms: while the expression $y + \frac{y}{r-1}$ denotes the sum of a complete series in which none of the terms are wanting, and that not because the least or lowest term is 0, the cause commonly assigned, or what amounts to the same because it has no least or lowest term, for it necessarily must have a lowest term and that term must necessarily have some real and determinate value, though from its extreme minuteness and its necessarily being an indivisible, the division terminating in it and therefore necessarily including the remainder that must have resulted from the further con-

tinuation

tinuation of the progression if it had been further divisible, that precise value may not be discoverable by natural means and human abilities: and it is surely highly inconsistent to regard and represent any decreasing series as *infinite*, and at the same time to make it *terminate*, and terminate in 0 or in nothing. As $y+\frac{y}{r-1}$ expresses the sum of the series $y+\frac{y}{r}+\frac{y}{r^2}+\frac{y}{r^3}+$, &c. when none of the terms are wanting, and the series is complete, so $y+\frac{y-a}{r-1}$ expresses the sum of the series when all the terms of it below or less than a are wanting; from $\frac{a}{r-1}$ being precisely equal in value to all the terms that are wanting or that would have succeeded a in the decreasing series if that series had been complete; and in the above expression $y+\frac{y-a}{r-1}$ it is not a but $\frac{a}{r-1}$ that is deducted from the sum of $y+\frac{y}{r-1}$; for if the a had not been deducted from the y of the second term, it would have been divided by $r-1$ as well as the y of that term; so that $\frac{a}{r-1}$, and not a would have remained, if the deduction of a from y had not been made, forming a part of the general amount of the sum $y+\frac{y}{r-1}$.

61. The above mentioned facts will perhaps appear plainer from the following simple numeral example, viz. if $r=4$, and $y=3072$; the complete decreasing progression comes to be $3072+\frac{3072}{4}+\frac{3072}{4^2}+\frac{3072}{4^3}+\frac{3072}{4^4}+\frac{3072}{4^5}+$, &c. or $3072+768+192+48+12+3+\frac{3}{4}+\frac{3}{4^2}+\frac{3}{4^3}+$, &c. $=4096=3072+\frac{3072}{3}$ $=y+\frac{y}{r-1}$. If this decreasing progression is not complete, but terminates with the term 48, then $a=48$, and $s=y+\frac{y-a}{r-1}=3072+\frac{3072}{3}=4080$; being 16, or $\frac{48}{3}=\frac{a}{r-1}$ less than 4096 the sum of the complete series, which deficiency of 16 is precisely the sum of the deficient terms, or precisely equal in value with the amount of the terms of the complete progression which in this case are cut off and are wanting, being those descending or decreasing, according to the common ratio, from the term 48, viz. $12+3+\frac{3}{4}+\frac{3}{4^2}+\frac{3}{4^3}+$, &c. $=16$.

62. Every series is necessarily finite; and therefore must necessarily have a precise and determinate value, and though these values cannot in many cases be discovered by any known means, yet many of those series

which are regarded as infinite and their values undetermined may be proved to be finite and of determinate values. No series formed by involving any bionomial by means of the binomial theorem can possibly be infinite; since every such series is necessarily limited by the power by which it is by that means raised; or by the value of n the exponent expressing it; and hence unless n or the exponent is infinite, which is impossible, the series must necessarily be finite. Thus, for instance, on converting $\overline{a+x}^n$

into the series $a^n + na^{n-1}x + \frac{n.n-1}{2}a^{n-2}x^2 + \frac{n.n-2}{2}.\frac{n-2}{3}a^{n-3}x^3 + \frac{n.n-1}{2}.\frac{n-2}{3}.\frac{n-3}{4}a^{n-4}x^4 + \frac{n.n-1}{2}.\frac{n-2}{3}.\frac{n-3}{4}.\frac{n-4}{5}a^{n-5}x^5 + \frac{n.n-1}{2}.\frac{n-2}{3}.\frac{n-3}{4}.\frac{n-4}{5}.\frac{n-5}{6}a^{n-6}x^6+$, &c. if $n=2$, the three first terms give $a^2 + 2ax + x^2$; and here the series must necessarily terminate, since $a^2 + 2ax + x^2 = \overline{a+x}^{n=2}$. If $n=3$; then the four first terms equal $a^3 + 3a^2x + 3ax^2 + x^3 = \overline{a+x}^{3=n}$; and here the series terminates, all the remaining terms of it vanishing. If $a=2$, $x=3$, and $n=2$; then $\overline{a+x}^2 = 5^2 = 25$; and $a^2 + 2ax + x^2 = 2^2 + 2\times6 + 3^2 = 4 + 12 + 9 = 25$ also. If $n=3$, then $\overline{a+x}^3 = 5^3 = 125$; and $x^3 + 3a^2x + 3a^2x^2 + x^3 = 8 + 36 + 54 + 27 = 125$ likewise: and so of other cases. The series formed in the evolution of binomials by the binomial theorem are also necessarily limited; as necessarily terminating either in the true root or result; or in a near approximation to it.

63. Series formed by the common method of the extraction of roots are likewise not infinite, for the values of some of these which are regarded as such are finite and may be accurately determined in many cases; and if the values of such series are finite in these cases they must necessarily be finite in other cases also; though methods of accurately determining their values in those other cases may not be known. Thus, according to that method, the square root of $a^2 + x^2$ is the series $a + \frac{x^2}{2a} - \frac{x^4}{8a^3} + \frac{x^6}{16a^5} -$, &c. But, if $a=4$, and $x=3$; or if $a=8$, and $x=6$; if $a=12$, and $x=9$; if $a=16$, and $x=12$, &c. or vice versa; the square root of $a^2 + x^2$ is not an infinite series but the finite quantity $a + \frac{x}{3}$, or $x + \frac{a}{4}$; being in numbers 4+1, or 3+2, =5; or 8+2, or 6+4, =10; or 12+3, or 9+6, =15;

or

or $16+4$, or $12+8=20$; the square roots of the quantities 25, 100, 225, and 400, respectively; or of the different values of a^2+x^2 according to the different values of a and x as stated above.

64. Besides, it must be altogether impossible for quantities or magnitudes to be *infinite* which admit of *finite geometrical* delineation; and consequently the square root of a^2+x^2 cannot possibly be an infinite quantity, or an infinite series, as it admits of being always accurately delineated and represented either by radius, when a is the co-sine, and x the sine, of an arc; and in that case the co-sine is that part of the radius, or root of a^2+x^2, which by the common method of extraction is expressed by the term a, and the versed sine is that part of it which by that method is expressed by an indefinite series; or, as it is always accurately delineated or represented by the secant, when a is the radius, and x the tangent of the arc; and in that case the radius is that part of the root, or secant, which is expressed by the term a, and that part of the secant which lies without the circle is that which by that method is expressed by an indefinite series.

65. When there are so many different ways of analysis there seems not to be much propriety in applying the term analytical in a manner exclusively to Algebra in denominating it the analytical art: and it is to be regretted that mathematicians, from mistaking the true nature of mathematical evidence, should so often, with the intention of establishing facts on a more valid basis, and of rendering the doctrines concerning them more perspicuous and obvious, have recourse to what is falsely conceived to be and is regarded as rigid demonstration of these facts deduced *a priori* from sources purely intellectual, and therefore, it is supposed, purely mathematical and unexceptionable; and still more that they should deem this procedure absolutely necessary even in cases where there is direct proof the most clear and convincing deduced by induction from the undeviating results of numerous, varied, and repeated trials, or experiments—as if these demonstrations, when they possess any validity, did not necessarily derive that validity from facts and experiments, and these necessarily more remote from apprehension and less applicable to the purpose than those on which the direct proof by induction rests—since this mode of procedure is calculated to produce effects the very reverse of those intended by it, as it seldom fails to perplex, bewilder, and mislead, and has a direct and certain

tendency

tendency to involve in obscurity doctrines that are of themselves clear and obvious. Newton, with much propriety, attempted no such demonstrations of several of his important discoveries; as of his justly celebrated binomial theorem, which admits of no other proof than that of trial and induction, or that of direct experiment with respect to its expressing justly the several powers and roots of quantities; as being, in reality, only a different way of expressing these, though for various purposes much more commodious and useful, than that by which they had before its discovery been expressed.

66. Lastly, it may not be improper to observe, as some seem to entertain too high an opinion of the generalizing power of Algebra, that the substitution of what are called general signs or symbols, as letters, in theorems, does not of itself give generality to these propositions; as these propositions may not apply to all the various quantities of which these letters may be symbols or representations :—what of its own nature is particular cannot by this means be rendered general. It is only from experiments and an induction of facts that generality can in any case be rationally and justly inferred. It is only from the agreement of the results of various different trials or experiments that the generality of the conclusion can with any degree of certainty be deduced; or that it can justly be concluded that the proposition holds generally or is an universal truth. If a proposition is not general in its own nature the using of general symbols in annunciating it will not make it so; but, if it is of its own nature general, the employing of general symbols, in place of particular quantities, in expressing it, will preserve that generality in as far as it depends on the annunciation or manner of expressing it; and will by that means prevent its being applied particularly only.

PART

PART III.

OF FLUXIONS, AND THE INFINITESIMAL CALCULUS.

1. THE following account of the discovery of the method of Fluxions is given by that eminent mathematician Dr. Hutton, of Woolwich, viz. " The method of Fluxions is one of the greatest, most subtle, and sublime " discoveries of perhaps any age: it opens a new world to our view, and " extends our knowledge, as it were, to infinity; carrying us beyond the " bounds that seemed to have been prescribed to the human mind, at least " infinitely beyond those to which the ancient geometry was confined.

" The history of this important discovery, recent as it is, is a little dark, " and embroiled. Two of the greatest men of the last age have both of " them claimed the invention, Sir Isaac Newton, and M. Leibnitz; and " nothing can be more glorious for the method itself, than the zeal with " which the partisans of either side have asserted their title.

" To exhibit a just view of this dispute, and of the pretensions of each " party, we may here advert to the origin of the discovery, and mark where " each claim commenced, and how it was supported.

" The principles upon which the method of fluxions is founded, or which " conducted to it, had been laying, and gradually developing, from the " beginning of the last century, by Fermat, Napier, Barrow, Wallis, Slusius, " &c. who had methods of drawing tangents, of maxima and minima, of " quadratures, &c. in certain particular cases, as of rational quantities, " upon nearly the same principles. And it was not wonderful that such a " genius as Newton should soon after raise those faint beginnings into a " regular and general system of science, which he did about the year 1665, " or sooner.

" The

" The first time, however, that the method appeared in print, was in
" 1684, when M. Leibnitz gave the rules of it in the Leipsic Acts of that
" year; but without the demonstrations. The two brothers however, John
" and James Bernouilli, being greatly struck with this new method, applied
" themselves diligently to it, found out the demonstrations, and applied
" the calculus with great success.

" But before this, M. Leibnitz had proposed his differential method, viz.
" in a letter dated Jan. 21, 1677; in which he exactly pursues Dr. Barrow's
" method of tangents, which had been published in 1670: and Newton
" communicated this method of drawing tangents to Mr. Collins, in a letter
" dated Dec. 10, 1672; which letter, together with another, dated June 13,
" 1676, were sent to M. Leibnitz by Mr. Oldenburgh, in 1676. So that
" there is a strong presumption that he might avail himself of the informa-
" tion contained in these letters, and other papers transmitted with them,
" and also in 1675, before the publication of his own letter, containing the
" first hint of the differential method. Indeed it sufficiently appears that
" Newton had invented his method before the year 1669, and that he ac-
" tually made use of it in his Compendium of Analysis and Quadrature of
" Curves before that time. His attention seems to have been directed that
" way, even before the time of the plague which happened in London in
" 1665 and 1666, when he was about twenty-eight years of age."

" This is all that is heard of the method, till the year 1687, when Newton's
" admirable Principia came out, which is almost wholly built on the same
" calculus. The common opinion then was, that Newton and Leibnitz
" had each invented it about the same time: and what seemed to confirm
" it was, that neither of them made any mention of the other; and that
" though they agreed in the substance of the thing, yet they differed in
" their ways of conceiving it, calling it by different names, and using dif-
" ferent characters. However, foreigners having first learned the method
" through the medium of M. Leibnitz's publication, which spread the me-
" thod through Europe, those geometricians were insensibly accustomed to
" look upon him as the sole, or principal inventor, and became ever after
" strongly prejudiced in favour of his notation, and mode of conceiving it.

" The two great authors themselves, without any seeming concern, or
" dispute, as to the property of the invention, enjoyed the glorious pro-
" spect

" spect of the progresses continually making under their auspices, till the
" year 1699, when the peace began to be disturbed.

" M. Facio, in a Treatise on the Line of swiftest Descent, declared, that
" he was obliged to own Newton as the inventor of the differential Calculus,
" and the first by many years; and that he left the world to judge, whether
" Leibnitz, the second inventor, had taken any thing from him. This pre-
" cise distinction between the first and second inventor, with the suspicion
" it insinuated, raised a controversy between M. Leibnitz, supported by
" the editors of the Leipsic Acts, and the English mathematicians, who
" declared for Newton. Sir Isaac himself never appeared on the scene;
" his glory was become that of the nation; and his adherents, warm in the
" cause of their country, needed not his assistance to animate them.

" Writings succeeded each other but slowly, on either side; probably on
" account of the distance of the places; but the controversy grew still
" hotter and hotter: till at length M. Leibnitz, in the year 1711, complained
" to the Royal Society, that Dr. Keil had accused him of publishing the
" method of Fluxions invented by Sir Isaac Newton, under other names
" and characters. He insisted that nobody knew better than Sir Isaac him-
" self, that he had stolen nothing from him, and required that Dr. Keil
" should disavow the ill construction which might be put upon his words.

" The Society, thus appealed to as a judge, appointed a committee to
" examine all the old letters, papers, and documents, that had passed
" among the several mathematicians, relating to that point; who, after a
" strict examination of all the evidence that could be procured, gave in
" their report as follows: ' M. Leibnitz was in London in 1673, and kept
" a correspondence with Mr. Collins, by means of Mr. Oldenbrugh, till
" Sept. 1676, when he returned from Paris to Hanover, by way of London
" and Amsterdam: that it did not appear that M. Leibnitz knew any thing
" of the differential calculus before his letter of the 21st of June, 1677, which
" was a year after a copy of a letter, written by Newton in the year 1672,
" had been sent to Paris to be communicated to him, and above four years
" after Mr. Collins began to communicate that letter to his correspondents,
" in which the method of Fluxions was sufficiently explained to let a man
" of his sagacity into the whole matter: and that Sir I. Newton had even
" invented his method before the year 1669, and consequently fifteen years

" before M. Leibnitz had given any thing on the subject in the Leipsic
" Acts.' From which they concluded that Dr. Keil had not at all injured
" M. Leibnitz in what he had said.

" The Society printed this their determination, together with all the
" pieces and materials relating to it, under the title of Commercium Epis-
" tolicum de Analysi Promota, 8vo. Lond. 1712. This book was carefully
" distributed through Europe, to vindicate the title of the English nation
" to the discovery; for Newton himself, as already hinted, never appeared
" in the affair: whether it was that he trusted his honour with his compa-
" triots, who were zealous enough in the cause; or whether he felt himself
" even superior to the glory of it.

" M. Leibnitz and his friends, however, could not shew the same indif-
" ference: he was accused of a theft; and the whole Commercium Episto-
" licum either expresses it in terms, or insinuates it. Soon after the publi-
" cation, therefore, a loose sheet was printed at Paris, in behalf of M.
" Leibnitz, then at Vienna. It is written with great zeal and spirit; and
" it boldly maintains that the method of Fluxions had not preceded the
" method of differences; and even insinuates that it might have arisen out
" of it. The detail of the proofs, however, on each side, would be too
" long, and could not be understood without a large comment, which must
" enter into the deepest geometry.

" M. Leibnitz began to work upon a Commercium Epistolicum, in oppo-
" sition to that of the Royal Society; but he died before it was completed.

" A second edition of the Commercium Epistolicum was printed at
" London in 1722; when Newton, in the preface, account, and annota-
" tions, which were added to that edition, particularly answered all the
" objections which Leibnitz and Bernouilli were able to make since the
" Commercium first appeared in 1712; and from the last edition of the.
" Commercium, with the various original papers contained in it, it evi-
" dently appears that Newton had discovered his method of Fluxions
" many years before the pretensions of Leibnitz. See also Raphson's
" History of Fluxions.

" There are however, according to the opinion of some, strong pre-
" sumptions in favour of Leibnitz; i. e. that he was no plagiary: for that
" Newton was at least the first inventor, is past all dispute; his glory is
" secure;

" secure; the reasonable part even among the foreigners allow it: and the
" question is only, whether Leibnitz took it from him, or fell upon the
" same thing with him; for, in his Theory of distinct Notions, which he
" dedicated to the Royal Academy in 1671, before he had seen any thing
" of Newton's, he already supposed infinitely small quantities, some greater
" than others; which is one of the great principles of his system."*

2. M. Carnot observes that " no discovery ever produced so happy
" and so sudden a revolution in the mathematical sciences as the infinite-
" simal analysis; nor has any improvement furnished us with such simple
" and efficacious methods of arriving at a knowledge of the laws of nature.
" By decomposing, so to speak, magnitudes into their constituent ele-
" ments, that analysis seems, as it were, to have detected their internal
" structure and organization."† And Mr. Emerson observes of the method of fluxions that " any one who is acquainted with the sciences will
" allow it to be a method of calculation incomparably superior to all
" other methods that ever were known or found out; and beyond which
" nothing further is to be hoped or expected. It lends its aid and assist-
" ance to all the other mathematical sciences, and that in their greatest
" wants and distresses: It opens and discovers to us the secrets and re-
" cesses of nature, which have always before been locked up in obscurity
" and darkness. To this all the noble and valuable discoveries of the last
" and present age are entirely owing."‡ All the other mathematicians of
Europe have been equally lavish in their encomiums of these methods, as
those quoted above, with the solitary exception of the learned and amiable
Berkeley, the celebrated Bishop of Cloyne, who, not satisfied with the
solidity of their principles, in a small treatise entitled the Analyst, published in 1734, represents them as unfounded, erroneous, and delusive.

3. As every work of this eminent author---who had sagacity enough to
discover, many years before the fact was decisively proved by the couch-
ing of the young gentleman by Mr. Cheseldon, mentioned in Essay I,
that a person born blind on being made to see would at first by means of
sight have no knowledge of distance, and be by that means altogether

---

* Mathematical and Philosophical Dictionary, Vol. I. pages 484 and 485, article Fluxions.
† Carnot's Reflections on the Infinitesimal Calculus, page 1st, English Translation.
‡ Emerson's Doctrine of Fluxions, Preface, page 1st.

incapable

incapable of distinguishing one thing from another*---is highly interesting and merits every attention; and as the account he gives in that treatise of these methods is singularly accurate, just, and perspicuous, I shall transcribe, literally, from that treatise this account, together with the statement of his objections to these methods.

§ III.

" The method of fluxions is the general key, by help whereof the mo-
" dern mathematicians unlock the secrets of geometry, and consequently of
" nature. And as it is that which hath enabled them so remarkably to out-
" go the ancients in discovering theorems and solving problems, the exercise
" and application thereof is become the main, if not sole, employment of
" all those who in this age pass for profound geometers. But whether this
" method be clear or obscure, consistent or repugnant, demonstrative or
" precarious, as I shall inquire with the utmost impartiality, so I submit
" my inquiry to your own judgment, and that of every candid reader.
" Lines are supposed to be generated † by the motion of points, plains by
" the motion of lines, and solids by the motion of plains. And whereas
" quantities generated in equal times are greater or lesser, according to
" the greater or lesser velocity, wherewith they increase and are generated,
" a method hath been found to determine quantities from the velocities of
" their generating motions. And such velocities are called fluxions: And
" the quantities generated are called flowing quantities. These fluxions are
" said to be nearly as the increments of the flowing quantities, generated
" in the least equal particles of time; and to be accurately in the first
" proportion of the nascent, or in the last of the evanescent, increments.
" Sometimes, instead of velocities, the momentaneous increments or de-
" crements of undetermined flowing quantities are considered, under the
" appellation of moments.

* See Berkley's Minute Philosopher, and his Essay on Vision.
" † Introd. ad Quadraturam Curvarum.

§ IV.

§ IV.

" By moments we are not to understand finite particles. These are said
" not to be moments, but quantities generated from moments, which last
" are only the nascent principles of finite quantities. It is said, that the
" minutest errors are not to be neglected in mathematics: that the fluxions
" are celerities, not proportional to the finite increments though ever so
" small; but only to the moments or nascent increments, whereof the pro-
" portion alone, and not the magnitude, is considered. And of the afore-
" said fluxions there be other fluxions, which fluxions of fluxions are called
" second fluxions. And the fluxions of these second fluxions are called
" third fluxions; and so on, fourth, fifth, sixth, &c. *ad infinitum*. Now as
" our sense is strained and puzzled with the perception of objects extremely
" minute, even so the imagination, which faculty derives from sense, is very
" much strained and puzzled to frame clear ideas of the least particles of
" time, or the least increments generated therein: and much more so to
" comprehend the moments, or those increments of the flowing quantities in
" *statu nascenti*, in their very first origin or beginning to exist, before they
" become finite particles. And it seems still more difficult, to conceive
" the abstracted velocities of such nascent imperfect entities. But the ve-
" locities of the velocities, the second, third, fourth and fifth velocities, &c.
" exceed, if I mistake not, all humane understanding. The further the
" mind analyseth and pursueth these fugitive ideas, the more it is lost and
" bewildered; the objects, at first fleeting and minute, soon vanishing out
" of sight. Certainly in any sense a second or third fluxion seems an ob-
" scure mystery. The incipient celerity of an incipient celerity, the nas-
" cent augment of a nascent augment, *i. e.* of a thing which hath no mag-
" nitude: Take it in which light you please, the clear conception of it will,
" if I mistake not, be found impossible, whether it be so or no I appeal to
" the trial of every thinking reader. And if a second fluxion be incon-
" ceivable, what are we to think of third, fourth, fifth fluxions, and so
" onward without end ?

§ V.

§ V.

" The foreign mathematicians are supposed by some, even of our own, to
" proceed in a manner less accurate perhaps and geometrical, yet more intel-
" ligible. Instead of flowing quantities and their fluxions, they consider
" the variable finite quantities, as increasing or diminishing by the conti-
" nual addition or subduction of infinitely small quantities. Instead of
" the velocities wherewith increments are generated, they consider the in-
" crements or decrements themselves, which they call differences, and
" which are supposed to be infinitely small. The difference of a line is an
" infinitely little line; of a plain an infinitely little plain. They suppose
" finite quantities to consist of parts infinitely little, and curves to be po-
" lygones, whereof the sides are infinitely little, which by the angles they
" make one with another determine the curvity of the line. Now to con-
" ceive a quantity infinitely small, that is, infinitely less than any sensible
" or imaginable quantity, or than any the least finite magnitude, is, I con-
" fess above my capacity. But to conceive a part of such infinitely small
" quantity, that shall be still infinitely less than it, and consequently
" though multiplied infinitely shall never equal the minutest finite quan-
" tity, is, I suspect, an infinite difficulty to any man whatsoever; and
" will be allowed such by those who candidly say what they think; pro-
" vided they really think and reflect, and do not take things upon trust.

§ VI.

" And yet in the *calculus differentialis*, which method serves to all the same
" intents and ends with that of fluxions, our modern analysts are not con-
" tent to consider only the differences of finite quantities: they also con-
" sider the differences of those differences, and the differences of the dif-
" ferences of the first differences. And so on *ad infinitum*. That is, they
" consider quantities infinitely less than the least discernible quantity; and
" others infinitely less than those infinitely small ones; and still others in-
" finitely less than the preceding infinitesimals, and so on without end or li-
" mit. Insomuch that we are to admit an infinite succession of infinitesimals,

" each

" each infinitely less than the foregoing, and infinitely greater than the
" following. As there are first, second, third, fourth, fifth, &c. fluxions,
" so there are differences, first, second, third, fourth, &c. in an infi-
" nite progression towards nothing, which you still approach and never
" arrive at. And (which is most strange) although you should take a mil-
" lion of millions of these infinitesimals, each whereof is supposed infi-
" nitely greater than some other real magnitude, and add them to the least
" given quantity, it shall be never the bigger. For this is one of the mo-
" dest *postulata* of our modern mathematicians, and is a corner-stone or
" ground-work of their speculations.

§ VIII.

" It must indeed be acknowledged, the modern mathematicians do not
" consider these points as mysteries, but as clearly conceived and mas-
" tered by their comprehensive minds. They scruple not to say, that by
" the help of these new analytics they can penetrate into infinity itself:
" That they can even extend their views beyond infinity: that their art
" comprehends not only infinite, but infinite of infinite (as they express it)
" or an infinity of infinites. But, notwithstanding all these assertions and
" pretensions, it may be justly questioned whether, as other men in other
" inquiries are often deceived by words or terms, so they likewise are not
" wonderfully deceived and deluded by their own peculiar signs, symbols,
" or species. Nothing is easier than to devise expressions or notations for
" fluxions and infinitesimals of the first, second, third, fourth, and subse-
" quent orders, proceeding in the same regular form without end or limit
" $\dot{x}. \ddot{x}. \dddot{x}. \ddddot{x}.$ &c. or $dx. ddx. dddx. ddddx.$ &c. These expressions indeed are
" clear and distinct, and the mind finds no difficulty in conceiving them
" to be continued beyond any assignable bounds. But if we remove the
" veil and look underneath, if laying aside the expressions we set ourselves
" attentively to consider the things themselves, which are supposed to be
" expressed or marked thereby, we shall discover much emptiness, darkness,
" and confusion; nay, if I mistake not, direct impossibilities and contra-
" dictions. Whether this be the case or no, every thinking reader is in-
" treated to examine and judge for himself.

§ IX.

§ IX.

" Having considered the object, I proceed to consider the principles of
" this new analysis by momentums, fluxions, or infinitesimals ; wherein if it
" shall appear that your capital points, upon which the rest are supposed to
" depend, include error and false reasoning ; it will then follow that you,
" who are at a loss to conduct yourselves, cannot with any decency set up
" for guides to other men.　The main point in the method of fluxions is to
" obtain the fluxion or momentum of the rectangle or product of two inde-
" terminate quantities.　Inasmuch as from thence are derived rules for ob-
" taining the fluxions of all other products and powers ; be the coefficients
" or the indexes what they will, integers or fractions, rational or surd.　Now
" this fundamental point one would think should be very clearly made out,
" considering how much is built upon it, and that its influence extends
" throughout the whole analysis.　But let the reader judge.　This is given
" for demonstration.　* Suppose the product or rectangle AB increased by
" continual motion : and that the momentaneous increments of the sides A
" and B are a and b.　When the sides A and B were deficient, or lesser by one
" half of their moments, the rectangle was $\overline{A - \frac{1}{2}a} \times \overline{B - \frac{1}{2}b}$ i. e. $AB - \frac{1}{2}aB - \frac{1}{2}bA$
" $+ \frac{1}{4}ab$.　And as soon as the sides A and B are increased by the other two
" halves of their moments, the rectangle becomes $\overline{A + \frac{1}{2}a} \times \overline{B + \frac{1}{2}b}$ or $AB + \frac{1}{2}aB +$
" $\frac{1}{2}bA + \frac{1}{4}ab$.　From the latter rectangle subduct the former, and the re-
" maining difference will be $aB + bA$.　Therefore the increment of the rect-
" angle generated by the intire increments a and b is $aB + bA$. Q. E. D.　But
" it is plain that the direct and true method to obtain the moment or incre-
" ment of the rectangle AB, is to take the sides as increased by their whole
" increments, and so multiply them together, $A + a$ by $B + b$, the product
" whereof $AB + aB + bA + ab$ is the augmented rectangle ; whence if we
" subduct AB, the remainder $aB + bA + ab$ will be the true increment of the
" rectangle, exceeding that which was obtained by the former illegitimate and
" indirect method by the quantity ab.　And this holds universally be the
" quantity a and b what they will, big or little, finite or infinitesimal, incre-

* Naturalis Philosophiæ principia mathematica, l. 2. lem. 2.

" ments,

" ments, moments, or velocities. Nor will it avail to say that *a b* is a quan-
" tity exceeding small : since we are told that *in rebus mathematicis errores*
" *quàm minimi non sunt contemnendi.* * Such reasoning as this, for demonstra-
" tion, nothing but the obscurity of the subject could have encouraged or in-
" duced the great author of the fluxionary method to put upon his followers,
" and nothing but an implicit deference to authority could move them to
" admit. The case indeed is difficult. There can be nothing done till
" you have got rid of the quantity *a b.* In order to this the notion of
" fluxions is shifted : it is placed in various lights : points which should be
" clear as first principles are puzzled ; and terms which should be steadily
" used are ambiguous. But notwithstanding all this address and skill the
" point of getting rid of *a b* cannot be obtained by legitimate reasoning. If
" a man by methods, not geometrical or demonstrative, shall have satisfied
" himself of the usefulness of certain rules ; which he afterwards shall pro-
" pose to his disciples for undoubted truths ; which he undertakes to demon-
" strate in a subtile manner, and by the help of nice and intricate notions ; it
" is not hard to conceive that such his disciples may, to save themselves the
" trouble of thinking, be inclined to confound the usefulness of a rule with
" the certainty of a truth, and accept the one for the other ; especially if
" they are men accustomed rather to compute than to think ; earnest rather
" to go on fast and far, than solicitous to set out warily and see their
" way distinctly.

" § XI.

" The points or mere limits of nascent lines are undoubtedly equal, as hav-
" ing no more magnitude one than another, a limit as such being no quantity.
" If by a momentum you mean more than the very initial limit, it must be
" either a finite quantity or an infinitesimal. But all finite quantities are ex-
" pressly excluded from the notion of a momentum. Therefore the momen-
" tum must be an infinitesimal. And indeed, though much artifice hath been
" employed to escape or avoid the admission of quantities infinitely small,
" yet it seems ineffectual. For aught I see, you can admit no quantity as a
" medium between a finite quantity and nothing, without admitting infini-

" * Introd. ad Quadraturam Curvarum.

" tesimals. An increment generated in a finite particle of time, is itself a
" finite particle; and cannot therefore be a momentum. You must therefore
" take an infinitesimal part of time wherein to generate your momentum. It is
" said, the magnitude of moments is not considered : and yet these same mo-
" ments are supposed to be divided into parts. This is not easy to conceive, no
" more than it is why we should take quantities less than A and B in order to
" obtain the increment of $A B$, of which proceeding it must be owned the
" final cause or motive is very obvious; but it is not so obvious or easy to ex-
" plain a just and legitimate reason for it, or shew it to be geometrical.

" § XII.

" From the foregoing principle so demonstrated, the general rule for finding
" the fluxion of any power of a flowing quantity is derived.* But, as there
" seems to have been some inward scruple or consciousness of defect in
" the foregoing demonstration, and as this finding the fluxion of a given
" power is a point of primary importance, it hath therefore been judged
" proper to demonstrate the same in a different manner independent of
" the foregoing demonstration. But whether this other method be more
" legitimate and conclusive than the former, I proceed now to examine;
" and in order thereto shall premise the following lemma. ' If with a view to
" demonstrate any proposition, a certain point is supposed, by virtue of
" which certain other points are attained ; and such supposed point be it-
" self afterwards destroyed or rejected by a contrary supposition ; in that
" case, all the other points, attained thereby and consequent thereupon, must
" also be destroyed and rejected, so as from thence forward to be no more
" supposed or applied in the demonstration.' This is so plain as to need
" no proof.

" § XIII.

" Now the other method of obtaining a rule to find the fluxion of any
" power is as follows. Let the quantity x flow uniformly, and be it proposed

" * Philosophiæ naturalis principia Mathematica, lib. 2. em. 2.

" to

" to find the fluxion of x^n. In the same time that x by flowing becomes
" $x+o$, the power x^n becomes $\overline{x+o}|^n$, i. e. by the method of infinite series
" $x^n+nox^{n-1}+\frac{nn-n}{2}oox^{n-2}+ \&c.$ and the increments o and $nox^{n-1}+\frac{nn-n}{2}$
" $oox^{n-2}+ \&c.$ are one to another as 1 to $nx^{n-1}+\frac{nn-n}{2}ox^{n-2}+ \&c.$ Let
" now the increments vanish, and their last proportion will be 1 to nx^{n-1}.
" But it should seem that this reasoning is not fair or conclusive. For when
" it is said, let the increments vanish, i. e. let the increments be nothing, or
" let there be no increments, the former supposition that the increments were
" something, or that there were increments, is destroyed, and yet a conse-
" quence of that supposition, i. e. an expression got by virtue thereof, is re-
" tained. Which, by the foregoing lemma, is a false way of reasoning.
" Certainly when we suppose the increments to vanish, we must suppose
" their proportions, their expressions, and every thing else derived from the
" supposition of their existence to vanish with them.

" § XIV.

" To make this point plainer, I shall unfold the reasoning, and propose it
" in a fuller light to your view. It amounts therefore to this, or may in other
" words be thus expressed. I suppose that the quantity x flows, and by
" flowing is increased, and its increment I call o, so that by flowing it be-
" comes $x+o$. And as x increaseth, it follows that every power of x is like-
" wise increased in a due proportion. Therefore as x becomes $x+o$, x^n will
" become $\overline{x+o}|^n$: that is, according to the method of infinite series, x^n+
" $nox^{n-1}+\frac{nn-n}{2}oox^{n-2}+ \&c.$ And if from the two augmented quantities
" we subduct the root and the power respectively, we shall have remaining
" the two increments, to wit, o and $nox^{n-1}+\frac{nn-n}{2}oox^{n-2}+ \&c.$ which in-
" crements, being both divided by the common divisor o, yield the quotients
" 1 and $nx^{n-1}+\frac{nn-n}{2}ox^{n-2}+ \&c.$ which are therefore exponents of the ra-
" tio of the increments. Hitherto I have supposed that x flows, that x hath
" a real increment, that o is something. And I have proceeded all along on

" that

" that supposition, without which I should not have been able to have made
" so much as one single step. From that supposition it is that I get at
" the increment of x^n, that I am able to compare it with the increment of x,
" and that I find the proportion between the two increments. I now beg leave
" to make a new supposition contrary to the first, *i. e.* I will suppose that there
" is no increment of x, or that o is nothing; which second supposition de-
" stroys my first, and is inconsistent with it, and therefore with every thing
" that supposeth it. I do nevertheless beg leave to retain $n x^{n-1}$, which is
" an expression obtained in virtue of my first supposition, which necessarily
" presupposeth such supposition, and which could not be obtained without
" it : all which seems a most inconsistent way of arguing, and such as would
" not be allowed of in divinity.

" § XV.

" Nothing is plainer than that no just conclusion can be directly drawn
" from two inconsistent suppositions. You may indeed suppose any thing
" possible : but afterwards you may not suppose any thing that destroys what
" you first proposed. Or if you do, you must begin *de novo*. If therefore
" you suppose that the augments vanish, *i. e.* that there are no augments, you
" are to begin again, and see what follows from such supposition. But no-
" thing will follow to your purpose. You cannot by that means ever arrive
" at your conclusion, or succeed in, what is called by the celebrated author,
" the investigation of the first or last proportions of nascent and evanescent
" quantities, by instituting the analysis in finite ones. I repeat it again : you
" are at liberty to make any possible supposition : and you may destroy one
" supposition by another : but then you may not retain the consequences, or
" any part of the consequences of your first supposition so destroyed. I ad-
" mit that signs may be made to denote either any thing or nothing : and
" consequently that in the original notation $x + o$, o might have signified either
" an increment or nothing. But then which of these soever you make it sig-
" nify, you must argue consistently with such its signification, and not pro-
" ceed upon a double meaning : which to do were a manifest sophism. Whe-
" ther you argue in symbols or in words, the rules of right reason are still the
                                                              " same.

" same. Nor can ft be supposed, you will plead a privilege in mathematics
" to be exempt from them.

"§ XVI.

" If you assume at first a quantity increased by nothing, and in the ex-
" pression $x + o$, o stands for nothing, upon this supposition as there is no in-
" crement of the root, so there will be no increment of the power; and con-
" sequently there will be none except the first, of all those members of the
" series constituting the power of the binomial: you will therefore never come
" at your expression of a fluxion legitimately by such method. Hence you
" are driven into the fallacious way of proceeding to a certain point on
" the supposition of an increment, and then at once shifting your suppo-
" sition to that of no increment. There may seem great skill in doing
" this at a certain point or period. Since if this second supposition
" had been made before the common division by o, all had vanished at
" once, and you must have got nothing by your supposition. Whereas by
" this artifice of first dividing, and then changing your supposition, you re-
" tain 1 and $n x^{n-1}$. But, notwithstanding all this address to cover it, the
" fallacy is still the same. For whether it be done sooner or later, when once
" the second supposition or assumption is made, in the same instant the for-
" mer assumption and all that you got by it is destroyed, and goes out toge-
" ther. And this is universally true, be the subject what it will, throughout
" all the branches of humane knowledge; in any other of which, I believe,
" men would hardly admit such a reasoning as this, which in mathematics
" is accepted for demonstration.

"§ XVII.

" It may not be amiss to observe, that the method for finding the fluxion
" of a rectangle of two flowing quantities, as it is set forth in the Treatise of
" Quadratures, differs from the abovementioned taken from the second book
" of the Principles, and is in effect the same with that used in the *calculus*
" *differentialis.*

" *differentialis.** For the supposing a quantity infinitely diminished and
" therefore rejecting it, is in effect the rejecting an infinitesimal; and indeed
" it requires a marvellous sharpness of discernment, to be able to distinguish
" between evanescent increments and infinitesimal differences. It may per-
" haps be said that the quantity being infinitely diminished becomes nothing,
" and so nothing is rejected. But according to the received principles it is
" evident, that no geometrical quantity can by any division or subdivision
" whatsoever be exhausted, or reduced to nothing. Considering the various
" arts and devices used by the great author of the Fluxionary Method: in
" how many lights he placeth his fluxions: and in what different ways
" he attempts to demonstrate the same point: one would be inclined to
" think, he was himself suspicious of the justness of his own demonstrations;
" and that he was not enough pleased with any one notion steadily to adhere
" to it. Thus much at least is plain, that he owned himself satisfied con-
" cerning certain points, which nevertheless he could not undertake to de-
" monstrate to others.† Whether this satisfaction arose from tentative me-
" thods or inductions; which have often been admitted by mathematicians,
" (for instance by Dr. *Wallis* in his Arithmetic of Infinites) is what I shall not
" pretend to determine. But, whatever the case might have been with re-
" spect to the author, it appears that his followers have shewn themselves
" more eager in applying his method, than accurate in examining his principles.

" § XVIII.

" It is curious to observe, what subtilty and skill this great genius employs
" to struggle with an insuperable difficulty; and through what labyrinths he
" endeavours to escape the doctrine of infinitesimals; which as it intrudes
" upon him whether he will or no, so it is admitted and embraced by others
" without the least repugnance. *Leibnitz* and his followers in their *calculus*
" *differentialis* making no manner of scruple, first to suppose, and secondly
" to reject quantities infinitely small: with what clearness in the apprehen-
" sion and justness in the reasoning, any thinking man, who is not preju-

" * Analyse des infiniment petits, part 1. prop. 2.
" † *See letter to* Collins, Nov. 8, 1676.

" diced

" diced in favour of those things, may easily discern. The notion or idea
" of an infinitesimal quantity, as it is an object simply apprehended by the
" mind, hath been already considered.* I shall now only observe as to the
" method of getting rid of such quantities, that it is done without the least
" ceremony. As in fluxions the point of first importance, and which paves
" the way to the rest, is to find the fluxion of a product of two indeterminate
" quantities, so in the *calculus differentialis* (which method is supposed to have
" been borrowed from the former with some small alterations) the main point
" is to obtain the difference of such product. Now the rule for this is got
" by rejecting the product or rectangle of the differences. And in general it
" is supposed, that no quantity is bigger or lesser for the addition or subduc-
" tion of its infinitesimal: and that consequently no error can arise from
" such rejection of infinitesimals.

" § XIX.

" And yet it should seem that, whatever errors are admitted in the pre-
" mises, proportional errors ought to be apprehended in the conclusion, be
" they finite or infinitesimal: and that therefore the ἀκρίβεια of geometry
" requires nothing should be neglected or rejected. In answer to this you
" will perhaps say, that the conclusions are accurately true, and that there-
" fore the principles and methods from whence they are derived must be so
" too. But this inverted way of demonstrating your principles by your
" conclusions, as it would be peculiar to you gentlemen, so it is contrary
" to the rules of logic. The truth of the conclusion will not prove either
" the form or the matter of a syllogism to be true: inasmuch as the illa-
" tion might have been wrong or the premises false, and the conclusion ne-
" vertheless true, though not in virtue of such illation or of such premises.
" I say that in every other science men prove their conclusions by their
" principles, and not their principles by the conclusions. But if in yours
" you should allow yourselves this unnatural way of proceeding, the con-
" sequence would be that you must take up with induction, and bid adieu
" to demonstration. And if you submit to this, your authority will no
" longer lead the way in points of reason and science."

" * *Sect.* 5 and 6.

4. The

·4. The reasonings, and the conclusions deduced, in the last eleven of these sections, in which the principles of these methods are examined, have experienced much opposition: and the opposers of them have succeeded so completely in persuading mankind of their having refuted them, as to have silenced all opposition to their opinions; no one having supported those of Berkeley, or publicly avowed their adoption of them, for more than half a century past.----Of the opposers of these reasonings the most eminent is the celebrated Colin Maclaurin, who endeavours to evade, if not refute them, first by arguing as follows, viz. " In the method of infi-
" nitesimals, the element, by which any quantity increases or decreases, is
" supposed to be infinitely small, and is generally expressed by two or
" more terms, some of which are infinitely less than the rest, which being
" neglected as of no importance, the remaining terms form what is called the
" *difference* of the proposed quantity. The terms that are neglected in this
" manner, as infinitely less than the other terms of the element, are the
" very same which arise in consequence of the acceleration, or retardation
" of the generating motion, during the infinitely short time in which the
" element is generated; so that the remaining terms express the element
" that would have been produced in that time, if the generating motion
" had continued uniform. Therefore those *differences* are accurately in
" the same ratio to each other as the generating motions or fluxions. And
" hence, though in this method infinitesimal parts of the elements are neg-
" lected, the conclusions are accurately true without even an infinitely
" small error, and agree precisely with those that are deduced by the me-
" thod of fluxions. For example, in prop. 2, when DG (see fig. 8th) the
" increment of the base AD of the triangle ADE, is supposed to be-
" come infinitely little, the trapezium $DGHE$ (the simultaneous incre-
" ment of the triangle) consists of two parts, the parallelogram EG, and
" the triangle EIH; the latter of which is infinitely less than the for-
" mer, their ratio being that of ½ DG to AD. Therefore, according to
" this method, the part EIH is neglected, and the remaining part, viz.
" the parallelogram EG is the *difference* of the triangle ADE. Now
" it was shown above (art. 93) that EG is precisely that part of the in-
" crement of the triangle ADE which is generated by the motion with
" which this triangle flows; and that EIH is the part of the same increment

" crement which is generated in consequence of the acceleration of this
" motion, while the base by flowing uniformly acquires the augment DG,
" whether DG is supposed finite, or infinitely little."*

5. This argument, however, it is presumed, must necessarily be allowed
to be of no avail; when it is considered, that it is perfectly impossible for
the triangle AGH or any other triangle to be generated in the manner here
represented—the common way in which they are according to the doctrine
of fluxions represented to be generated—or by the uniform motion of the
line DE, parallel to itself, along the base AG, in the direction AG; or
for a triangle to be generated by any line flowing or moving in any ONE
direction along any base; whether in the direction of its length, in a direction perpendicular to it, or in any other particular direction; and whether
that motion is uniform, or is accelerated or retarded: a square or parallelogram may thus be formed; but to form a triangle by this means is utterly
impossible. To form the triangle AGH by the flowing of any quantity
along the given base AG, from A to G, that quantity must necessarily flow
in two directions at once perpendicular to each other, the one the direction
AG, and the other that of GH; and that quantity when it commences its
motion at A must necessarily be a point, or indivisible, which expands itself
into a line, in the direction GH, gradually increasing in length in its
progress along AG. And it is equally impossible for any acceleration or
retardation of any motion to be in any other direction than that of the
motion; and, consequently, for the line IH, and the triangle EIH, to be
produced in the manner here represented, or in consequence of any acceleration of the motion of the line DE in the direction AG, or along the base
AG, since the line IH in place of being in that direction is manifestly in
a direction perpendicular to it. The same objections are applicable to the
generation of squares, parallelograms, curvilineal figures, &c. by the flowing or motions of lines, as represented by the doctrine of fluxions: a surface, whether a square or a product, may be generated by the motion of a
line, moving parallel to itself, along a given base; and a solid by the motion of a surface along a given base; but it is absolutely impossible for
them to be generated in the manner and by the means supposed in the
doctrine of fluxions.

* M'Laurin's Fluxions, Vol. II. page 1, last edit. by Davies, art. 495.

6. He afterwards, having premised in art. 706 that " it is of no import-
" ance how great or small soever those measures" (of the ratios according to
which quantities increase or decrease) " are, if they be in the just propor-
" tion to each other," attempts to refute the reasoning of the Analyst by
endeavouring to prove art. 707, that the fluxion of A being a, that of AA
will be $2Aa$, and not $2Aa+aa$, in the manner following; viz. " Prop. The
" fluxion of the root A being supposed equal to a, the fluxion of the square
" AA will be equal to $2A+a$.

" Let the successive values of the root be $A-u$, A, $A+u$, and the corre-
" sponding values of the square will be $AA-2Au+uu$, AA, $AA+2Au+uu$,
" which increase by the differences $2Au-uu$, $2Au+uu$, &c. and because those
" differences increase, it follows from art. 704, that if the fluxion of A be
" represented by u, the fluxion of AA cannot be represented by a quantity
" that is greater than $2Au+uu$, or less than $2Au-uu$. This being premised,
" suppose, as in the proposition, that the fluxion of A is equal to a; and
" if the fluxion of AA be not equal to $2Aa$, let it first be greater than $2Aa$
" in any ratio, as that of $2A+0$ to $2A$, and consequently equal to $2Aa+0a$.
" Suppose now that u is any increment of A less than 0; and because 0 is
" to u as $2Aa+0a$ to $2A+0u$, it follows (art. 706) that if the fluxion of A
" should be represented by u, the fluxion of AA would be represented by
" $2Au+0u$, which is greater than $2Au+uu$. But it was shewn, from
" art. 704, that if the fluxion of A be represented by u, the fluxion of AA
" cannot be represented by a quantity greater than $2Au+uu$. And these
" being contradictory, it follows that the fluxion of A being equal to a,
" the fluxion of AA cannot be greater than $2Aa$. If it can be less than
" $2Aa$, when the fluxion of A is supposed equal to a, let it be less in any
" ratio of $2A-a$ to $2A$, and therefore equal to $2Au-0u$. Then because
" a is to u as $2Aa-0a$ is to $2Au-0u$, which is less than $2Au-uu$ (u being
" supposed less than 0, as before), it follows that if the fluxion of A was
" represented by u, the fluxion of AA would be represented by a quantity
" less than $2Au-uu$, against what has been shewn from art. 704. There-
" fore the fluxion of A being supposed equal to a, the fluxion of AA must
" be equal to $2Aa$."*

* M'Laurin's Fluxions, Vol. II. page 169.

7. On

7. On perusing this supposed demonstration of the above proposition, the strange indirect manner in which it proceeds must strike every one, in giving to the root A three different values, and in effect three different fluxions; and in giving the fluxions of the square of all these different values of the root, except the fluxion of the square according to the proper value of it as stated in the proposition of which it is represented as the demonstration; or in place of giving the fluxion of the square of $A+a$, when a is the fluxion of the root, giving the fluxion of the square of the quantities $A+u$, and $A-u$, in which $+u$, and $-u$, are the fluxions of A; and of which the former quantity is stated to be greater and the latter to be less than the root. The confusion of thought necessarily resulting from this indirect procedure; from the employing of so many different suppositions in the demonstration; from some of the conclusions being manifestly erroneous, as when it is stated that the fluxion of the square of $A+u$ is not $2Au+uu$, but $2Au+0u$, if 0 is greater than u; and *vice versâ* if 0 is less than u; and from the substitution of 0, or cypher, for a real quantity, and stating real quantities as less than 0; must also be experienced by every one: the cypher was first brought into Europe by the Arabians, who ascribe the invention and use of it to the Indians; and it is one of the happiest devices imaginable as used in the notation of numbers, but to make it a representative of real quantity is an unwarrantable abuse of character, productive of ambiguity and equivocation, and liable to create a suspicion of intended deception.

8. There is one error, however, enters into the premises of this demonstration that would necessarily vitiate and invalidate all the subsequent reasonings and conclusions in it, were they otherwise unexceptionable, which there can be no doubt has escaped even the author himself; that is, a mis-statement of facts; 1st, in represesenting the square of A, or AA, as being increased by decreasing the root A by $-u$, and by squaring it when so decreased, whereby it becomes $AA-2Au+uu$; when AA in place of being decreased, as here stated, is in reality decreased by the difference $-2Au+uu$: and, 2dly, in directly after stating this difference to be $+2Au-uu$ in place of $-2Au+uu$; by which means, indeed, it is converted from a decrement into an increment, as in this case the first term of the square AA is also positive. That the changing of the signs of the

terms

terms whereby this effect is produced must have been the effect of inad-
vertency, in consequence of too great a predilection for and faith in a favourite system, there can be no doubt, for of designed deceit Mr. Maclaurin was incapable; nor are the above modes of reasoning peculiar to him---
who, though the statement of the last article is no doubt very embarrassed,
in general expresses himself with more perspicuity and elegance, and with
equal fairness and more ingenuity of argument, than the other defenders
of these systems---but are common to all who adopt and zealously maintain untenable doctrines.

9. Euclid demonstrates, (Book 2d, Prop. 4th) that, if a straight line
be divided into any two parts, the square of the whole line is equal to the
two squares of the two parts, together with twice the rectangle contained
by the parts. Algebra concurs in the same conclusion; or in making the
square of the binomial $A+a=AA+2Aa+aa$, in place of $=AA+2Aa$
only, as it is supposed to be in the doctrine of fluxions; and the product
of $A+a\times B+b=AB+Ba+Ab+ab$, as stated by the Analyst, in place
of $AB+Ba+Ab$ only, as by the fluxional doctrine: and, if real quantities are substituted for these symbols, this doctrine so repugnant both to
geometrical and algebraical conclusions, will be proved to be erroneous by
arithmetic also. Thus, if $A=7$, $A^2=49$; and if $a=3$, $\overline{A+a}|^2=49+42+$
$9=100=\overline{7+3}|^2$; and the difference between A^2 and $\overline{A+a}|^2$, or between
49 and 100, is $51=42+9=2Aa+aa$, in place of $=2Aa=42$ only. And
if $A=6$, $a=3$, $B=8$, $b=4$, then the rectangle or product $AB=48$; while
the product $A+a\times B+b=AB+Ba+Ab+ab=48+24+24+12=108$;
and the difference between $A\times B$, and $A+a\times B+b$, or between 48 and
108, $=60=24+24+12=Ba+Ab+ab$, as stated by the Analyst, in place
of $=48=Ba+Ab$ only, as stated in the doctrine of fluxions.

10. The fallaciousness of this doctrine, however, affects not the validity
of the infinitesimal calculus, but that of the method of fluxions only; for,
in the former, though such equations as $\overline{A+a}|^2=AA+2Aa$; and $A+a\times B$
$+b=AB+Ba+Ab$, are adopted in the calculations, yet they are admitted not to be true, but to be imperfect equations only: at the same time,
that with much inconsistency, they are employed, reasoned on, and conclusions

clusions are deduced from that reasoning, in that calculus on all occasions, with as great confidence as if they were true equations. The cypher, in that calculus as well as in the fluxional, is also often employed to denote either something or nothing, or both by turns, as best suits the system and purposes of the operator, in similar manners with that of the other attempted proof of the above principle so effectually refuted by the Analyst, in sects. 12th, 13th, &c. of the treatise bearing that title.

11. But though the Analyst not only denies the justness of the fundamental principles of these methods, but also proves in a perspicuous and satisfactory manner that they are erroneous and false, he nevertheless, in common with all others, allows the conclusions deduced by their means, to be rigidly accurate and just; and, with the intention of accounting rationally for this seeming paradox of true conclusions being deducible from false premises, he proceeds as follows, viz.

" § XX.

" I have no controversy about your conclusions, but only about your
" logic and method. How you demonstrate? What objects you are con-
" versant with, and whether you conceive them clearly? What principles
" you proceed upon; how sound they may be; and how you apply them?
" It must be remembered that I am not concerned about the truth of
" your theorems, but only about the way of coming at them; whether it
" be legitimate or illegitimate, clear or obscure, scientific or tentative. To
" prevent all possibility of your mistaking me, I beg leave to repeat and
" insist, that I consider the geometrical analyst as a logician, i. e. so far
" forth as he reasons and argues; and his mathematical conclusions, not
" in themselves, but in their premises; not as true or false, useful or in-
" significant, but as derived from such principles, and by such inferences.
" And for as much as it may perhaps seem an unaccountable paradox,
" that mathematicians should deduce true propositions from false princi-
" ples, be right in the conclusion, and yet err in the premises; I shall en-
" deavour particularly to explain why this may come to pass, and shew
" how error may bring forth truth, thou it cannot bring forth science.

" § XXI.

"§ XXI.

" In order therefore to clear up this point, we will suppose for instance
" that a tangent is to be drawn to a parabola, and examine the progress
" of the affair, as it is performed by infinitesimal differences. [See fig. 9th.]
" Let A B be a curve, the abscisse $AP = x$, the ordinate $PB = y$, the dif-
" ference of the abscisse $PM = dx$, the difference of the ordinate $RN = dy$.
" Now by supposing the curve to be a polygon, and consequently BN, the
" increment or difference of the curve, to be a straight line coincident with
" the tangent, and the differential triangle B R N to be similar to the triangle
" T P B, the subtangent PT is found a fourth proportional to RN : R B :
" P B : that is to $dy : dx : y$. Hence the subtangent will be $\frac{y\,dx}{dy}$. But
" herein there is an error arising from the forementioned false supposition,
" whence the value of PT comes out greater than the truth : for in reality
" it is not the triangle RNB but RLB, which is similar to PBT, and
" therefore (instead of RN) RL should have been the first term of the
" proportion, i. e. $RN + NL$, i. e. $dy + z$: whence the true expression for
" the subtangent should have been $\frac{y\,dx}{dy+z}$. There was therefore an error of
" defect in making dy the divisor: which error was equal to z. i. e. N L
" the line comprehended between the curve and the tangent. Now by the
" nature of the curve $yy = px$, supposing p to be the parameter, whence
" by the rule of differences $2y\,dy = p\,dx$ and $dy = \frac{p\,dx}{dy}$. But if you multiply
" $y + dy$ by itself, and retain the whole product without rejecting the square
" of the difference, it will then come out, by substituting the augmented
" quantities in the equation of the curve, that $dy = \frac{p\,dx}{2y} - \frac{dy\,dy}{2y}$ truly. There
" was therefore an error of excess in making $dy = \frac{p\,dx}{2y}$, which followed from
" the erroneous rule of differences. And the measure of this second error
" is $\frac{dy\,dy}{2y} = z$. Therefore the two errors being equal and contrary destroy
" each other; the first error of defect being corrected by a second error of
" excess.

"§ XXII.

"§ XXII.

" If you had committed only one error, you would not have come at a
" true solution of the problem. But by virtue of a twofold mistake you
" arrive, though not at science, yet at truth, For science it cannot be
" called, when you proceed blindfold, and arrive at the truth not knowing
" how or by what means. To demonstrate that z is equal to $\frac{dy\,dy}{2y}$, let B R
" or dx be m and R N or dy be n. By the thirty-third proposition of the
" first book of the conics of *Apollonius*, and from similar triangles, as $2x$
" to y so is m to $n+z=\frac{my}{2x}$. Likewise from the nature of the parabola $yy+$
" $2yn+nn+xp+mp$, and $2yn+nn=mp$: wherefore $\frac{2yn+nn}{p}=m$: and be-
" cause $yy=px$, $\frac{yy}{p}$ will be equal to x. Therefore substituting these values
" instead of m and x we shall have $n+z=\frac{my}{2x} \cdot \frac{2yynp+ynnp}{2yyp}$: $i.\,e.\; n+z=$
" $\frac{2yn+nn}{2y}$: which being reduced gives $z=\frac{nn}{2y}=\frac{dy\,dy}{2y}$ Q. E. D.

"§ XXIII.

" Now I observe in the first place, that the conclusion comes out right,
" not because the rejected square of dy was infinitely small; but because
" this error was compensated by another contrary and equal error. I ob-
" serve in the second place, that whatever is rejected, be it ever so small,
" if it be real and consequently makes a real error in the premises, it will
" produce a proportional real error in the conclusion. Your theorems
" therefore cannot be accurately true, nor your problems accurately
" solved, in virtue of premises, which themselves are not accurate, it being
" a rule in logic that *Conclusio sequitur partem debiliorem*. Therefore I ob-
" serve in the third place, that when the conclusion is evident and the pre-
" mises obscure, or the conclusion accurate and the premises inaccurate,
" we may safely pronounce that such conclusion is neither evident nor ac-
" curate, in virtue of those obscure inaccurate premises or principles; but
" in virtue of some other principles which perhaps the demonstrator him-
" self never knew or thought of. I observe in the last place, that in case
" the

" the differences are supposed finite quantities ever so great, the conclusion
" will nevertheless come out the same: inasmuch as the rejected quanti-
" ties are legitimately thrown out, not for their smallness, but for another
" reason, to wit, because of contrary errors, which destroying each other
" do upon the whole cause that nothing is really, though something is ap-
" parently thrown out. And this reason holds equally, with respect to
" quantities finite as well as infinitesimal, great as well as small, a foot or
" a yard long as well as the minutest increment."

12. That perspicuity and great depth of penetration for which this ingenious author is so eminently conspicuous on most occasions seems to have
forsaken him in this instance; for the two propositions here adduced with
the intention of proving that the result is just, only from each being erroneous in its particular conclusion, and from the errors of these conclusions
vanishing by their destroying or compensating each other from their being of
contrary natures and in each of equal amount. For these two propositions
are perfectly different and perfectly independent of each other, are formed
upon perfectly different premises, and give perfectly different conclusions,
the one giving the value of the subtangent for its result, and the other the
value of what is regarded as the differential or the fluxion of the ordinate
for its conclusion; and neither of these conclusions are erroneous, but
each, in itself independent of the other, accurately true as expressed in
the original propositions. Thus the expressions $\frac{y\,dx}{dy}$, or, as by the flux-
ional notation, $\frac{y\dot{x}}{\dot{y}}$, $=\mathrm{P\,T}$, the subtangent; and $dy=\frac{p\,dx}{2y}$, or $\dot{y}=\frac{p\dot{x}}{2y}$ are each
perfectly independent of the other, and each accurately just; while the
expressions proposed to be substituted for them respectively, namely,
$\frac{y\,dx}{dy+x}=\mathrm{P\,T}$; and $dy=\frac{p\,dx}{2y}-\frac{dy\,dy}{2y}$; are not true equations, or such as express
just results, on the presumption of the same meaning or value being as-
signed to dy, or $\dot{y}$, in both statements; and, if that is not the case, and
different meanings and values are assigned to the same expression, as suits
the particular object in view, the argument degenerates into a sophism and
becomes altogether nugatory.—The reasons of this will be given in the se-
quel.—Moreover, if such errors did actually exist in these particular conclusions,

clusions, it does not appear how they could be the means of either destroying or of compensating each other, and thereby of giving true results, or that they are ever employed for that purpose, that they are ever compared together, that any mean is ever taken between them, or that any other method is ever tried with them with that intention, which no doubt would be the case if true conclusions could be obtained by these means, and these particular conclusions were erroneous and required it.

13. None of the Bishop's opponents, whose works I have seen, have observed this error in his reasoning; and not having observed it, have made no attempt to expose or refute it; but have confined their arguments to the refutation of his with respect to the erroneousness of the principle mentioned above, and in that they have completely failed: they do not assail him where vulnerable but where invincible; and, in too warmly espousing the opinions he refutes, are themselves deceived by the artifices they unsuspectingly employ to elude or evade the strength and effect of his reasoning.

14. In a small but well wrote treatise entitled Reflections on the Theory of the Infinitesimal Calculus, by the learned M. Carnot, ex-minister of war in France, there is a most perspicuous statement of the principles of the infinitesimal calculus.—According to this author the infinitesimal calculus is a method of approximating to the solution of a question by neglecting quantities which embarrass the combinations, if it be foreseen that such quantities, on account of their small value, may be neglected without producing any sensible error in the result of the calculation:—and, in this statement, the justness of the conclusions obtained by means of the infinitesimal calculus is also attributed to a compensation of errors; but errors of another kind from those supposed by the Analyst. Here, the assuming and employing of the infinitesimals or infinitely small triangles on the supposition of curves being polygons is represented as the first error in the calculus, from its being absolutely impossible that a circle can be a true polygon; and the ellimenating of these infinitesimals, or the values they represent, from the conclusions, whereby they become perfectly accurate, which they were not before, is represented as the second error, and that whereby the first error is compensated. But this procedure can with no propriety and justice be regarded as a method of obtaining true conclusions by means of a compensation of errors; for if it was an error to admit these infinitesimals into

the calculation, it surely can be no error to expunge them from it again, especially when a true result may be obtained by that means. It seems strange indeed that assumptions confessedly erroneous, and which require to be expunged, should ever be admitted, and be proceeded upon as data; and that the inferences and consequences obtained by their means, or deduced from that false data, should be retained after these assumptions or the data themselves have been rejected and expunged from the calculations as being false, in any rational investigation the professed purpose of which is the obtaining of just results by means of just premises.

15. The infinitesimal calculus, however, has the advantage of the fluxional, in not representing the square and the product of a binomial as being complete without comprehending the square or the product of what is called the difference or fluxion; and there is no greater absurdity in rejecting a finite quantity as an infinite or infinitesimal, than in rejecting it under the pretence of its having no existence, as forming no part of the square or product. There is also no greater absurdity in regarding curves as polygons of an infinite number of sides, agreeable to the infinitesimal doctrine, than in regarding certain sides of plane right-angled triangles as curves, that they may be coincident with other curves, and that they may contain areas precisely equal to those contained by other right-angled triangles having the same base and altitude with a curve line in place of a straight for the hypothenuse; or that the areas of right-angled triangles whereof the bases and altitudes are equal but of which the hypothenuse of the one is a straight, and that of the other a curve line, may be regarded as equal to each other, as the fluxional doctrine requires. Besides, in the infinitesimal hypothesis there is no necessity for having recourse to the mysterious and untenable doctrine of prime and ultimate ratios, or limits, as its principles as originally given by Leibnitz do not depend upon it, as those of the fluxional do, though it has been adopted by the disciples of Leibnitz.

16. The FACT, however, is, that the justness of the conclusions, by either of these methods of computation, has no dependence whatever on COMPENSATIONS OF ERRORS. And, however strange it may appear, or however contrary to the universally received opinion, it is also a FACT, that neither of these methods are what they are represented to be; and, though they have never been viewed in this light, that they have no dependence

whatever

whatever upon infinitesimals, moments, or limits : the infinitesimal calcu*
lus neither proceeding upon infinitesimals or differentials, nor deducing its
conclusions by means of these ; and the fluxional neither proceeding upon
prime and ultimate ratios, moments, or fluxions ; nor deducing its conclusions by means of these :---what in these methods are represented as infinitesimals, differentials, moments, fluxions, increments, or decrements,
&c. of certain particular quantities, being not so in reality. And it is besides a FACT---and a mortifying fact it is, as demolishing the basis on which
several beautiful but delusive theories with their supposed demonstrations
are supported, as depriving science of what has been regarded as the principal means of its progress and improvement, and as evincing the vanity
of human pursuits even in cases where they have been deemed most suc-
cessful---that no discovery ever was made, or ever possibly can be made,
by either of these methods :---each of them, in reality, being nothing but
a most refined and most ingenious species of algebraical finesse---so refined
and ingenious indeed as to have imposed even upon the authors of these
methods themselves, though perhaps inferior to none of the human race in
clearness of apprehension and soundness of judgment---a kind of scientific
legerdemain by means of which many extraordinary feats may be performed, and many deceptions may be, and have been successsfully, but
unintentionally and unknowingly, practised, to the wonder, astonishment,
and admiration of mankind.

17. It is impossible, without regret, to abandon prepossessions long entertained, to renounce favourite opinions and favourite systems ; and to reject as incompetent or deceptious what was regarded as a certain criterion
of truth, and the surest means of discovering and demonstrating it : and
still greater must be the reluctance to forsake the flattering prospects these
doctrines offered, and the means and methods they held out to view as the
most effectual for the further successful prosecution of science; more especially of those who have been accustomed to regard and to represent these
means as infallible, and to pride themselves on the knowledge and practice of them. Yet such are the sacrifices which truth, utility, and the interest of science, in this case demands; and which may require more can-
dour and magnanimity to accomplish and acknowledge, however irresistible
and decisive the arguments adduced, than falls to the lot of the generality

of

of the human race. It is supposed, however, that the following observations, in addition to what has been already advanced on this subject, will be deemed by the candid and unprejudiced as affording a proof sufficiently satisfactory and conclusive with respect to the facts stated above.

18. The erroneous principle on which the doctrine of exhaustions of the ANCIENTS is founded, in representing quantities as equal whose difference is less than any assignable quantity; as if quantities, or the ratio of quantities, which *differ*, however small the difference may be, could be *equal* to each other: and the erroneous conclusions thence deduced of the infinite divisibility of magnitude, &c. which it is hoped have been satisfactorily refuted in the preceding parts of this Essay, seem sufficiently inconsistent, contradictory, and incomprehensible; yet it must be acknowledged that these doctrines of the ancients are far exceeded in these respects by those of the moderns, who have carried these principles to the utmost excess of extravagance; and---under the designations of the doctrines and arithmetic of infinites---of prime and ultimate ratios---of infinitesimals, and fluxions---have, from geometry, introduced them into philosophy; and, by that means involved the first principles of science in obscurity and mystecism.

19. The doctrine of limits, or of prime and ultimate ratios, is inconsistent and incomprehensible; and, necessarily, erroneous and absurd, since it is founded on principles which are contradictory and impossible---as those of the doctrine of exhaustions mentioned above, and those of the doctrine and arithmetic of infinites---and since it terminates in conclusions that are contradictory and absurd, as in stating certain quantities to be neither finite nor infinite; that a velocity which continues for no finite time may describe space; that quantities which are annihilable in a finite time by being gradually diminished are yet divisible and diminishable in infinitum or for an infinite time without being annihilated; that certain ratios are ultimately equal which it is acknowledged may approach to equality in infinitum without ever attaining it; that the ultimate ratio of straight and curve lines is that of equality; that the ultimate ratio of bounding lines and of the areas of all figures, however different from each other, and notwithstanding of their retaining their respective forms till they vanish, is that of equality; that ratios exist after those quantities of which they were

the

the ratios are annihilated, or that there are actually existing ratios between non-entities, with several others equally marvellous, some of which will be mentioned occasionally.

20. The principal difficulty in refuting doctrines the fallacy of which lies hid under ambiguous expressions consists in the discovering what ought to have been the proper meaning of these expressions by freeing them from these ambiguities; and, indeed, this of itself is a complete refutation of them. In the doctrine of prime and ultimate ratios, or of limits, much ambiguity arises from representing the *ultimate ratio,* at one time, as the *limit;* and at other times, as suits the then purposes, in representing the *limit or limiting ratio* as a ratio to which the *ultimate ratio approaches but never attains.* Thus, the following attempt at an explanation and proof of these doctrines is so ambiguously expressed as not to be intelligible till freed of such ambiguities, and then it refutes itself, viz. " It has been said that " when the increments are actually vanished, it is absurd to talk of any " ratio between them. It is true; but we speak not here of any ratio then " existing between the quantities, but of that ratio to which they have ap- " proached as their *limit;* and that ratio still remains. Thus, let the incre- " ments of two quantities be denoted by $ax^2 + mx$ and $bx^2 + nx;$ then the " *limit* of their ratio, when $x = o$, is $m:n;$ for, in every state of these quan- " tities, $ax^2 + mx : bx^2 + nx :: ax + m : bx + n ::$ (when $x = o$) $m:n$. As the " quantities therefore approach to nothing, the ratio approaches to that of " $m:n:$ as its *limit.* Hence, if $m = n$, the *limit* of this ratio is a ratio of " equality. We must therefore be careful to distinguish between the ratio " of two evanescent quantities, and the *limit* of their ratio; the former ra- " tio never arriving at the latter, as the quantities vanish at the instant that " such a circumstance is about to take place."*

21. This article is commented upon by the author in section 20th, pages 15th and 16th, but this comment tends rather to render the subject more obscure than to elucidate it; as, among other things equally inconceivable, we are there informed, " When we therefore deduce the *limit* by making " the increments vanish, the *effect* of the prior existence of the terms x, y, " of the ratio still remains in the terms m, n, which express the *limit* of the

---

* Vince's Principles of Fluxions, page 5th, sect. 8th.

" ratio."

" ratio." Or, in other words, that that which *limits* the ratio is *effected* by quantities, or the ratio of quantities, which have vanished and exist not. The purport of article 8th, quoted above, when divested of ambiguities, amounts to this. That though there is no ratio between quantities that have vanished; yet that ratio to which they approached as their *limit* remains after they have vanished; and that it is necessary to distinguish between the evanescent or *ultimate ratio*, and the *limiting ratio*, of quantities; the former ratio never arriving at the latter, as the quantities vanish at the instant that such a circumstance is about to take place. And, when thus plainly expressed, it is manifest that, according to the doctrine here propounded, the *ultimate ratio* of quantities differs in every case from their *limiting ratio*; and, consequently, that though the *limiting ratio* should be that of equality, yet—in direct contradiction to the general inference deduced from this doctrine of ultimate ratios being that of equality—the *ultimate ratio* of the quantities, or increments, could never be that of equality; as vanishing at the instant that such a circumstance is about to take place: this statement, besides, involves the absurdity of supposing the ratio of the quantities to be limited, and not limited, at the same time; as never acquiring that ratio which is represented as their limit, or to which they are said to be limited. It is also to be observed that though it is in article 8th, the *limiting ratio* only that is stated to remain after the quantities have vanished; yet, that in the comment on it, article 20th, the *ultimate ratio* of the quantities that are vanished, or what amounts to the same the *effect* of that ratio, is stated also to remain after the quantities of which it was the ultimate ratio have vanished, in contradiction to the assertion, article 8th, that we speak not of ratios existing between quantities that are vanished.

22. The supposed proof of these positions, article 8th. viz. " Let the " increments of two quantities be denoted by ax^2+mx and bx^2+nx; " then the *limit* of their ratio, when $x=0$, is $m:n$; for in every state of " these quantities, $ax^2+mx : bx^2+nx :: ax+m : bx+n :: $ (when $x=0$) $m:n$. " As the quantities therefore approach to nothing, the ratio approaches to " that of $m:n$ as its *limit* Hence, if $m=n$, the *limit* of this ratio is a ra- " tio of equality" is unsatisfactory and insufficient; for, in the first statement of $ax^2+mx : bx^2+nx$, if $x=0$, m and n, as being co-efficients of x

or

or o, must likewise $=o$; since when x vanishes all the powers and co-effi-cients of x must necessarily vanish with it, and consequently $m:n=o:o$, if such a ratio can be supposed: so that, in this case, it is manifest that no ratio can remain after the terms, increments, or quantities, have va-nished. In the second statement of $ax+m:bx+n$, the case is entirely altered, and differs so essentially from the first as to have nothing in com-mon with it; for, in the first, all the terms, or quantities, were affected by the vanishing of x, or its gradual approach to nothing, as x entered as a principal into all of them; and the evanescent or ultimate ratio was to be attained by the gradual diminution or vanishing of all, and not of some only, of the terms; and thereby the ultimate ratio not of some of the terms, or quantities, only, but of all the terms or quantities; whereas, in this case, there are terms, or quantities, which include not x, or the vanish-ing quantity in them, viz. m and n; and which, therefore, not only neither vanish themselves, either in whole or in part, but also no way *limit* the va-nishing quantities or terms, or those into which x enters; as no way affect-ing them, or being affected by them: and, consequently, if any ratio, ul-timate or limiting, is obtained in this case by the vanishing of those terms, that ratio, or the ultimate ratio of the terms that vanish cannot possibly be that of $m:n$, since their vanishing is no way affected or limited by the terms m and n, or by the ratio of these terms; and, as $m:n$ is not the ultimate ratio of the terms or quantities which vanish, so it cannot possibly be an ultimate ratio obtained by the vanishing of terms or quantities which are supposed, and by the data are admitted, not to vanish or decrease the terms or quantities m and n. And, hence, though the ratio of $ax+m$ to $bx+n$ will gradually approach nearer and nearer to that of m to n, as the terms or quantities ax and bx gradually decrease, and when they entirely vanish will become that of m to n, it is not because the vanishing of these terms or quantities, or of the ratio of these terms or quantities, is in any respect *limited* or affected by the terms or quantities, or the ratio of the terms or quantities m and n; but because neither these terms or quantities, nor the ratio of these terms or quantities m and n, are any way affected by the vanishing, either of those other terms or quantities, or by the vanishing of their ratio: and the ratio obtained in this case by the vanishing of ax

and

and $b\,x$, or that of $m:n$, can never be a ratio of equality, though called an ultimate ratio, but when $m=n$; nor can the ultimate ratio of the terms that vanish ever be that of equality, when their ratio was not originally that of equality: so that it is manifest there is no limitation even in this case, except in the vanishing of a quantity consisting of two terms being limited, and that by the data or hypothesis only, to the vanishing of one of these terms only; and hence that the ratio thus obtained can with no propriety or justice be regarded as the ultimate or evanescent ratio of these compound quantities; and, that, though regarded as such, it can never be a ratio of equality but in the single instance of the original assumption in the data of $m=n$, or of those terms in the quantities which are permanent being equal to each other.

23. The above manner of reasoning on this subject is by no means peculiar to Professor Vince, and this statement of it is selected in preference to others merely on account of his treatise being, I believe, the most recent of the Elementary Treatises on Fluxions, for even the great author of this method, himself, to whom the world is indebted for so many important discoveries, and who, on most other occasions, is so eminently distinguished for accurate discrimination and soundness of judgment, on this subject, from too great an attachment to a favourite hypothesis and to this fascinating art by means of which computations are apparently effected with so much facility, loses, as has been proved by the Analyst, his usual precision and justness of inference, and reasons not only inaccurately but inconsistently: and, of this, Lemma 1st, with its demonstration, which forms the basis of this doctrine of prime and ultimate ratios or of limits, together with the scholium by which these lemmas are succeeded, afford pertinent examples. This lemma, with its demonstration, are as follow, viz.

" *LEMMA* 1st.

24. " *Quantities, and the ratio of quantities, that in any finite time converge* " *continually to equality, and before the end of that time approach nearer the* " *one to the other than by any given difference, become ultimately equal.*"

" If

" If you deny it, suppose them to be ultimately unequal, and let D be
" their ultimate difference. Therefore they cannot approach nearer to equa-
" lity than by that given difference D; which is against the supposition."*

25. It is manifest that this lemma with its demonstration rests upon supposition only, and that what ought to have been proved is assumed and
taken for granted: the demonstration amounting precisely to this, that the
ultimate ratios are equal because they are assumed as such; and that they
cannot be otherwise, as that would be contrary to the supposition—which
is in effect nearly the same with the demonstration given by Euclid of the
justness of the Doctrine of Exhaustions, in his 10th book. And, in the
scholium by which the lemmas are succeeded, it is said, " And in like
" manner, by the ultimate ratio of evanescent quantities is to be understood
" the ratio of the quantities not before they vanish, nor afterwards, but
" with which they vanish;" and in the immediately succeeding paragraph
in the same page, it is added, " For those ultimate ratios with which
" quantities vanish are not truly the ratios of ultimate quantities, but
" limits towards which the ratios of quantities decreasing without
" limit do always converge; and to which they approach nearer than
" by any given difference, but never go beyond, nor in effect attain
" to, till the quantities are diminished *in infinitum*."† According to
the first of these quotations the ultimate ratios are those with which
quantities vanish; while, according to the last, they are limits towards
which the ratios of quantities approach nearer than by any given difference, but never attain to, till the quantities are diminished *in infinitum;* assertions which it is impossible to reconcile: what is meant in this
case by diminished *in infinitum* is not explained; if it be till the quantities
have vanished, it is necessarily absurd, as there cannot then be any ratio;
if immediately before they vanished, they then necessarily must have attained it.

26. According to this doctrine the ultimate ratio is that of equality; but
in the developing of it this equality is often represented in different man-

* Mathematical Principles of Natural Philosophy, vol. i. page 30. Motte's translation, last edition,
by Davis.

† Ibid. page 39.

ners and by different characters; as sometimes by $m = n$, sometimes by 0 or nullity, and sometimes by unity, creating much ambiguity which it is frequently difficult to decypher. And it is also common to suppose that a ratio subsists not only between quantities that have vanished, but also between quantities which have coalesced so as to become one and the same quantity, and to denominate it a ratio of equality; which is in fact only saying that a quantity is either equal to itself, or equal to a quantity that has vanished.

27. Thus, it is said, in M. Carnot's Reflections on the Infinitesimal Calculus, page 16, art. 12, " With a view to fix those ideas the more firmly in the " mind, and to give to the principles thence derived the necessary degree " of precision and generality, I shall remark, that the quantities which we " have occasion to consider in the subject before us, may be distinguished " into two classes. The first class consists of quantities which are either " given, or determined by the conditions of the problem, such as MC, " MP, PT, MT (see fig. 10). The second class is composed of quantities, " such as RS, RT', ST', which depend on the arbitrary position of the point " R, and which, as the point R approaches to the point M, do respectively " approach their corresponding quantities in the first class. Thus MP, for " example, is the limit of RS, that is, the fixed term to which it continually " approaches, or, if you will, its last or *ultimate value*. In like manner, " MT is the limit or ultimate value of RT', and PT that of ST'. For the " same reason, it is clear that the limits or ultimate values of MZ, RZ, " MR, TT, are, every one of them, 0. In fine, it is also evident, that the " *ultimate* ratio of RS to MP, (that is, the ultimate value of $\frac{RS}{MP}$,) is the " ratio of equality, and such is the ratio of RT' to MT, of ST' to PT, or, " in a word, such is that of any other quantity to its limit." According-ing to this statement, the limit and the ultimate value is the same; and the limit or ultimate value of the quantities that vanish, in this case, is represented to be either that of 0, as in the case of MZ, RZ, MR, and TT; or those of MP, MT, PT, in the cases of RS, RT, and ST; and the ultimate ratio, in each case, is said to be that of equality.

28. It is said, page 18th of this Treatise, " Since, in the mathematics, " two lines, two surfaces, two solids, in short two quantities of any kind " whatever, are supposed continually to approach each other by insensible
                                                                    " degrees;

" degrees; so that their proportion, or the quotient representing that pro-
" portion, differs less and less, and as little as we please, from unity, we
" say, that the last, or ultimate, ratio of those two quantities is a ratio of
" equality.

" If one of the quantities be assigned, and the other auxiliary, the first
" is called the *limit* or *ultimate value* of the second. Thus a limit is nothing
" else than an assigned quantity, to which an auxiliary quantity is sup-
" posed continually to approach, in such a manner that their difference
" may be rendered as small as we please, and that their ultimate ratio may
" be a ratio of equality.

" Thus auxiliary quantities alone can be properly said to have limits;
" for assigned quantities, being supposed constant and unchangeable, and
" to be themselves the terms, or ultimate values of auxiliary quanti-
" ties, cannot, in strictness, be said to have any limits; unless we choose
" to say, that every assigned quantity is its own limit, a liberty of speech
" which cannot be refused us; since the ultimate value of any determinate
" quantity whatever can be nothing else than that quantity itself.

" Hence, in general, we give the names of ultimate values and ultimate
" ratios of quantities, to the values and ratios which are, in fact, the last,
" or ultimate, ones assigned to those quantities and their relations, by the
" law of continuity, when each of them is supposed to approach, by con-
" tinued and insensible degrees, to its corresponding assigned quantity.

" We generally give the name of an *infinitely small* quantity, to the dif-
" ference between any auxiliary quantity whatever and its limit. Thus,
" for instance, RZ, which is the difference between RS and MP, is what
" we call an infinitely small quantity."

According to the above representation, a limit is an assigned quantity
to which an auxiliary quantity continually approaches; and the ultimate
values and ultimate *ratios* of quantities are the same.

In page 20th, it is said, " Hence it follows farther, that every infinitely
" small quantity may be considered as the difference between two auxiliary
" quantities, which have the same third assigned quantity for their limit.
" For, let X and Y be two different auxiliary quantities, whose limit is the
" same third quantity A, I say, that $X - Y$ is an infinitely small quantity.
" For, since the limit, or ultimate value of X is A, and that of Y is also A,
" it follows that the ultimate value of $X - Y$ will be $A - A$, or 0. There-

M M 2   " fore

" fore the limit of $A+(X-Y)$ is A; and consequently we may consider
" $X-Y$ as the difference between an auxiliary quantity $A+(X-Y)$ and
" its limit A, and this difference (by art. 19.) is an infinitely small quantity.
" It may therefore be affirmed, in general, that *an infinitely small quantity*
" *is the difference between two auxiliary quantities which have the same limit :*"
which is only saying, in other words, that *no difference* at all is an infinitely
small difference ; or that where there is *no difference* there is *a difference :* as
thus attempted to be proved, when $X=A$, and $Y=A$, then $X=Y$; and
$X-Y=A-A=0$; and, hence, " I say that $X-Y$ is an infinitely small
" quantity."

29. This is preceded by a good deal of similar reasoning, contradictory
in its assertions, and erroneous in its conclusions—for the purpose of proving
that 0, or nothing, is an infinitely small quantity, and that unity divided
by nothing, or $\frac{1}{0}$, is an infinitely great quantity, on the absurd assumption
of 0 being a quantity, or nothing something, and of something being divisible by nothing—which it would be only loss of time to attend to. In a
note, page 17th, a distinction is attempted to be drawn between what is
here called mathematical infinity and metaphysical infinity, and between
mathematical and real quantities; but no such distinction can be made,
no line can be drawn between them, for mathematical quantities abstracted
from real quantities are non-entities, since mathematical quantities neither
have, nor can have, any existence but as being the relations or properties
of entities or real quantities: akin to this is the attempt, in page 33d of
this treatise, to distinguish nothing into different kinds, as into absolute
and relative; and what is here called mathematical infinity, into sensible
and absolute, as being also directly repugnant to the proper meanings of
the terms, to right reason, and the nature of things.

30. In page 21st, it is said, " Two quantities cannot have the same third
" quantity for their limit, unless the ultimate ratio between those two quan-
" tities themselves be a ratio of equality. For, since, by the supposition,
" the limit, or ultimate value of $\frac{X}{A}$ is 1, and that of $\frac{Y}{A}$ is also 1, it is evident
" that the limit, or ultimate value of $\frac{\left(\frac{X}{A}\right)}{\left(\frac{Y}{A}\right)}$ is likewise unity. Now $\frac{\left(\frac{X}{A}\right)}{\left(\frac{Y}{A}\right)}=\frac{X}{Y}$;
" and therefore the limit, or ultimate value of $\frac{X}{Y}$ is 1; that is, the ultimate
" ratio

" ratio of X to Y is a ratio of equality :" which amounts precisely to this ; that each of two quantities cannot be equal to a third quantity unless they are equal to each other ; and the proof given here of this long-established axiom founded on experience is, because the one quantity divided by the other gives unity for the quotient ; as if their equality was a consequence of their quoting unity, and not their quoting unity a consequence of their equality :—and 1, or this quotient of unity, which is denominated their limit or ultimate ratio, is here improperly employed to denote the ratio of equality, no doubt in place of 1 : 1, because the ratio of any quantity to that of any other dividing it without a remainder is as the quotient to unity ; and, in this case, the ratio of the quotient to unity is that of 1 : 1. But the expressions 4 : 4, 7 : 7, &c. or the ratio of any equal quantities whatever, thus expressed, are without any reference to their quotients, or what is here improperly denominated their limits, equally indicative of the ratio of equality with the expression 1 : 1.

30. It is said, in art. 41st, page 33d, " Absolute nothing I also distin-
" guish by the name of an *evanescent* quantity ;" and in art. 47th, page 39th,
it is said, " So far from its not being logical to consider infinitely small
" quantities, either as real beings, or as nothings, they may, on the con-
" trary, be treated at pleasure, either as nullities or as true quantities.
" For they who wish to consider them as nullities, may answer, that what
" they call infinitely small quantities are not any nullities taken at random,
" but nullities assigned by the law of continuity which determines their
" relation ; that among all the relations of which these quantities are
" susceptible as nullities, they only consider those which are determined
" by this law of continuity ; and, in a word, that these relations are not
" vague and arbitrary, because the law of continuity does not assign several
" different relations between the differentials, for example, of the abscisse
" and ordinate of a curve, when these differentials vanish, but one only,
" which is that of the subtangent to the ordinate."—These are surely very
strange positions which state certain quantities to be either something or
nothing : and that when these quantities or differentials which were something have vanished or become nothing, that this nothing is not only possessed of relations, but of relations which are determined by certain laws ;
and which states these conclusions to be strictly logical ; though it is manifest

fest that if they become absolutely nothing, as here stated, it must be absolute absurdity to suppose they or nothing possess ratio or any power or property whatever. And, in the above case of the subtangent and the ordinate, if they are supposed to vanish, not from becoming nothing, but from coalescing and becoming identical with the subtangent and the ordinate, then it is manifest that, in place of having vanished, they still exist, only under new characters and designations, as having actually become the subtangent and the ordinate; and, consequently, that this doctrine of evanescent or ultimate ratios, and of non-entities, is no ways applicable to them and their ratios.

31. This doctrine not only includes the absurdities resulting from the adoption of the doctrine and arithmetic of Infinites; as of there being infinitesimals of infinitesimals *in infinitum*, and infinites of various kinds and qualities, including among others 0, and $\frac{1}{0}$, and different kinds of 0's; as also finite infinites possessing parts, ratios, and limitations, as one end or termination, and which admit of addition and subtraction, and of being multiplied and divided, &c. either by finite quantities, or by other such infinites, &c. but also from abstracting the ratios from the quantities of which they are the ratios, and of thereby investing them with existence after the quantities themselves have vanished; a fact which, in some of the above statements of the doctrine is both denied and admitted and when denied is yet proceeded upon in the calculations the conclusions being invariably deduced from and established on the ratios of the quantities which have vanished after they have vanished in both these methods of computation, and which confers, contrary to nature and right reason, on attributes or relations an independent and therefore necessary and eternal existence. This doctrine also involves the absurdity of quantities of every kind, even substantial existence, being diminishable by division or otherwise even to annihilation; as if substantial existence could be annihilated any otherwise than by the will of its Creator: and likewise of that which is annihilable, by being gradually diminished, in a finite time, being yet diminishable *in infinitum*, or for an infinite time, without being annihilated. It is attributes, relations, or modifications, only, of substances or bodies that are annihilable by that means; as their respective motions, forms, distances, &c. and the relations or ratios of these different modifications of the different bodies among

themselves,

themselves, as their relative motions, distances from each other, &c. which admit of being diminished till they vanish : and though they admit of being diminished till they vanish, they do not admit of being diminished *in infinitum*, since vanishing necessarily precludes all further diminution.

32. But however unfounded and fallacious the doctrine of prime and ultimate ratios or of limits may be, neither the fluxional nor the infinitesimal calculus are any way affected by that circumstance; as the justness of their conclusions has no dependence on it; nor is there any use made of it in these, except in assuming, what is utterly impossible, certain mixtilinear triangles as exactly similar to certain rectilinear triangles, in the one method, on the supposition of their ultimate figures being exactly similar, though it is admitted that they retain their original forms to the last; and, in the other, on the supposition of the infinitesimal parts of curves being right lines, and they of course polygons of an infinite number of sides. And, on either of these assumptions, RN and RL (see fig. 9th) are equal; and, hence, the fluxion or infinitesimal of the ordinate is dy, or $\dot{y}$, and not $dy + z$, as supposed by Bishop Berkeley; and hence it is that the conclusions are accurately true, when the infinitesimal or fluxion is in this case denoted by dy, or $\dot{y}$; and that they become erroneous when $dy + z$ is substituted for dy, as he proposes. The real matter of fact, however, is; that the justness of the conclusions by these methods has no dependence whatever on the justness of these assumptions, or on the doctrine of prime and ultimate ratios, or of limits.

33. Neither has it any dependence whatever on a compensation of errors, either in the manner supposed by Bishop Berkeley, or in that supposed by M. Carnot: nor has it, though perhaps the assertion may seem strange and paradoxical, any dependence whatever on either of these methods themselves; which, though differing in theory, are, except in name and notation, the same in practice. Such, however, is the fact. It is by other means, and on other principles, that the truths supposed to be obtained by these methods have been discovered and ascertained. For, invariably, in these methods, the questions to be resolved, or quantities required, are either previously known, or are assumed in the premises; and it is in consequence, merely, of this previous knowledge, or of these gratuitous assumptions, that the different diagrams, and the different formulas, according to

their

their several modes of notation, representing or expressing these quantities or values, or the solutions of the questions, are obtained. It is neither to the attenuation of the infinitesimals or fluxions, nor to a compensation of errors, that what is called the success of the calculus is owing. It is merely to the previous knowledge of what is pretended to be unknown and sought, and the consequent just delineation of a diagram, or triangle, truly representing it, and to the drawing of other triangles precisely similar to that triangle; and the deducing from this similarity, thus obtained, results previously known, and assumed in the premises in delineating the original triangle according to them; and in denominating these similar triangles differentials, increments, infinitesimals, or fluxions, not indeed of the triangles to which they are formed similar, and on the similarity to which the whole reasoning in these cases proceeds, but of certain polygons or curves to which they have no similarity whatever, and to which of course the reasoning deduced from the similarity is in no respect applicable; and in expressing the equation giving the previously known results or facts by means of a different notation from that used in algebra, as seemingly obtained by means of this obscure, circuitous, and retrograde process, which is represented as a new, accurate, and most important mode of calculation, far superior to all others. If the triangles, or other figures, representing the known facts are justly delineated, it is of no importance what the magnitudes of the triangles, &c. drawn similar to them may be, with regard to what is called the success of the calculus, or to the reasoning founded on that similarity; for that will be just, if the similarity is just, however great, or however small, the similar triangles, &c. or falsely supposed differentials, increments, infinitesimals, or fluxions, of a curve or polygon, may be.

34. These triangles, &c. supposed to be, and denominated infinitesimals or fluxions, are introduced into the calculus merely as auxiliaries for the purpose of obtaining from their *similarity* to the original triangles, &c. which express and give those results, which, though known, are in these cases sought, that proportion required for expressing them according to these modes of notation; and this being obtained by their means, they are dismissed; but without dismissing the ratio deduced from their similarity to the original triangle, &c. expressing them, by means of the proportion thus obtained.

25. Thus,

35. Thus, for example, in the case of drawing a tangent to a parabola, (see fig. 9th, or that taken from the Analyst) a diagram, including what is sought or the ratio of the ordinate to the subtangent and thereby the tangent itself or quantity required, is, from the previous knowledge of that which is pretended to be unknown and sought, first geometrically and justly delineated; and next, since in this diagram the subtangent PT, with the ordinate PB, and tangent BT, form a right-angled plane triangle TPB, another small plane triangle BRL, directly similar to it in every respect, is, under the pretence of its being an infinitesimal or fluxion of a curve, drawn at the point B; that, from this direct similarity to the triangle TPB, which gives the ratio of the ordinate to the subtangent, the proportion $LR : RB :: BP : PT$, may be obtained; and, consequently, the equation $PT = \frac{y\,dx}{dy}$, or according to the fluxional notation $= \frac{y\dot{x}}{\dot{y}}$; or an expression, according to the several notations of these methods, giving what is represented as the result of this process by these methods; and which result is pretended to be discovered and ascertained by means of those infinitesimals or fluxions, or the auxiliary quantities or triangles thus procured and the proportion deduced by their means; though it is manifest that a triangle could not have been drawn, arbitrarily, having these ratios, or having the ratio of the ordinate to the subtangent, as the triangle TPB, without that ratio having been previously known; and that the similar triangle to it could not have been drawn without a triangle including that ratio being known according to which it is made similar, and by that means the above proportion obtained. It is, however, from this latter triangle that this ratio is pretended to derived and deduced, and it is represented as having been introduced for the express purpose of discovering and ascertaining it: and in the fluxional calculus this small triangle is represented as not being rectilinear but mixtilinear as having one side a curve; and yet, inconsistently with that circumstance, is represented as being directly similar to the plane triangle to which it is annexed; while, with equal inconsistency, it is represented to have been generated by the flowing of the curve, though it is manifest that if it had been generated by the flowing of any quantity at all, it necessarily must have been by the flowing of that triangle to which it is in every respect similar.

VOL. II. N N 36. It

36. It is known from geometry that the subtangent PT of a parabola is equal to twice x the abscisse; and, from geometry and algebra, that the equation of this curve is $Px = y^2$, when P is the parameter, and y an ordinate of it: truths which never could have been discovered by means of processes such as the above, which in reality are founded upon and proceed on the knowledge of them, or by the method either of fluxions or of infinitesimals: and, since it is easy by common algebra to form a formula expressing this ratio of the abscisse to the subtangent, as $PT = 2x$; or, from the ratio of the co-ordinates in a value of y the ordinate in a function of x the abscisse, as $PT = \frac{2xy}{y}$, and consequently $PT = \frac{yz}{\frac{1}{2}y}$; the only object of the infinitesimal calculus, and the method of fluxions, in this case can be the giving a new formula in place of this; or, more properly, the expressing of this formula by a different notation, and by that means impressing a belief of the result or truth expressed by it, having been discovered by these methods. And even in this, they, in this case, fail; as $\frac{yds}{dy}$, or $\frac{y\dot{z}}{\dot{y}}$, is not a just expression for $\frac{yz}{\frac{1}{2}y}$ and therefore does not give the true result, unless dy, or $\dot{y}$, $= \frac{y}{2}$, and on the absurd supposition of fluxions and their fluents, and of differentials and their integrals, being quantities which are at the same same time both different and identical; or that dx, and $\dot{x}$, $= x$.

37. In like manner, in the case of drawing a tangent to a circle, (see fig. 10th), a diagram including what is sought or the ratio and quantity required, is, from the previous knowledge of it, first delineated, in the triangle MTP; and, then, a small triangle precisely similar to it, mno, is drawn at the point m; that the proportion $mo : no :: TP : MP$ may be obtained by this means, from which apt expressions, agreeable to the several notations of these methods, for the well and long known algebraical equation of $PT = \frac{y^2}{a - x}$, for the subtangent of a circle, when PT is the subtangent, a the axis, x the abscisse, and y an ordinate of a circle, may be obtained: and even this humble and unnecessary attempt has not, in this case, been attended with success. The only differences between the processes in this case by the infinitesimal method, and the method by fluxions, consists in the difference of their respective modes of expression; and that, in the infinitesimal method, the additional small triangle mno is said to be a differential or first difference of the curve, in place of a fluxion of it, though

it

it has evidently no dependence whatever on it, but on the triangle only to which it is made similar; and that it is, in that method, said to have been introduced into the calculation for the express purpose of generating a small error in it, that the error may be corrected again by again withdrawing the quantity it expresses from the conclusions; which, to say the least of it, seems to be but a very unprofitable procedure. The above results were discovered and known long before either of these methods were known or thought of: and they never could have been discovered and known by their means; which, in place of deducing and proving them, assume them. No discovery ever was or can be made by means of these supposed sciences, and, indeed, it would be absurd in the extreme to imagine that just conclusions could ever be rationally deduced from erroneous principles.

38. Procedures similar to the above take place in every other case by these methods of analysis as they are called. But these are not the only modes of deception adopted and practised by them. For it is a fact—though never suspected or attended to before, and though the assertion may appear still more strange and paradoxical than that announcing those just now described—that not only what are called the infinitesimals, differentials, increments, and fluxions, of simple quantities, are generally nothing else but these simple quantities themselves; but also that what is called the infinitesimal or fluxion of an area, as of a rectangle, a square, &c. is, in reality, the area, rectangle, square, &c. itself in masquerade, as exhibited under the disguise of another form and another name, by means of which it can be made to disappear and re-appear, to vanish and to re-assume its former state and character, as suits the will and the purposes of the performer, merely by the artifices of what are called the direct and inverse methods of fluxions, and the methods of the infinitesimal and the integral calculus.

39. This fact I shall now attempt to prove; by deducing it, as an inevitable consequence, from the common rules for the finding of fluxions and their fluents, and of infinitesimals and their integrals. In this proof I shall make use of the fluxional notation only, as being the most obvious and as it is easy to change it to the infinitesimal by placing d's before those letters which have points placed over them and obliterating these points; and as

the

the appreciating and ascertaining of the true values of the fluxions of powers and products that eventually lead to and terminate in the ascertaining of the true values of all fluxions whatever, and that often by mere ocular inspection. I shall begin with these.

40. According to the common rule for finding of fluxions, the fluxion of a square, as of xx, for instance, is $\dot{x}x + x\dot{x} = 2x\dot{x}$. Now, from the rule for finding the fluent of any power of a simple quantity multiplied by the fluxion of that quantity---viz. of adding unity to the index, dividing by the index so increased, and also by the fluxion of the root---it follows as a necessary consequence that the value of the fluxion in this case is precisely one half of that of the fluent or quantity of which it is the fluxion, that is $\dot{x} = \frac{1}{2}x$. For by adding, agreeable to the rule, unity to the index of x, in the rectangle or product $x\dot{x}$, it becomes $x^2\dot{x}$; and dividing this by $\dot{x}$ the fluxion, and then by 2 the index, it ultimately becomes $\frac{x^2}{2}$, or $\frac{1}{2}x^2$; but $\frac{1}{2}x^2 = x \times \frac{1}{2}x = x\dot{x}$: and hence $\dot{x} = \frac{1}{2}x$ in this case; so that $x\dot{x}$ is the product of x multiplied by $\frac{x}{2}$, and $x\dot{x} + x\dot{x} = x \times \frac{x}{2} + x \times \frac{x}{2}$. Or otherwise, more directly, thus, by applying the rule to $2x\dot{x}$, and then exemplifying the case by giving appropriate values to the symbols; when, by adding unity to the index of the root, x, and then dividing it by 2, the index thus increased, and by $\dot{x}$, the fluxion of the root, $2x\dot{x}$ becomes x^2, $= 16$, if x, the root, $= 4$; but $2x\dot{x}$ cannot become $= 16$, if $x = 4$, unless $\dot{x} = 2 = \frac{1}{2}x$ or one half of the root, when $2x\dot{x} = 2 \times 4 \times 2 = 16 = x^2$, or $\dot{x}x + x\dot{x} = 2x\dot{x} = x^2 = x \times \frac{1}{2}x + x \times \frac{1}{2}x = 4 \times 2 + 4 \times 2 = 8 + 8 = 16$, and $\dot{x}x + x\dot{x}$ or $2x\dot{x}$ and x^2 become identical in every thing except in name and notation. In the same manner and on the same principle if x, the root, $= 6$; $\dot{x}$, the fluxion, $= 3$; $x\dot{x} = 18$, $x\dot{x} + x\dot{x} = 2x\dot{x} = 36 = x^2$; if $x = 10$, $\dot{x} = 5$, $x\dot{x} + \dot{x}x = 2x\dot{x} = 100 = x^2$; and so of other cases :---and hence it is manifest that the fluxion of the root of the second power of every quantity is, in every case, precisely equal in value to the one half of that root ; and, consequently, that what is called the FLUXION of that power is, in reality, the POWER itself, the power and its nominal fluxion being identical in every thing but in name and notation.

41. In the same manner, the fluxion of x^3 is $xx\dot{x} + x\dot{x}x + \dot{x}xx = 3x^2\dot{x}$; and $3x^2\dot{x}$ is precisely of equal value with x^3, the quantity of which it is

said

said to be the fluxion; the fluxion of the █████ █████ ████ █████ in the third power precisely one-third of the valu█ ██ ████ root? ██, by adding unity to the index, &c. as by the rule, it beco████ █████ ██ resume ██ pristine form and character; and by substituting █ for instance, for the root, or making $x=6$, $x^2=36$, and $x x \times \dot{x}=36 \times 2$ or one-third of x or 6 the root $=72$, and three times $x x \dot{x}$, or three times 72, $=216=x^3$; or $x^2 \times \dot{x} \times 3=3 x^2 \times \dot{x}$, and $=36 \times 6$, or 108, multiplied by $\dot{x}$ or 2, one-third of the root, $=216=x^3$, as before. In the same manner it may be proved that what is called the fluxion or differential of x^4, or $4 x^3 \dot{x}$, is precisely of equal value with x^4, and is in every respect, except in name and notation, identical with it; and that, in this case of the fourth power of the root, $\dot{x}$, or what is called the fluxion of the root, is precisely of one-fourth the value of x, the root; also that $5 x^4 \dot{x}$ is precisely equal in value to x^5, and is therefore only another way of expressing it; and that $\dot{x}$ in this case is precisely of one-fifth the value of x the root. And in this manner it may be shown that what are called the fluxions and increments of all other powers and products are, in every case, of precisely the same value with the quantities of which they are said to be the fluxions or increments; and, consequently, that these supposed fluxionary quantities are, in reality, nothing but these quantities disguised under another form and another name; and, also, that what are called the fluxions of the roots of the powers, in these cases, are always of precisely equal value with the root divided by the index of the power: being, respectively, equal to $\frac{1}{2}x$, to $\frac{1}{3}x$, to $\frac{1}{4}x$, to $\frac{1}{5}x$, to $\frac{1}{6}x$, to $\frac{1}{n}x$, the root, according as they are fluxions of the 2d, the 3d, the 4th, the 5th, the 6th, the nth, power of the root: and hence it is that the above-mentioned rule for finding the fluent, integral, or original quantity, when the co-efficient of the fluxionary expression of it is by any means wanting, is applicable for ascertaining the value of the expressions thus mutilated; as, for instance, when $2 x \dot{x}$ is deprived of its co-efficient 2 and is thus reduced to $x \dot{x}$, by adding unity to the index it becomes $x^2 \dot{x}$, and then, by dividing by the index thus increased, and also by the fluxion of the root, it becomes $\frac{x^2}{2}$, or $\frac{1}{2}x^2$; which it could not do if $\dot{x}$ did not exactly equal $\frac{1}{2}x$; $x \times \frac{1}{2}\dot{x}$, only, being equal to $\frac{1}{2}x^2$; when $3 x^2 \dot{x}$ is reduced to $x^2 \dot{x}$, on applying the above-mentioned rule it becomes $\frac{1}{3}x^3$, which it could not

do

do if $\dot{x}$ in this case was not equal $\frac{1}{3}x$ precisely, $x^2 \times \frac{1}{3}x$, only, being $=\frac{x^3}{3}$ or $\frac{1}{3}x^3$; thus, for instance, if $x=6$, $x^2 \times \frac{1}{3}x = 72 = \frac{216}{3} = \frac{1}{3}x^3$. And when $\frac{1}{4}x^3\dot{x}$ is reduced to $x^3\dot{x}$, by applying the rule it becomes $\frac{x^4}{4}$ or $\frac{1}{4}x^4$, which could not be if $\dot{x}$ in this case did not equal $\frac{1}{4}x$ precisely, $x^3 \times \frac{1}{4}x$, only, being equal to $\frac{1}{4}x^4$, or $\frac{x^4}{4}$; and the same rule holds for ascertaining the values of the fluxions of the roots of all other powers; so that in this manner also they can be proved to be respectively as stated above.

42. The value of what is called the *fluxion* of a logarithm is necessarily determined by the value of the *fluxion* of the number of which it is the logarithm relatively to the *number* itself; or, in other words, by the ratio of the fluxion of the number to the number: and, consequently, if y is any number, and x its logarithm; if $\dot{y}$, the assumed fluxion of y, equal y, as is often the case, then $\dot{x}$, the assumed fluxion of its logarithm x, must necessarily $=x$; and since in this case $\frac{\dot{y}}{y}=\frac{y}{y}=1$, the value of $\dot{x}$, the fluxion of the logarithm which is determined by this ratio, must also be 1; if $\dot{y}$, the fluxion of the given number y, $=\frac{1}{2}y$, then $\frac{\dot{y}}{y}=\frac{1}{2}$, and consequently $\dot{x}=\frac{1}{2}x$; if $\dot{y}=\frac{1}{3}y$, $\dot{x}=\frac{1}{3}x$; if $\dot{y}=\frac{1}{4}y$, $\dot{x}=\frac{1}{4}x$; and so of other cases. Agreeable to the rules given for finding the fluents of the fluxions of logarithms, it is usual in the practice, and in the examples, to assume in this, as in other cases, that which is sought, the fluent or logarithm itself, as a constant quantity, and to denominate it the modulus of the system and represent it as such by the symbol m, though it had been represented before as a varying quantity under the appropriate symbols x and its fluxion $\dot{x}$; so that in these cases it is made to assume and act under different characters and names at the same time: thus, it is evident that if x, the logarithm, $=\frac{my}{y}$, $x=m$, and the modulus and logarithm are the same; and that if $\dot{x}$, the fluxion of x the logarithm, is, as commonly supposed and represented, $=\frac{m\dot{y}}{y}$, $\dot{x}$ must equal either $\frac{1}{2}$, or $\frac{1}{3}$, or $\frac{1}{4}$, &c. m, or its equivalent x, according as $\frac{\dot{y}}{y}$ is either $\frac{1}{2}$, $\frac{1}{3}$, or $\frac{1}{4}$, &c. The logarithm of each particular quantity, is according to every system, a constant quantity, and may be accurately expressed by the equation $x=\frac{y\dot{x}}{\dot{y}}$, provided $\dot{x}$ has the same ratio to x, that $\dot{y}$ has to y, but not otherwise; thus, if x the log. $=8$, and its fluxion $\dot{x}=4,$

$\dot{x}=4$, and if $y=6$, and $\dot{y}=3$, then $x=\frac{y\dot{x}}{\dot{y}}$ is equivalent to $8=\frac{6\times4}{3}$, or $8=\frac{24}{3}$; or if $x=12$, $\dot{x}=4$, $y=15$, and $\dot{y}=5$, then $x=\frac{y\dot{x}}{\dot{y}}$ is equivalent to $12=\frac{15\times4}{5}$: and, from the above it follows, that $\dot{x}=\frac{x\dot{y}}{y}$. But this very equation for the given logarithm x, of $x=\frac{y\dot{x}}{\dot{y}}$, is, according to this method, which gives the very same equation for the subtangent of the parabola, &c. the equation for the modulus of a system of logarithms;* or $m=\frac{y\dot{x}}{\dot{y}}$, a conclusion entirely inadmissible: and it appears, from what is advanced above, that an operator by this method may assume as what is called the fluxion of a logarithm, either the logarithm itself, or various other values, as may best suit his purposes.

43. The fluxions or differentials of simple quantities not regarded as the roots of any powers, and not determined in value by any equation as in some of the cases above, generally differ in nothing from the quantities of which they are said to be the fluxions or differentials, except in name, and in having either a dot or point placed over them or a d prefixed to them, to distinguish them from their fluents or integrals; and hence it is that nothing further is required to restore them to their pristine form and character than to deprive them of these distinguishing marks, and to restore their former names, the value of the fluxion and of its fluent, of the differential or infinitesimal and of its integral, being in these cases commonly precisely the same; and the fluxional and differential notations and nomenclatures of them only different expedients for exhibiting them under the disguise of different appearances and different characters from those under which they used to appear and are known.

44. What is called the fluxion or differential of a fraction is said to be thus found: let the fraction be $\frac{x}{y}$, viz. " Put $z=\frac{x}{y}$, then $zy=x$, and $z\dot{y}$

" $+y\dot{z}=\dot{x}$; $\therefore \dot{z}=\frac{\dot{x}-z\dot{y}}{y}=\frac{\dot{x}-\frac{x}{y}\times\dot{y}}{y}=\frac{y\dot{x}-x\dot{y}}{y^2}$."† But $z\dot{y}+y\dot{z}=zy$, as is proved by the rule given for the fluxions of products; and, consequently, $\dot{x}=x$, or the fluxion and fluent are the same. What are here called the fluxions of

* See Vince's Fluxions, article 44th, page 59th.
† Ibid, article 17th, page 11th.

z and

z and of y, or $\dot{z}$, $\dot{y}$, are mere arbitrary assumptions agreeable to the rules of this fallacious art for the finding of what is called the fluxion of a product or of the second power of a root; or, in other words, for the finding of an apt but different expression for the product itself, which, being identical with it except in name and notation, may be substituted for it or replaced by it at pleasure without producing any error in the results; and, consequently, are each equal to one half the values of those quantities of which they are respectively said to be the fluxions; or $\dot{z} = \frac{1}{2}z$, and $\dot{y} = \frac{1}{2}y$. According to the values thus arbitrarily assumed of those nominal fluxions $\dot{z}$ and $\dot{y}$, the succeeding equations of $\dot{z} = \frac{\dot{x} - z\dot{y}}{y}$, &c. as here stated, if x was substituted for $\dot{x}$ in them, would be just, in as far as they give $\frac{1}{2}\frac{z}{y} = \frac{1}{2}z$ $= \dot{z}$ as here arbitrarily assumed as the fluxion of $\frac{z}{y}$, or z; though $\frac{1}{3}\frac{z}{y}$, $\frac{1}{10}\frac{z}{y}$, &c. might in this case with equal propriety have been assumed as the fluxion of $\frac{z}{y}$, or z. But, as here stated if $\dot{x}$ is not equivalent to x but of half its value only, $\dot{z}$, or its equivalent $\frac{y\dot{x} - z\dot{y}}{y^2}$ the supposed fluxion of the fraction $\frac{z}{y}$, $=0$, in place of $\frac{1}{2}\frac{z}{y}$; since $y\dot{x} - x\dot{y}$, in this case, $=0$.

45. It now must be sufficiently manifest from the preceding reasoning, that true results could not be obtained by either of these methods of analysis if the fundamental errors in them observed by the analyst were corrected as he proposes; since such corrections would, necessarily, infallibly ruin the whole; as the quantities called fluxions or differentials thus corrected would no longer be proper for answering the purposes of these methods, from their then not being equivalent, or identical in every thing except in notation and name, to their respective fluents or integrals; and, therefore, not qualified for acting properly the parts assigned these fluents or integrals by these methods, under their masquerade habits, and their new assumed titles of fluxions or differentials: it being evident that if $2x\dot{x} = x^2$, $2x\dot{x} + \dot{x}\dot{x}$ cannot also equal it; or if $x\dot{y} + y\dot{x} = xy$, that $x\dot{y} + y\dot{x} + \dot{x}\dot{y}$ cannot also $= xy$, and so of other cases. And it necessarily must have been this inaptness of $2x\dot{x} + \dot{x}\dot{x}$, and $x\dot{y} + y\dot{x} + \dot{x}\dot{y}$, &c. for performing the parts of x^2, and of xy, &c. with such accuracy and effect as it is performed in these methods by the quantities adopted as the fluxions or differentials of these powers, and products, &c. by these methods, or by

$2x\dot{x}$,

$2x\dot{x}$, and $x\dot{y}+y\dot{x}$, &c. that so much pains have been taken, and so much address employed, to get rid of the last term of the second power of a binomial and of the product of two binomials, or of the square and the product of the differences: the infinitesimal calculus rejecting them as infinitely small; though with much inconsistency as admitting of other quantities which it represents as infinitely smaller; while the fluxional rejects them, not as being infinitely small, but on the supposition of its being demonstrated that they actually exist not in any case, the square or the product of a binomial being complete without them.

46. It is also evident from what has been advanced, that this hitherto strange, mysterious, unintelligible character, called an infinitesimal or fluxion, which was neither something, nor nothing; but either the one or the other as best suited the purposes of the practitioner, now proves to be in every case a real entity, a certain definite quantity as determined by the circumstances of each particular case.

47. Thus, then, it appears that the quantities here treated of are neither flowing quantities, nor are generated by fluxions and their increments or by the flowing of quantities, as of points, lines, and surfaces; since what are called the fluxions and increments of these quantities are nothing else than the quantities themselves concealed under the disguise of another dress and designation. And, also, that what have been denominated fluxions and increments, or differentials and infinitesimals, are, in place of being as they have hitherto been represented to be quantities infinitely small, in reality finite quantities of precise determinate values; and, hence, it is manifest that the doctrine of prime and ultimate ratios, though it could have stood the test of reason, could not with any propriety have been applied to any method of calculation of this kind where all the fluxions and infinitesimals, as they are denominated, when they are the representatives or fluxions or infinitesimals of finite quantities, fluents, or integrals, as in every case they necessarily must be, are themselves necessarily finite and determinate quantities.

48. The conclusions or results obtained by these methods are true, only, unless by chance, when these conclusions or results were previously known, and they had been discovered and their truth ascertained by other means: in other cases, many false conclusions or results have been deduced, and

many erroneous and delusive theories have been supported, by means of these methods. Many apparent wonders, however, have been, and may, with facility, be wrought by means of these subtile species of seeming mathematical magic, of the doctrine of infinities, of the use and abuse of symbols, and of THESE accommodating modes of *apparent* computation; and hence it is that mankind have been so lavish in their encomiums on these methods as not perhaps to be surpassed even by those bestowed on the philosophy of a Plato, or an Aristotle: to which indeed it is presumable the singular ingenuity of their contrivance, their intricacy, obscurity, and in some respects incomprehensibility, may have very much contributed. And hence it is that doctrines however erroneous and deceitful when vested in the garb of these modes of calculation, and conducted agreeable to the rules they prescribe, have in general not only escaped detection and passed with impunity, but have been highly applauded and have contributed much to the celebrity of their authors: error or deceit not being in these cases so much as suspected even by the authors themselves.

49. The method of indeterminates, as given in the Reflections on the Theory of the Infinitesimal Calculus, is as follows, viz.

" *The Infinitesimal Analysis is only an Application or Extension of the Method* " *of proceeding in Indeterminate Problems.*

" 37. From what has been said, it will be easy to perceive that the infinite-" simal analysis is nothing else than an application, or, if you will, an ex-" tension of the method of indeterminates. For agreeably to that method, " I say, that when we neglect an infinitely small quantity, we do nothing " more, properly speaking, than *understand* it, and do not suppose it to be " nothing. Thus, when instead of the two exact equations found in article " 9, namely, $TP + TT = MP\frac{MZ}{RZ}$, and $\frac{MZ}{RZ} = \frac{2y + RZ}{2a - 2x - MZ}$, I employ the two im-" perfect equations, $TP = MP\frac{MZ}{RZ}$, and $\frac{MZ}{RZ} = \frac{y}{a-x}$; I know very well that I " am committing an error, and I put the equations, *mentally*, so to speak, " into this form, $MP\frac{MZ}{RZ} = TP + \varphi$, and $\frac{MZ}{RZ} = \frac{y}{a-x} + \varphi'$; φ and φ' being such " quantities as the former equations want to render them exact. In like " manner, in the equation $\frac{TP}{MP} = \frac{y}{a-x}$, resulting from the above two imper-" fect

" fect equations, I *understand* the quantity φ'', being such that $\left(\frac{TP}{MP} - \frac{y}{a-x}\right)$
" $+\varphi''=0$, may be an exact equation. But I know well enough, that this
" last quantity φ'' is equal to zero; or, at least, that it is only an infinitely
" small quantity, since no infinitesimal enters into the first term. Now
" this cannot happen, unless each of the terms taken separately be equal
" to nothing; whence I conclude that I have exactly $\frac{TP}{MP} = \frac{y}{a-x}$; so that
" the quantities φ, φ' and φ'' have not been suppressed as nullities, but only
" *understood*, in order to simplify the calculation.

" Again: if X, for example, be an arbitrary quantity, which may be
" rendered as small as we please, and if there were given an equation of
" this form, $A + BX + CX^2 + \&c. = 0$, A, B, C, &c. being independent on
" X, this equation cannot exist, unless it be $A=0$, $B=0$, $C=0$, &c.;
" that is, unless each term, taken separately, whatever be their number,
" be equal to zero. And, for the same reason, if we have an equation
" of this general form, $P + Q = 0$; so that P may be a function of the
" quantities given or determined by the conditions of the problem; and,
" on the other hand, Q, a quantity which we may suppose as small as we
" please, we shall necessarily have $P=0$, and $Q=0$. But such is pre-
" cisely the nature of the equation in the last article, namely, $\left(\frac{TP}{y} - \frac{y}{a-x}\right) +$
" $\left(\frac{TT}{y} - \frac{2y'.(RZ : MZ)+a RZ - s RZ}{(a-x).(2a-2x-MZ)}\right) = 0$. Therefore each of the terms of this
" equation, taken separately, is equal to zero; and consequently, the
" quantities TT, MZ and RZ, which enter into the first term, may be
" neglected, in the course of the calculation, without altering that first term.

" The infinitesimal analysis, therefore, differs from the method of inde-
" terminates only in this, that in the former, quantities which, were they
" allowed to remain, would, in the end, always destroy one another, are
" treated as nothing, or rather are *understood* throughout the calculation;
" while, in the method of indeterminates, we wait till the end of the cal-
" culation, and then cancel the arbitrary quantities which ought to be eli-
" minated. This last method may therefore very easily be made to supply
" the use of the infinitesimal calculus, without the help of imperfect equa-
" tions, and without committing any error in the course of the calcula-
" tion."

This

This method as here described, if I understand it right, of which I confess I am somewhat doubtful, as I am at a loss to conceive what can be the true meaning of the expression: "we do nothing more, properly "speaking, than *understand* it, and do not suppose it to be nothing,"— that is a quantity which is afterwards acknowledged to be equal to zero— appears to me to have been conceived in error, and to terminate either in error or in deception. For if the quantity φ'' is equal to zero, it is not from each of the terms taken separately being $=0$ of the equation $\left(\frac{TP}{MP} - \frac{y}{e-z}\right) + \varphi'' = 0$; as they $=0$ from $\frac{TP}{MP}$ being equal $\frac{y}{e-z}$, or from these terms being equal and in that equation having opposite signs, and it is the equation, and not any of its terms when taken in their true values as expressed by the proposition and denoted by the diagram, that $=0$. Also, if $A + BX + CX' +$, &c. $= 0$, X and the powers of X must $= 0$ as well as A, B, C, &c.

50. The method of limits, as explained in the same Treatise, is thus stated, viz.

" 38. There is yet another method of coming at the results of the infinite-
" simal analysis, without overpassing the bounds of ordinary algebra; and
" that is by the method of limits or ultimate ratios. For though this ana-
" lysis be founded entirely on the properties of limits and ultimate ratios,
" it differs nevertheless from what is properly called the method of limits,
" in this, that in the latter, the quantities which we call infinitesimal, do
" not enter separately into the calculation, nor even their ratios, but only
" the ultimate values of these ratios, which being finite quantities, do not
" so properly constitute this method a particular calculus, as a simple ap-
" plication of ordinary algebra.

" The business before us, then, is by barely introducing into ordinary
" algebra, not infinitesimal quantities themselves, but the ultimate ratios
" of these quantities, to supply the means which the infinitesimal analysis
" furnishes, for discovering any properties, ratios and relations whatsoever,
" of the magnitudes which constitute any proposed system; and this is
" that which is properly called the method of limits.

" To explain the procedure, and give some idea of the spirit, of this
" method, we shall again resume the example before treated of.

" *Explanation*

" Explanation of the Method of Limits, properly so called.

" It is evident, from what was delivered in article 9, that though $\frac{MZ}{RZ}$ be
" not equal to $\frac{TP}{MP}$, yet the first of these quantities differs much less
" than the second, as R S approaches nearer to M P, or, in other words,
" that $\frac{MZ}{RZ}=\frac{TP}{MP}$ is an imperfect equation; but that (putting L. for the limit,
" or the ultimate value,) L. $\frac{MZ}{RZ}=\frac{TP}{MP}$ is a perfect, or rigorously exact equa-
" tion.

" In like manner, L. $\frac{MZ}{RZ}=\frac{y}{a-x}$ is proved to be a perfect, or rigorously exact,
" equation. Equating then these two values of L. $\frac{MZ}{RZ}$, there arises, as be-
" fore, $\frac{TP}{MP}=\frac{y}{a-x}$, or (M P being $=y$) TP$=\frac{y^2}{a-x}$. Thus, this new calculus
" contains neither the infinitely small quantities M Z and R Z, nor even
" their ratio $\frac{MZ}{RZ}$; but only the limit or ultimate value of that ratio, namely,
" L. $\frac{MZ}{RZ}$, which is a finite quantity.

" If this method could be always as easily put in practice as the ordinary
" infinitesimal analysis, it might even appear the most eligible of the two:
" for it would have the advantage of conducting us to the same results, by
" a path which is always direct and luminous; whereas the other conducts
" us to the truth, only after having made us traverse, so to speak, the re-
" gions of errors.

" But it must be owned that the method of limits is attended with a
" considerable difficulty, which has no place in the ordinary infinitesimal
" calculus. In the former, the infinitely small quantities cannot, as in the
" latter, be separated from each other; and these quantities being always
" connected two and two, afford no opportunity of introducing into the
" combinations the properties of each in particular, or of subjecting the
" equations into which they enter to those transformations which may
" assist in their elimination. This difficulty is much less felt in the opera-
" tions themselves, than in the preparatory and supplemental propositions
" and reasonings."

From the above it is evident that this method is also only a method of
deception by introducing any *known* as an *unknown* quantity, and passing

it

it for such on the unwary, under the disguise of another form and another name, by employing different symbols to represent it from those under which the known quantity is usually exhibited and known; and by equating it thus disguised to the equivalent known quantity undisguised, that is in effect to itself, and then to another known quantity known to be equal to the former known quantity, and therefore also in effect to itself; and from these two equations, or from these two quantities being each equal to it, deducing the conclusion that these two quantities are equal to each other. Thus, in the example given, that which is sought, or the result of $\frac{TP}{MP} = \frac{y}{a-x}$, or (M P being $=y$) $TP = \frac{y'}{a-x}$ is previously known: and making the arbitrarily assumed expression $L.\frac{MZ}{RZ}$ equal the known quantity $\frac{TP}{MP}$ is only giving another expression for the known quantity $\frac{TP}{MP}$, under the disguise of which it may, as seeming to represent some other quantity, be made to carry on the deception; for the quantity thus expressed is neither an unknown, nor an indeterminate quantity, $L.\frac{MZ}{RZ} = \frac{TP}{MP}$ being declared to be a a perfect equation, rigorously exact, but is the identical quantity $\frac{TP}{MP}$ in every thing except in the manner of expressing it: it is then stated that $L.\frac{MZ}{RZ} = \frac{y}{a-x}$ is also a perfect equation; of this, however, no other proof is given, or can be given, but because it equals the quantity $\frac{TP}{MP}$, or more properly is that quantity in disguise, which quantity was previously known to equal $\frac{y}{a-x}$; yet, it is inferred from these equations, that the previously known fact---though in this very case admitted and proceeded on as one of the data of the supposed demonstration, of the equality of $\frac{TP}{MP}$ to $\frac{y}{a-x}$--- has been discovered merely by the equating of both of these quantities $\frac{TP}{MP}$ and $\frac{y}{a-x}$, separately, with the pretended unknown and indeterminate quantity $L.\frac{MZ}{RZ}$.

51. The method of increments of the learned Dr. Brooke Taylor is akin to those of infinitesimals and fluxions; or, more properly, is only these under the disguise of another name and the garb of a more intricate and perplexing notation, as differing but little from them in other respects.

52. The

52. The passion for abstraction, and thereby for investing attributes, or properties and relations, with an independent existence, and the too ardent desire for generalising, has proved exceedingly prejudicial to mathematical as well as to metaphysical science; since in consequence of them visionary existences, non-entities, and incomprehensibles, have been introduced into it as realities; and as such have had all the rules of arithmetic and algebra applied to them; while real quantities, with the intention of generalising their relations or properties, have been so disguised by the too frequent use and abuse of symbols—as if what of its own nature is particular could by the mere substitution of a symbol for it be rendered general—that both they and their relations have often been entirely lost sight of in mathematical investigations even by the investigator himself, who, entangled in the mysterious web of his own weaving, and anxious only about conducting his symbols agreeable to the rules of art, concerning the justness of which he entertains no doubt, is imperceptibly led into error; and when, proceeding on the erroneous principle of imaginary beings or quantities being realities, he exhibits them as such bodied forth under the only form in which they can be rendered cognoscible to sense the proxies he appoints them of appropriate symbols and an appropriate notation and applies to them in this state all the rules of arithmetic and algebra as if they were actual existences, overlooking the fallaciousness of the principles on which he proceeds in his eagerness to render this application as perfect and complete as possible, is inevitably conducted from error to error till the whole, though deemed ingenious and profound, necessarily terminates in false conclusions, obscurity, and mystery; though, from the investigations having been conducted with much dexterity and address and perfectly agreeable to the rules of art, this is not so much as suspected even by the authors themselves; and this I am persuaded is always the case when philosophers and mathematicians happen to promulgate doctrines which upon a more mature and accurate investigation prove to be unfounded:—truth being invariably the object of philosophy; and those who cultivate it with any degree of success being commonly far superior to practising the arts of voluntary deception.

53. Principles, which are represented as of the most extensive use, and the foundation of a sublime geometry, ought to be clear and satisfactory. There

There is no deviating from nature without deviating from truth; and therefore to divest science of obscurity and mystery it becomes necessary to reject incomprehensibles for intelligibles, delusions for realities; to abandon the alluring but devious and deceitful path of fancy for the study of nature, and the deducing from thence by rational investigation conclusions which safely may be relied upon, and which are truly useful and important. The attainment of these ends is one of the principal objects of these Essays; and if the principles they develope shall prove to be well founded and just, they must effect a complete revolution in the sciences of which they treat in these and other respects; and it is hoped that by means of the preceding plain and simple observations and operations respecting the doctrines of infinitesimals and fluxions, the veil of delusion under which these doctrines were disguised is withdrawn, the obscurity dispelled, and the whole mystery of the art laid open to view; that the spell is now broken, the charm has lost its power; and that mankind, no longer trusting to these so highly celebrated modes of calculation for the extension, proof, and perfection of their knowledge, will employ their time more profitably and pleasantly than in a study so irksome and unavailing from which nothing but misrepresentation and error can possibly result.

54. Nothing but too great confidence in the supposed infallibility of what are called mathematical demonstrations, and in the erroneous doctrine of mathematical science being the result of pure intellection only---opinions universally entertained from too great a veneration for the ancients by whom they were first promulgated---could possibly have induced such a character as Sir Isaac Newton, who in all other cases proceeds so warily and surely in his investigations, to have adopted the doctrine of exhaustions and fanciful theory of infinites, and on such a basis to have attempted the erecting of a new system of computation, in direct deviation from his usual practice of trusting to nature and realities, to experiment and induction for the principles from which he rationally deduces his conclusions and the data on which he founds his calculations; and who, by these means and extraordinary powers and application of mind, became, whatever may be the fate of some analytical speculations to the invention of which he had only a disputed claim, the author of by much the most profound and important discoveries in physics that ever were made.

55. Since

55. Since attempts to reconcile contradictions, or what is in the nature of things irreconcilable, and to render what is incomprehensible intelligible, must necessarily be vain; it can be matter of no surprise that those who have endeavoured to explain, elucidate, and extend these methods of analysis, should, though many of them persons of great abilities, have succeeded so ill in these attempts. It was intended in a supplement to this part of the Essay to have attempted a proof of the doctrines here developed in a manner more in detail than that given in the Essay, as deduced from an investigation into the principles and practice of the science, or rather art, as given by the most eminent of those who have treated of this subject, of which the materials are prepared, and at present lie before me; but I now do not think it necessary, as I imagine there has been enough advanced in the Essay to prove the insufficiency and inefficacy of these methods of computation, and to enable any one to detect the errors in the principles and practice, and in the examples given by these authors; and I do not hesitate to affirm, from what lies before me, that in every case it will be found on an accurate investigation, that the result is either included in the premises, or is deduced from previously known facts by some unwarrantable abuse of symbols, or other analytical manœuvre. And I am happy to think this supplement is unnecessary as exempting me from the invidious and disagreeable task of pointing out the errors of others; and thereby, perhaps, of wounding the feelings of those who merit not such treatment, and to whom science and mankind are in other respects under obligations; those to whom these mistakes are not peculiar, and who in place of intending to deceive have themselves been deceived by these specious and alluring but most deceptious of sciences, if sciences they may be called.

APPENDIX.

THE ancients for long, with much propriety and a just regard to accuracy, admitted no lines into geometry but those described on a plane surface by the application of a pencil or pen to a ruler or compass, and which were of consequence necessarily determined by the position of the ruler or compass in all their points or parts, and by that means were adequate to and completely qualified for the purpose of delineating the diagrams proposed with the requisite correctness. But geometrical lines being by this means restricted to the right line and the circle, and the ancients being exceedingly solicitous to give geometrical solutions of the famous problems of—The quadrature of the circle—The cubature of the sphere—The duplication of the cube—The finding of two continued geometrical mean proportionals to two extremes given—and—The trisection of an angle; which they found they could not effect by means of these lines, they first admitted the conic sections into geometry, and afterwards had recourse to other mechanical constructions and mechanical instruments for that purpose, whereby lines are formed and figures constructed which are deficient in that essential circumstance of not having the positions of their several points or parts necessarily determined, and thereby the figures produced by their means accurately delineated, nothing further than a near approach to correctness being in these cases either professed or attempted :---as in the construction of the CONCHOID of NICOMEDES, of the CISSOID of DIOCLES, and of the QUADRATRIX of DINOSTRATES, &c. where certain points of the curves being determined, a mere approximation to the others by their means is all that is attempted, expected, and obtained.

Sir Isaac Newton, in his Treatise on the Linear Construction of Equations, near the end of his universal Arithmetic, says : " We approve of the " trisection of an angle by a conchoid, which Archimedes in his Lemmas,

" and

" and Pappus in his Collections, have preferred to the inventions of all
" others in this case, because we ought either to exclude all lines, besides
" the circle and right line, out of geometry, or admit them according to
" the simplicity of their descriptions, in which case the conchoid yields to
" none, except the circle:" and he soon after adds, " That is arithmetically
" more simple which is determined by the more simple equations, but that
" is geometrically more simple which is determined by the more simple
" drawing of lines; and in geometry, that ought to be reckoned best
" which is geometrically most simple: wherefore I ought not to be blamed,
" if, with that prince of mathematicians Archimedes and other ancients,
" I make use of the conchoid for the construction of solid problems." And,
surely, there can be no good reason for restricting the delineation of lines to
the use of the common ruler and compass only in cases where the lines required can be delineated with more facility by other instruments and by
means as simple and equally correct; and more especially when it is impossible to delineate them by means of these instruments, as in the case
of its being required to draw a right line equal to the circumference of a
circle of which the diameter is given.

Neither the zeal nor the industry of the moderns has fallen short of that
of the ancients for the obtaining of accurate geometrical solutions of these
celebrated problems, though they have hitherto been attended with no
better success. Such solutions being still desiderata in this science. There
seems, notwithstanding, to be nothing in the nature of these problems
which necessarily imposes an impossibility of solution: and if, agreeable
to the opinion of Sir Isaac Newton, that construction is to be reckoned
the best which is geometrically most simple; if it is admitted that it is possible for the length of a right line to be delineated with correctness by other
means besides that of the application of compasses; and if facility of description, a necessary determination of the positions of all the points or
parts, and that accuracy thence necessarily resulting, are allowed to constitute the essentials of geometrical lines and figures, and to form that distinguishing characteristic of the science, on which the precision of its proofs
principally depend; perhaps the following solutions of them, distinguished
as much by their simplicity as by their perspicuity and conciseness, may
be deemed accurately geometrical and just:---viz.

PROBLEM

PROBLEM I.

To Quadrate the Circle.

By the revolution of a wheel, having a fine point fixed any where in its periphery, on a plane surface along a ruler, obtain two small marks on the plane, as formed by the point in the periphery on the revolution of the wheel; join these two marks by a right line by means of a ruler and pen or pencil; and thus, by a very easy method of description, will a right line equal to the periphery of the wheel, or to the circumference of the circle represented by the wheel, be obtained as correctly as the length of any right line is obtained by applying a compass to it and marking the length thus ascertained by the points of the compass on a plane surface and joining those marks by a line described by means of a ruler and a pen or pencil, or as the circumference of a circle is described on a plane surface by means of a compass; at the same time that the position of all the points or parts of the right line measuring the circumference of the circle are in this case necessarily determined, and accurately described, by means of the generating circle or wheel itself. A straight line, equal to the circumference of the circle, being thus geometrically obtained, or at least as much so as the lengths of right lines are in the usual way obtained by the application of a compass to them, the method of quadrature is obvious, since nothing further can be required for that purpose than squaring the mean geometrical between one half of the radius and the circumference thus ascertained, the square thus obtained being equal to the rectangle under the circumference and half the radius, and therefore equal to the circle.

Corollary. By similar methods, and on similar principles and proofs, may the lengths and areas of aliquot parts of the circle, and geometrical quadratures, &c. of certain other curves, with much accuracy be geometrically obtained and ascertained.

Scholium. Lines giving the length of a diameter of a circle, and of its circumference obtained as above described, might with propriety and advantage be marked on scales, since the circumference of any other circle of which the diameter is given could by this means easily be obtained, as being a fourth proportional to these two lines on the scale and the given diameter.

PROBLEM

PROBLEM II.

To find two Continued Geometrical Mean Proportionals to two Extremes given.

Let the two extremes given (See fig. 11th) be the lines A and B; draw the line C D equal A, and the line D E, at a right angle to it at the point D, equal B; extend the line C D towards G indefinitely, and the line E D towards F indefinitely :---then apply two square rulers H F G, and I G F, to the points C and E of the lines C D and D E, respectively, in such a manner as that their angular points shall fall on the lines D F and D G, each upon each respectively, and that their sides or arms F G, G F, may exactly coincide; then with a pen or pencil applied to the rulers describe the lines C F, F G, and G E, cutting the lines C D and E D extended, in the points F, and G, when the definite lines D F, and D G, will be the two continued geometrical mean proportionals required :---as is manifest from the nature of right-angled triangles.

N. B. It is to be observed that in this case right lines only are used.

PROBLEM III.

To Double the Cube.

This is the famous Delian problem, the solution of which was an object of so much anxious solicitude to the geometricians of antiquity, and was so called from having been first proposed by the oracle of Apollo at Delphos on being consulted as to the means of stopping the progress of the plague then raging at Athens, by returning for answer, that the plague should cease when Apollo's altar, which was cubical, should be doubled. It was discovered by Hippocrates of Chios that this might be geometrically effected if two continued geometrical proportionals to two extremes given could be geometrically found. But the ancients failing in their attempts to obtain these, were necessitated to have recourse to approximations to them by means of the conchoid of Nicomedes, and other curves in which certain of the points or parts were necessarily determined, and the others

assumed

assumed as near approximations only to what they ought to be. This necessity no longer subsisting, the two means required being by the immediately preceding proposition obtainable with great facility of description, and with much geometrical accuracy and precision from the position of each point or part being in this case necessarily determined, the exact duplication of the cube can now be effected geometrically by means of a very simple process founded on simple principles. As I have not been able to obtain the proper information with respect to the means by which Hippocrates discovered that the duplication of the cube depended upon the finding of two geometrical mean proportionals to two extremes given, and on what principle he founded his demonstration of this fact, I shall here develope the circumstances which naturally led me to the same discovery, before I knew that Hippocrates had made it before me, as well as the principles on which it may be demonstrated :---but whether these circumstances are the same with those which led Hippocrates to the same discovery, or whether these principles are the same with those on which he founded his demonstration of the same fact, I am altogether ignorant. When I first applied my thoughts to the subject of the geometrical duplication of the cube, it naturally occurred to me in the first place to consult those parts of the Elements of Geometry of Euclid which treat of solids, with the view of obtaining some useful information with regard to this subject, and on an attentive perusal of the 11th and 12th books, I found one proposition which naturally leads to the discovery of this truth and its demonstration, and thereby to the solution of this problem, though this natural consequence of it, this discovery and demonstration, has escaped Euclid. The particular proposition here alluded to—a proposition that perhaps was unknown to Hippocrates—is the 36th Proposition of the 11th book of Euclid's Elements, viz. " If three straight lines be proportionals, " the solid parallelopiped described from all three as its sides, is equal to " the equilateral parallelopiped described from the mean proportional, one " of the solid angles of which is contained by three plane angles equal, " each to each, to the three plane angles containing one of the solid angles " of the other figure." Simson's Euclid, page 238. On reflecting on the nature of this proposition, it soon occurred to me, that if two continued geometrical mean proportionals could be found to two extremes given, of

which

which the one is precisely double the length of the other, that the cube of the first or shortest of these means must necessarily, from the above quoted proposition and its demonstration, be precisely equal in solid contents to twice the cube of the first or shortest of these extremes: that is, to twice the given cube, and that this is actually the case may thus be demonstrated:---It having been demonstrated, Proposition 16th, book 6th, of Euclid's Elements---that if four right lines be proportional, the rectangle contained by the means is equal to the rectangle contained by the extremes; and it having also been demonstrated---Proposition 31st, book 11th, of the same Elements---that solid parallelopipeds having equal bases and the same altitude are equal to each other; it necessarily follows that if a cube is given which is required to be doubled, and a parallelopiped is formed by the junction of two cubes, each equal to the given cube, with each other, and therefore of precisely double the solid contents of the cube given, the altitude of which is the same with that of the given cube, and the base equal to double the base of that cube, as being contained under a rectangle of which one of the sides is a right line equal in length to one of the sides of that cube and the other to a right line of double that length, the parallelopiped thus formed of double the solid contents of the given cube must be precisely equal to another parallelopiped of the same altitude, and having a base contained under a rectangle of which the sides are two mean geometrical proportions to the sides of the rectangle under which the base of the other is contained, and therefore of equal area with that of the other, since the bases and altitudes being equal, the parallelopipeds must, from the above-mentioned Propositions, necessarily be also equal. But, since the parallelopiped contained under the two means is equal, the altitudes being the same, to the other, or to that formed by the junction of two cubes, each equal to the given cube, with each other; and since the first or shortest of these means is a geometrical mean between the altitude, or length of a side of the given cube, or between the first and shortest extreme, and the second or longest mean, it follows from this 36th Prop. of the 11th book of the Elements, that the cube of this first or shortest mean is equal to this parallelopiped; and, therefore, to double the cube of the shortest extreme, that is to double the cube given, and consequently that cubing this mean gives the required duplication. *Q. E. D.*

PROBLEM

           APPENDIX.

PROBLEM IV.

To Cube the Sphere.

By Problem 1st of this square a great circle of the sphere, and then form a parallelopiped having this square for its base, and two-thirds of the diameter of the sphere for its altitude, and it will be equal in solid contents with the sphere. Cube this parallelopiped by cubing the longest of two geometrical means of which the altitude, and a line equal to the length of one of the sides of the base of the parallelopiped, form the extremes; and a cube of equal solid contents with the given sphere will of consequence be obtained. This is manifest from the last proposition, as being only a particular case of it, depending on the same principles, and demonstrable by the same means, and differing from the former only in *cubing* the longest in place of the shortest of the two *means*, from its being the longest of the two *extremes* that is *squared* in this case in place of the shortest as in the last of the double cube.

PROBLEM V.

To Trisect an Angle.

Let A BC (fig. 12th) be the given angle; with B for a center and the radius A B describe the arch A C; draw the line D E (fig. 13th) equal in length to three times A B, and with the point E as a centre, and D E as a radius, describe the arch D F, having a line for a cord equal in length to the cord of the arch A C of fig. 12th, join F E; then with E for a centre, and a radius equal A B, (fig. 12th), describe the arch G H; take A o, and n C, each equal to G H, join o B and n B, and I say the angle A B C is trisected by these lines o B and n B. For arches, or the cords of arches, of the same circle being the proper measure of angles; and the circumferences, and any determinate parts or portions of the circumferences of the same length of cord, of different circles, being to each other in the ratio of their respective radii to each other; it necessarily follows, that when the length of
line

line for the cords of the arches measuring the angles is the same or equal, while the radii of the different circles, of which these are severally arches, are to each other in the ratio of one to three, that the angles these different arches respectively measure must also be to each other in the same ratio of one to three; and, consequently, that the angle D E F, or G E H, of fig. 13, must be precisely one-third of the angle A B C of fig. 12; that the arch G H must be precisely one-third of the arch A C, as it is an arch of a circle of equal radius, and as the angle it measures is only one-third of the angle measured by the arch A C; and that the angle A B C is trisected by the lines o B and n B, drawn from the points o and n, to B, since the arches A o, o n, and n C, are each equal to the arch G H, and the triangles A B o, o B n, and n B C, are consequently each equal to the triangle G E H; and that any other angle whatever may be trisected by the same means, or according to the manner and principles above described.

Corollary. By taking radii in the same ratio to each other with that of the given angle to the angle required, and proceeding as above described, may any given angle, with the utmost ease and accuracy, be geometrically divided according to any ratio required.

Since the above solution of this problem must have been allowed by the most scrupulous of the ancient geometricians to be strictly and rigidly geometrical, it cannot but excite admiration that a solution which, now that it is discovered, seems so simple, should have foiled the efforts of all preceding ages.

In the constructions and solutions of all these problems no lines are made use of but the right line and the circle; and the only difference between the method here employed and the common is, that in one of these problems the circumference of a circle, or what is the same thing, a right line equal to it, in place of being mechanically described by a compass, is mechanically described by the periphery of a wheel; and that in another of them a square or angular ruler in place of a straight one is employed for drawing certain right lines by.

THE END.

www.ingramcontent.com/pod-product-compliance
Lightning Source LLC
Chambersburg PA
CBHW062036090426

42740CB00016B/2924